DIASPORA BY DESIGN:
MUSLIMS IN CANADA AND BEYOND

Haideh Moghissi, Saeed Rahnema, and Mark J. Goodman

Few groups face as many misconceptions within their new countries as do Muslim immigrants. This book challenges the common misperceptions of Muslim immigrants as a homogeneous, religiously driven group, and identifies the tensions they experience within their host countries.

A comparative, multi-ethnic study based on over two thousand interviews, *Diaspora by Design* examines Muslim populations that have settled in Canada, Britain, Iran, and Palestine. Utilizing hard socio-economic data as well as qualitative analysis, the authors show the remarkable diversity and divisions between Muslim immigrant populations along urban-rural, cultural, class, and gender lines. They argue that integration is a two-way exchange that requires a readiness on the part of the host society to remove barriers that prevent the full social and economic participation of immigrant populations.

Extensively researched and thoughtfully provocative, *Diaspora by Design* is a much-needed work that provides an accurate and dynamic depiction of the lives of Muslim immigrants away from their homelands.

HAIDEH MOGHISSI is a professor in the Department of Sociology at York University.

SAEED RAHNEMA is a professor in the Department of Political Science at York University.

MARK J. GOODMAN is the undergraduate program director of the School of Social Sciences at York University.

HAIDEH MOGHISSI, SAEED RAHNEMA,
AND MARK J. GOODMAN

Diaspora by Design

Muslims in Canada and Beyond

UNIVERSITY OF TORONTO PRESS
Toronto Buffalo London

© University of Toronto Press Incorporated 2009
Toronto Buffalo London
www.utppublishing.com
Printed in Canada

ISBN 978-0-8020-9787-3 (cloth)
ISBN 978-0-8020-9543-5 (paper)

Printed on acid-free paper

Library and Archives Canada Cataloguing in Publication

Moghissi, Haideh, 1944–
    Diaspora by design : Muslims in Canada and beyond / Haideh Moghissi,
Saeed Rahnema, and Mark J. Goodman.

    Includes bibliographical references and index.
    ISBN 978-0-8020-9787-3 (bound). ISBN 978-0-8020-9543-5 (pbk.)

    1. Muslims – Canada.   2. Muslim diaspora.   I. Rahneema, Saeed, 1942–
II. Goodman, Mark J., 1941–   III. Title.

FC106.M9M64 2009   305.6'970971   C2008-904080-5

This book has been published with the help of a grant from the Canadian
Federation for the Humanities and Social Sciences, through the Aid to Scholarly Publications Programme, using funds provided by the Social Sciences
and Humanities Research Council of Canada.

University of Toronto Press acknowledges the financial assistance to its
publishing program of the Canada Council for the Arts and the Ontario Arts
Council.

University of Toronto Press acknowledges the financial support for its
publishing activities of the Government of Canada through the
Book Publishing Industry Development Program (BPIDP).

This book is dedicated to women and men who generously shared their knowledge and experiences with us in the process of our research. They work hard in their adopted country, encouraging their children, and trying, as best they can, to adjust to their new life – without complaints, and without bowing to helplessness and despair. Zeib and Ata are just two among many:

In the midst of the turmoil of the Afghan Civil War, Zeib ... was still a teenager when an Afghan Mujahed fighter – a tough, abusive man, twenty years her senior – approached her father, asking for her hand in marriage. Fearing for Zeib, her father refused the proposition. He was killed; later, it came out that the man who would become her husband was, in fact, the very one who had murdered him. Zeib was forced to marry the man, giving birth to two daughters and two sons. When the older daughter was eleven, the father and his friend, also an old man, got it in their heads that they would swap daughters – still, just children – and take them as new wives. Filled with panic that her own horror would be doubled, Zeib fled. She could only manage to take her daughters and was forced to leave her sons to follow on their own. But, tragically, at the border, in great confusion, the boys were pulled apart. The older one, seventeen, was lost. He was never seen again. Zeib made it to Canada with the girls and younger son. She has worked hard as a cleaning lady in Toronto, taking care of her children. Her older daughter, the same girl rescued from the terrible forced marriage, is now Valedictorian in her graduating class. Zeib, having survived a massive stroke, continues her search for her older son, working hard, adjusting to a new life.

As a young member of the pro-Soviet Tudeh Party in 1940s Iran, Ata Safavi daringly crossed into the USSR, fleeing Iranian political persecution and drawn, with great hopes and illusions, to live in freedom in a land he had come to admire. Instead, he was jailed and subjected to lengthy trials and sent to Siberia to work in the dark coal mines of Magadan, suffering ten years of fierce slave labour, hunger, and cold. Only with Stalin's death in 1953 was Ata given the choice to either return to Iran or move somewhere else in the Soviet Union. Given the CIA coup in Iran the same year and the total suppression of the Tudeh and other parties, Ata moved to Tajikistan, where he attended medical school and became a successful and popular surgeon. In the wake of the 1979 Revolution, he returned to Iran, once again with great hopes and illusions of freedom, this time in the land of his birth. But he was soon disillusioned. Dr Ata and his wife (also a physician), having no other choice, went back to Tajikistan. When his son moved to Canada, and with a civil war in Tajikistan, they moved to Canada as refugee claimants. The son, also a physician, works in a Toronto factory to support his aging parents. In Canada, Dr Ata, at 81, is left undisturbed to live his life in freedom, but with economic hardships and far from home.

Contents

Tables and Figures

Tables

Figures

Preface

The processes of thinking about, studying, and recording the experiences in the West of migrant populations with Muslim cultural backgrounds developed several years ago. The intellectual and political influences that gave birth to the project had little to do with the fact that two of us belong to the category of migrants, émigrés, and exiles that is unwittingly identified by the undifferentiated – and charged – term 'Muslim diaspora.' Instead, what was critical for our thinking was the increasingly disturbing turn in global politics affecting the Middle East and the consequences that were being felt in Western societies with relatively large Muslim populations. Haunted by the spectre of Islamic fundamentalism and the horrific acts of terror committed in the name of re-establishing Islamic piety against Western cultural and political encroachments, European and North American societies had a hard time, even before 11 September 2001, in differentiating between fundamentalist rhetoric and behaviour and the ordinary Muslims living in their cities. Expressions, practices, and gestures that were openly anti-Muslim and that targeted anyone presumed to be Muslim gradually replaced hidden feelings of unease and the cold reception of migrants and refugees that had been the norm. These feelings and practices inevitably heightened the sense of alienation and marginalization felt by populations of Muslim cultural background. For too long they had suffered in silence the wounds of discrimination and social exclusion; and in many Western societies, particularly since the mid-1980s, this sense of frustration and alienation had from time to time led to acts of protest that were readily manipulated by self-proclaimed community leaders in pursuit of specific political ends. This was the case in the 1989 Rushdie affair and in several hijab controversies in Britain, Canada, and France. The expression of agency by Muslims increasingly took a discernible religious tone and, hence, included a renewed emphasis on Islam as a cultural identity, religion, or ideology of resistance, even for previously secular individuals.

Our study, the findings of which are presented in this book, is aimed at making sense of the interacting elements that sharpen awareness of cultural marginality and assessing its impact on the sense of belonging and on the harmonious integration into the new country for the individuals involved. We hoped that our findings, like other research that focuses on work with marginalized communities, would assist policymakers, in some modest way, in understanding what hinders communities of Muslim cultural heritage from accepting the social values and practices of their adopted country and what members of these communities find to be barriers to participation in its civic and political life. We also hoped that by probing these communities, our study might help provide its members with insight into their own social and cultural hang-ups and the mental blocks that prevent them from adjusting to life in settings which are culturally, socially, geographically, and temporally different from the ones they have left. Such knowledge can be an empowering tool in the development of a collective awareness about how to actively shape the social conditions of their lives.

Empirical research in the project focused on four displaced and immigrant communities from Islamic cultures – Iranians, Afghans, Pakistanis, and Palestinians – and as explained in chapter 1, each community was studied both in Canada and in a comparator country. In addition to formal questionnaires, intensive interviews with individuals, focus groups, and other research instruments were used. The questionnaire was pre-tested in both Canada and the comparator countries. To supplement the core funding of this research by the Social Science and Humanities Research Council of Canada's Major Collaborative Research Initiative (MCRI) program, a second grant was provided by the Ford Foundation to assist in the training of research partners and social science students from the Palestinian Occupied Territories.

Winning the trust of respondents is always an essential component of community-focused research. This was even more important for us in the aftermath of 11 September as the 'War on Terror' appeared to many to have become a war on citizens of non-European ethnicity. The build-up of surveillance and widespread questioning and detention of individuals of Middle Eastern origin, along with the blockage of bank accounts or businesses owned by persons from the Middle East and racist depictions by the media of the Middle East, Islam, and Muslims, continued to create fear and distrust among the groups who were the subjects of this study. This had crucial effects both on adults and on youth in these communities, the latter often characterized as those who were most likely to become terrorists. We had the daunting task of capturing the overlooked lives and realities, activities, ideas, and feelings of those whose voices we recorded and of recognizing and validating their agency. We had to accept the fact that many of those who participated in extended interviews or focus groups had had to deal with the practical difficulties of displacement. Some individuals do not wish to share the intimate details of their lives, let alone humiliating experiences or failures. This reluctance is more profound in cultures where 'saving face' and keeping up a public appearance are critical and where acceptance by and approval of the community defines the individual's psychological health and sense of security.

Equally important is the question of accountability to those who would be affected, directly or indirectly, by the research process or by its findings. In studying communities of Muslim cultural background, we were dealing with people whose realities have remained hidden beneath official refugee documents, resettlement reports, and statistics that more often than not are influenced by prejudicial ideas and perceptions. But we were very fortunate to succeed in securing the participation of a broad range of research partners from academe and particularly from the communities. The target groups became partners in the research rather than its object. This approach helped bridge the gap between researchers and researched and between Islamic and non-Islamic sources of knowledge, and thus helped to knock down the imaginary barriers that are sometimes proposed between Islamic moral values and those of the West. Nonetheless, from beginning to end – that is, from the moment of developing appropriate methodological tools to the collecting and analysing of data – we were repeatedly challenged by uncertainty, unanticipated nuances, and differing views and suggestions. We continually faced new circumstances and events that needed to be incorporated into the initial research plan, and so we needed to be prepared to make revisions to that plan on an ongoing basis.

One aim of the work was to help unhinge the grip of fixed ideological preconceptions in pursuing the empirical study of the lives and feelings of migrant groups. We are indebted to the men and women who agreed to participate in the study and share their experiences and knowledge with us. It is hoped that the study in its totality will prompt more investigations into the specific conditions and socio-economic factors that shape the experiences, attitudes, behaviours, and reactions of particular groups in the diaspora, rather than using purportedly fixed properties to explain them.

Even though the final results of the study presented in this book are authored by three researchers, they are the result of collaboration, intersecting intellectual communications, scholarly inputs, and many debates and discussions amongst the colleagues and friends who were part of the study from beginning to end and some of whom also coordinated and supervised data collections and arranged the training of interview personnel in their respective locations. We constantly benefited and were intellectually inspired by them. They are too many to name, but we particularly should express our deep gratitude to Haleh Afshar and Myfanwy Franks (for Pakistanis in the UK), Vida Nassehi-Behnam (for Iranians in the UK), Afsaneh Ashrafi (for Afghans in Iran), and Salam Hamdan (for Palestinians in Occupied Territories and in Jordan). Susan Babbitt's ideas and suggestions on ethical issues of research – questions of voice and authority, respect for diversity, moral responsibility and choice – were an integral part of the project from the beginning to the end.

The project could not have been completed without the enthusiastic contributions of the coordinators of data collection in Canada, working with teams in the four communities and supervising data collection in them: Ibrahim Nasser (for the Afghan community); Farshideh Nasrin (for Iranians); Jehad Aliweiwi and Lina Smoum (for Palestinians); Abdul Nasir Khan (for Pakistanis) in Toronto; Afsaneh Hojabri, coordinator of data collection in Montreal; and Behzad Ghotb, the input coordinator who oversaw day-to-day operations and monitored data entry protocol in Toronto. Special thanks are due to Madhat Majid, the project's computer applications manager, for his most valuable contributions to the project; he often went beyond the call of duty in attending to urgent technical issues in the research. Day-to-day administration of the project at different periods was managed by postdoctoral researchers, Nadia Sayed Ali, Marianne Vardalos and Nadia Habib. We are grateful for their contributions. Over fifty graduate and undergraduate students at York University and roughly an equal number of community researchers in Canada and other settings assisted in administering the questionnaires, conducting oral interviews and focus groups, inputting data and computer applications. They were invaluable colleagues, and their contributions are greatly appreciated. We also salute the support and intellectual guidance of the project's advisory group, comprising Jamshid Behnam, Cyrus Shahkhalili, Niloufar Pourzand, Parvin Samadzadeh, Peter Penz, and Vijay Agnew.

At York University, we would especially like to thank the members of the staff at the School of Social Sciences, in particular Paula Yanovsky and Mavis Griffin. Last and certainly not least, we gratefully acknowledge the financial support of Canada's Social Science and Humanities Research Council. At the Ford Foundation, our program officer, Dr Constance Buchanan, provided timely and invaluable help. Without such supports, research of this magnitude could not possibly have been conducted. We are thankful to the editorial staff at the University of Toronto Press, to our two anonymous reviewers for their valuable comments and suggestions, and to our copy editor, Beth McAuley, who made several shrewd and very helpful suggestions. It goes without saying that we are solely responsible for any shortcomings in the research and in reporting its results in this book.

H. Moghissi, S. Rahnema, and M.J. Goodman

DIASPORA BY DESIGN:
MUSLIMS IN CANADA AND BEYOND

1 Introduction

The identifier 'Muslim diaspora' is not as self-explanatory as it may appear, particularly when it is used in reference to the vast number of ethnically, culturally, linguistically, nationally, and religiously diverse migrant populations of Muslim cultural background in the West. But apart from these complicating realities, the uncertainty also reflects a shift in the notion of 'diaspora,' as this term, once a rather romantic, mystical notion – the source of nostalgic poetry and creative arts, reserved for groups forced to depart from a sacred place of origin – is increasingly used by academics and sometimes even by the media to refer simply to the mass migration of individuals from their homelands. In this more general usage, notions of exile and the idea of the émigré have been diluted, and the voluntary or involuntary character of the departure seems to have lost its significance. In the process, the question of who is and who is not a 'member of diaspora' or is 'in diaspora' has become contested terrain.

In the last two decades, several influential writings have theorized the concept of diaspora beyond the simple experiences of transnational migration, settlement, integration and adaptation, with some proposing common features that seem to draw boundaries around the experience (Safran, 1991; Clifford, 1997; Brah, 1996; Cohen, 1997; Anthias, 1998, 2001; Braziel and Mannur, 2003; Hall, 2003; Brubaker, 2005; among many others). The main concern has been the overuse of the concept and the need to distinguish it from other migratory experiences. 'Diaspora' is widely used today to refer to populations of refugees, migrants, guest workers, expatriates, and the exiled and self-exiled without much concern for the existence of common features or contextual applicability. In these accounts, it is assumed that globalization has created 'de-territorialized,' fluid, and 'transnational' identities, and that the concept allows an understanding of ethnicity, culture, and identity free from problems of essentialism (Hall, 2003). But others have expressed concern that 'diaspora' deploys a notion of ethnicity that privileges the point of origin in constructing identity and thus tends to homogenize the population referred to at the transnational level (Anthias, 1998: 558, 564).

The concept of diaspora sometimes generates resentful contestation, as if it is a badge of honour that is being denied to certain groups. For instance, in a department meeting at our university, in opposition to an initiative to create a 'diaspora studies' program, a colleague suggested that in Canada, except for the people of the First Nations, we are all 'in diaspora' and that one group does not have a greater entitlement to the concept over another. Being of Somali or Pakistani origin, she suggested, is no different from being of British or Scottish heritage – except for the time of migration. Following up on the challenge, another colleague asked how, then, would we define people of the First Nations forced onto reserves in Canada, or Palestinian refugees in camps on the West Bank and in Gaza? Even indigenous populations can have a sense of displacement from their historical location and cultural origins, and a feeling of being alienated and isolated in their own land.

To get hold of the real issues in this debate, the question of 'diaspora' cannot be treated as one of definition only, but must also be critically reconnected to the forces that have uprooted populations historically and pushed masses of peoples beyond known and familiar borders. These forces include colonialism, neo-colonialism, the formation of nation-states and the rise of hegemonic nationalist ideologies, regionalization, imperialism, and globalization.

Our intention here is not to further contest the purity of the diasporic experience of any dislocated or relocated population. Indeed, any proposed list of common characteristics for diaspora has its own critics. There exists no definitive model for drawing the boundaries of the concept and deciding who is in and who is out. As Michele Reis suggests, very few modern-day diasporas can be ascribed all of the characteristics that seem to be the basic tenets used to assess whether an ethnic group is 'diasporic' in nature. Rather, after the Second World War, the increased dislocation and fragmentation characteristic of the period created complex diasporic groups with manifold reasons for their formation. Reis (2004: 43–7) argues that the process of 'diasporization' and globalization are 'coeval processes, with globalization having the most impact on the contemporary phase.'

At the same time, the concept of diaspora cannot be used inter-changeably with, say, ethnicity, that is, simply a sense of 'group affinity' adopted by people who hold a subjective belief in shared historical ancestry and/or language (Weber, 1997: 18–19). 'Ethnicity' refers to social relations that, as John Rex (1996) suggests, are 'given,' or to which 'we all enter at birth,' and that provide members with emotional satis-faction or 'emotional warmth' (82–3). By contrast, experience 'in dias-pora' depends on a sense of existence in separation from one's group. Both 'ethnicity' and the condition of being 'in diaspora' are social con-structions, but the feelings they invoke are different. In contrast to the warmth and emotional support often associated with 'ethnic' belong-ing, being 'in diaspora' is marked by feelings of '*not* belonging,' of being an exile or suffering as a psychological outsider. The crucial element is the shared experience of being displaced, an experience located in a particular place and time; it is not, thus, a condition to which one is 'naturally' linked, but an experience to which specific groups are drawn by force of circumstance. However, the term cannot be applied so loosely that it would include all people who have moved from an originating county regardless of the specific historical context or without regard to their location and experience within the socio-eco-nomic and political structures of the receiving society. Because these are populations that are displaced, the creation of diaspora and their inser-tion into new countries always reflects the operation and consequences of social power. If 'globalization' denotes the bringing together of dif-ferent parts of the world, 'diaspora' points to the inequalities which this 'bringing together' articulates and energizes.

One key element, perhaps, is the concept of *difference* which, as Stuart Hall proposes, connotes not only Otherness, but also the condi-tion of 'instability, permanent unsettlement, the lack of any final reso-lution.' Hall (2003: 238–44) suggests that experience in diaspora is not defined 'by essence or purity, but by the recognition of a necessary het-erogeneity and diversity, by a conception of "identity" which lives with and through, not despite, difference.'

Going back to the question of people of the First Nations in Canada and camp refugees in Palestine, for example, if one of the features of experience in diaspora – that is, living in a country that is not one's birthplace – is not taken as the determining factor and one focuses, instead, on the experiences associated with the loss of an ancestral land and cultural heritage, of being driven to the margin of social, cul-tural, economic, and political power and being racialized, then we can say that both groups constitute diaspora living as outsiders in their own homeland. Or at least, they share many aspects of diaspora experience and, as such, are native diaspora.

Thinking along these lines, we are aware that sociocultural marginality, racialization, and denial of access to political and economic power are made the major components of diasporic experience. That is to say, some of the features of the concept are made to be determining. It then follows that the question of the British or Scottish diasporas in Canada cannot be addressed simply in terms of the mere experience of the departure from a 'home,' whether through force or choice, or by living outside one's ancestral homeland, or having a 'group affinity' to a population in a remote place, but also, and perhaps even more importantly, it should focus on relations of power and on the set of social practices and norms that operate to encourage or discourage a population from feeling 'at home.'

In the multicultural and multi-ethnic societies which have now become the norm in the West, the main questions to be addressed are, who is at the periphery of social and political power and who is disempowered because of her or his national origin and social location and cultural practices? As Avtar Brah (1996: 182–3) argues, when we look at migrants, at issue is not only the circumstances of the group's leaving but also those of arrival and of settling down – and of how and in what ways a group is inserted into the social relations of class, gender, racism, sexuality, or other axes of differentiation in the country to which it migrates. In sum, groups in diaspora are confronted with new realities and new opportunities, but these opportunities come at a cost. In moving from one country to another, identities are not simply merged or rendered unstable; they are merged under the sway of specific social relations. Indeed, one may argue that new identities are forged that are influenced by experience of difference, which is characteristically asymmetric.

Taking these concerns seriously means giving rather less emphasis to the voluntary or involuntary nature of a group's separation from its place of origin and emphasizing, instead, the mechanisms of differentiation the group encounters in the new country. These mechanisms consist of the codes, etiquettes, rules, and regulations that construct social as well as psychological borders and boundaries, underlining the ability to include or exclude ethnic communities from a sense of nationhood and belonging. If relations of power are given more prominence rather than real or imagined commonalities of geographical origin, or even common ancestry, it then follows, as Mary C. Waters (1998) suggests, that some groups in diaspora have the option of 'choosing' their ethnicity and displaying it, and some don't. Which is to say that some migrants (and we use the term 'migrants' in a historical sense) can have a 'symbolic ethnicity' which they may claim whenever they fancy or whenever it suits and serves them. But the assigned identity of others is not a matter of choice. It is not fluid. It is fixed by forces of racism and xenophobia, despite the possibility of social mobility and regardless of the individual's wishes or desires.

This is particularly true of groups that are 'visible' in their new country as a result of skin colour, religion, language, accent, dress code and observable cultural practices or simply because of their nationality and different way of life. The 'ethnicity' of such groups is absolute. This 'ethnic absolutism,' as Paul Gilroy (2003: 51–2) explains, maximizes cultural, social, and historical differences and assumes an unbridgeable, imaginary gap between specific groups of humans that no amount of counter-evidence can bridge. A classic instance of such absolutism is provided historically by the experience of Africans and by the powerful stigma attached to 'blackness' as an indelible racial marker recalling the weight of enslavement, the Atlantic slave trade, and colonial violence. In this way, Fanon, for example, writes about his own encounter with racism in *Black Skin, White Masks*, telling us that despite the black person's wish for a dignified individuality, he must become, not himself, but the descendant of ancestors who had been enslaved or lynched, and from whom this experience cannot be erased, this absolute objectification staining him 'like a dye' (Fanon, 1967: 109, 112; see Goodman, 2006).

The Making of Muslim Diasporas

The size of Muslim populations in the West is rapidly increasing. It is estimated that the Muslim population in Europe has reached 15 million, making Islam the continent's second-largest religion after Christianity (Hunter, 2002). The number is also growing in Canada, where the 2001 Census showed that although only 2 per cent of the population identified themselves as Muslims, Muslims and peoples from Islamic cultures were the fastest-growing religious and ethnic groups in the country. By 2001, within only one decade, the population had grown by 128.9 per cent.

Muslim diasporas are diverse because of a set of factors that, combined together, help determine their behavioural characteristics. Some of these factors relate to the internal configuration of the Muslim communities, and others to the characteristics of the receiving society. The internal configurations include factors such as ethnic, national, cultural, linguistic, sectarian, and class diversities and the length of each group's history in the new country, as well as the size of the communities. The receiving country's level of social, economic, and cultural development, along with its political system, its immigration and settlement policies, and the existence or non-existence of a tradition of cultural tolerance and acceptance of difference, also affect Muslim populations' experience in various Western societies. These internal and external factors have a combined, systemic effect, determining the condition and behaviour of the diasporic communities.

The larger the size and the longer the history of the Muslim population in a receiving country, the greater its internal homogeneity and politicization, and the more tolerant and pluralistic the new country's policies and practices are, the more cohesive, more visible, and more demanding is the diasporic community.

A remarkable aspect of the diversity of Muslim populations in the West relates to their religious affiliation, which is used as the most common element in their identification. Islam, contrary to simplistic views in the West – views shared, ironically, by the Muslim orthodoxy – is not a monolithic religion. Heresiographers have identified over seventy-two sects within the religion, each considering itself the 'saved sect' and the others as misguided (Watt, 1998: 3). Apart from the major division between the majority Sunnis and the minority Shi'as, there are major subsects and divisions within each sect. An authoritative source on Shi'a sects names over 200 different subsects (Mashkoor, 1980: 146–51, 168–86). Moreover, like any other religion and ideology, Islam has had a contingent nature, influenced by and influencing the various cultures and societies that it came to dominate. Followers of the four major Sunni schools – Hanafi, Maleki, Shafei, and Hanbali – and of different sects in the Shi'a world, notably the Twelvers, the Zeidis, and the Ismailies, each have their own interpretations of the religion (Rahnema, 2006).

Moreover, not every individual of Muslim cultural heritage is religious. The inhabitants of Muslim-majority countries and diasporic populations originating from them, like other populations, include orthodox believers, practising individuals, non-practising sceptics, secular and laic members, and atheists. Among practising Muslims there are radical Islamists (who constitute a very small minority) and a vast majority of peaceful and moderate adherents. This diversity is usually ignored, and in particular, the existence of a large number of secular and laic persons of Muslim cultural background is completely overlooked. These secular Muslims, identified on the basis of cultural origin, are recognized neither by devout Muslims nor by average citizens or mainstream media in the West. A recent 'Secular Islam summit' in Florida drew attention to the fact that a significant number of Muslims identify themselves with Islam culturally but not necessarily religiously. But unlike non-religious Jews and non-religious Christians who are recognized as such by their own religion and by others, 'cultural' or secular/laic Muslims are not acknowledged (Saunders, 2007).

Diversity within communities of Muslim origin is not limited to differing religious interpretations. They are also differentiated internally by diverse ethnicities and cultures of origin as well as by class differences. In a sense, Muslims in diaspora have at least triple identities (Rahnema, 2006: 32–3). Apart from the religious and sectarian identities mentioned above, they are distinct in terms of ethnic and national groupings (Arabs, Pakistanis, Indians, Turks, Kurds, Algerians, Nigerians, Iranians, Somalis, Indonesians, Albanians, Bosnians, Chinese, and many others), and many of them may identify themselves first as Iranians, Arabs, Pakistanis, Afghans, or Nigerians, for example, and then as Muslims. In fact, the national and ethnic divisions are often so strong that, other than occasional individual friendships or business dealings, there are no regular social relations and interactions among the various Muslim groups. They speak different languages, dance to different tunes, and have distinctively different cultures and tastes.

As citizens of their new countries of residence, populations of Muslim cultural background have yet another form of identity. They are, for instance, French, British, Dutch, Irish, Swedish, German, or Canadian, and to different degrees acquire characteristics of the dominant culture of these societies. This is particularly the case for the younger members of these communities who are either born or raised in these new societies. A growing number of Muslim youths, with some exceptions, as will be discussed later, tend to assimilate and absorb the identity of their new home country, considering themselves to be first or solely Canadian, for example, or British, or French rather than nationals of their parents' country of origin. The present study clearly shows this trend within the four communities surveyed.

Furthermore, the extent of the heterogeneity and lack of cohesiveness among these diverse populations differs from one Western country to the next. In most European countries, the majority of Muslims come from the same ethnic or national origin: mostly Pakistanis and Bangladeshis in England; Algerians and other North African (*Maghreb*) peoples in France; and Turks, Moroccans, and Kurds in Belgium, Germany, Sweden, and the Netherlands (which also has a relatively large population of Surinamese and Antilleans). In many European states, typically these populations have a longer history in diaspora, are larger in size, and are more cohesive both in terms of national origin and religious sect. By contrast, Muslim populations in Canada are not only smaller in size and younger historically, but also come from very diverse national backgrounds, including, among others, South Asia, the Arab world, Iran, Afghanistan, Africa, Latin America, and East and Southeast Asia. With these features, the Muslim population in Canada is more fragmented than its European counterparts.

Of course, there are other major differences within these diverse communities in terms of class, gender, and age and generational gaps that make them even more heterogeneous. No doubt, as the present study shows, these multiple identities work differently for different national communities, as some have a stronger affiliation with their religion than with their nationality. These multiple identities are also conflictual and, depending on the condition of diaspora, one identity may play a more dominant role than the others. At the same time, prevailing stereotypes about Muslims in the West result in the piling up of all these communities, which do not have much in common and are culturally very different, ignoring the existence of a large and growing number of non-religious and secular members within them. Saleh Bechir and Hazem Saghieh (2005: 2) rightly point to the 'essentialist view of the Other' in the West, which, within this context, considers people of diverse cultures and origins as simply 'Muslims' and in a sense, has 'invented' the 'Muslim community.'

The question is, then, can we refer to this diverse population as simply the 'Muslim diaspora'? After all, the vast populations of émigrés, exiles, and refugees of Muslim cultural background do not fully and unproblematically conform to the common features of diaspora proposed and debated by scholars in the field. In fact, the multiplicity and heterogeneity of migrants from Islamic cultures reflects the immensely complex history and diversity of the Middle East and the vast Muslim world itself. For example, what does a secular Ugandan man of Indian Muslim ancestry have in common with a practising Shi'a woman from Iraq or Pakistan, or a non-practising Muslim woman coming from former-Soviet Azerbaijan with an Ahmadi Muslim female from rural Pakistan, or both of them with a secular Iranian woman, or the devout Wahhabi/Hanbali man from Saudi Arabia?

Our findings in this study, in fact, show remarkable diversity in perspective, lifestyle, and religious identification of the four groups with whom we have worked. We suggest, therefore, that if the diverse communities of Muslim cultural heritage are to be identified as a diasporic group, it is not because they conform to all or a few of the proposed common features of diaspora. We have already suggested that common geographical origin or ethnicity might not be the single most important factor in the formation of a diaspora and the nostalgic connection to a land of origin. Nor can Muslim cultural heritage or even religious belief act as a binding factor for identification and solidarity among these groups, as we need to be mindful of the inflexible religious divisions among practising Muslims.

However, there are some distinguishable, unifying characteristics that differentiate an expatriate group from a diasporic group, whose most important feature is its collective consciousness about the group members' marginal location in the larger society in which they reside. In fact, the persistence of the dominant stereotypes about Muslims – as an essentially different, unified, and devout religious group – has turned an imagined attribute into a social reality. The tragedy of 11 September 2001, the subsequent U.S.-led invasion of Afghanistan, the total devastation of Iraq after the similar U.S. invasion of that country, Hezbollah's attack on Israel that led to the 2006 war in Lebanon, and the continued suffering of Palestinians under Israeli occupation, have all brought the vast communities of Islamic origin closer and have increasingly politicized them. It is this group-consciousness that brings them together, at least from time to time, in various acts of protest or in an expressive sense of connection and solidarity. For example, the greatest display of Muslim unity in Canada was displayed after 11 September when more than 140 organizations endorsed a submission to the federal government on Bill C-36, the *Anti-Terrorism Act* (Syeed, 2004: 25). In fact, the author of the submission, legal counsel to the Coalition of Muslim Organizations, was right in suggesting that until 11 September Muslim individuals and organizations in Canada rarely monitored or were concerned about the actions or words of community members. But they have begun to see how the words or actions of a few can implicate all and affect their perception by other Canadians. This is an undeniable reality. Indeed, we are increasingly witnessing in the West the formation of a diasporic impulse among the earlier and new migrants of Muslim cultures who collectively carry the insinuatingly negative identity marker of 'Muslim.' They are Muslims, regardless of the fact that many, at least until recently, did not care to identify themselves with Islam or be identified as such by others. Hence, the emergence of the notion of 'Homo-Islamicus,' as the Syrian philosopher Sadeq Jalal al-Azm would have it, a concept similar in its mystification to the Western concept of 'Homoeconomicus.'

The point is that Muslims in the West today, like Africans historically, have become another prime example of a population against whom 'ethnic absolutism' is applied, and with destructive effects. Under the stimulus of an intense political struggle, the maximization of cultural differences has very quickly turned into a dangerous essentialization, demonizing Muslim believers – indeed, anyone who comes from Muslim societies, regardless of the extent of their religious adherence and the nature of their beliefs, their variability as individuals, and the variety of cultures from which they originate. One of our respondents clearly points to this frustrating fact:

> [Since] September 11, we are all identified with Islam. Islam targeted my identity as a human being to reduce it to Islam only, but I do not identify with that. And I have tremendous difficulty with this because I see [that], after September 11, our younger generations are being forced or made to become Muslims. I mean they have found their identity in Islam as a way to oppose the U.S. policies. I have a dear friend who is gay. After these events he now says, 'I am a Muslim too.' How on earth can that be? I tell him, 'If you go to Iran now, they'll put you in a bag and throw you over a cliff. What kind of Muslim are you?' And this is only because he feels his opposition to [the mainstream] is best shown through identifying with Islam. (Iranian male)

The point is that, as Phil Cohen (1999: 2) suggests, 'race' can become 'ethnicized' and ethnicity 'racialized' so that these factors 'can be used interchangeably in a way that allows their respective elements of fixity and permeability to be conjugated into more subtle idioms of attribution than either, on their own, could achieve.' In the same way the notion of a monolithic and unchanging 'Islam' can become psychologically fixed as the anchor of opposition, fitting the needs of an aggressive agenda among political leaders in the West.

As in the case of Africans who became identified with physical misery, degradation and slavery, the long, intimate, and violent history of Islam's encounters with the West is now condensed into a symbolic construction with enormous psychological power – Islam as a wellspring of backwardness and religious fanaticism, hateful of women, and yet a shimmering seduction: a permanent enemy. Hence, while the primordialist idea of identities embedded permanently in specific populations has been pretty much abandoned in most writings on ethnicity, it survives, oddly, in writing on cultural groups linked to Islam (Moghissi, 2006). This reflects, perhaps, the influence of a persistent Orientalism as well as the mounting 'politicization of cultures,' as Mahmoud Mamdani (2004) calls it.

It is this situation of ideological polarization that has propelled efforts towards identification and the formation in the West of a group identity among migrant populations who originate from Muslim-majority societies. In other words, we are witnessing the rapid formation of an overarching, collective identity or group affiliation that disarticulates each of these communities from its specific origins, instead uniting them all as a nominally homogeneous 'Muslim' population. The marked national and ethnic diversity of these groups, along with their distinct political histories, cultures, and languages, suggests that it is neither nostalgia for a homeland, real or imaginary, nor the sudden discovery of Islam's moral and ethical values that motivates these populations to join together, but rather a commonality in the sense of being deported to the culture of not belonging, of becoming a permanent target for stereotyping and bigotry. It is this deep sense of insecurity and wounded pride that sometimes leads to reactions – in some cases blown out of proportion, as we saw most recently, in the case of the infamous Danish cartoons that lampooned Prophet Mohammed and outraged some Muslims – or the development of a culture of victimhood that is skillfully manipulated by Muslim extremists. This process is further deepened and made even more troubling for persons of Islamic background when coinages such as 'Islamic fascism' are flaunted in a cynical way to polarize populations and to wring from these anxieties political advantages for leaders in the West (Pollitt, 2006; Cloud, 2006).

We are suggesting that rather than being an expression of cultural nostalgia, the formation of a collective identity and solidarity in the diaspora more often manifests a response to political frustration and the blossoming of deep-seated resentment to the continuing colonial and neocolonial aggression against Muslim societies, accentuated by an inhospitable climate in the new country. Perhaps this explains the emergence of a new enthusiasm for 'Islam' among some diaspora youth, many of whom have never seen their ancestral homeland and whose parents, despite a hesitant or hostile reception in the new country, have often found a positive side to the migration experience. An observer of the growth of youth attraction to Islam and the flourishing of Muslim associations and mosques in Toronto asserts, for example, that teenagers coming from secular or nominally Muslim parents are increasingly influenced at school by fellow students with rigid fundamentalist views. Hence, it is not unusual to see students from Shi'a backgrounds drawn to Sunni fundamentalist views (Soltanpour, 2005).

The tendency among this younger generation, even among those living under economically favourable conditions, to identify with an idealized 'Islamic world' or 'Islam' that is much more conservative, unforgiving, and intolerant than that actually practised by the overwhelming majority of Muslims, reflects a sense of belonging that grows from an urgent need to connect with people who, despite their internal differences and divisions as individuals or communities, share political objections to the West's hegemonic role, as well as the experience of social and cultural exclusion. In this way, under the pressure of their own isolation, and angered by the aggressive turn in global politics, including the unapologetic foreign interventions in the Middle East, a growing number of Muslims in the West have become participants in the shaping of a frightening and distorted 'Islam' that is then presented back to them as their own identity. That is to say, the shift to a heightened 'Muslim' identity does not represent increasing adherence to Islam as an answer to spiritual and religious needs, but to Islam as a powerful ideological tool of resistance – indeed, in the absence of a viable, anti-racist, and leftist movement, it is practically the only force that appears to effectively challenge global power structures and systems of domination.

Within this context, the racialization of Muslims creates the need for connections, support and solidarity. But one must be cautious because not all communities of Islamic culture and, certainly, not all individuals within each community respond to social pressures and racism uniformly. As our study shows, some communities express the need for group connections and support of the collective more than others. For some, it can prompt devotion to Islamic identity; and along with that, goes the possibility that the commitment can be manipulated by Islamists in pursuit of their own political goals. Another approach is to try to create self-sufficient and self-sustaining support services and networks and to minimize one's encounter with the dominant culture and its institutions, without feeling the need to accent one's 'Islamic' identity. This can lead to affirming ethnic identifications, but without a religious spin. However, as participants in the study often say, the secular response is less widely known. There is pressure on those who never thought of themselves as religious at home to brand themselves as Muslims or to allow this identity to be forced upon them. The result is frustration – and, for some, self-imposed isolation and debilitating exclusion from the larger society. Opposition develops to moderating ideas and practices that otherwise might help break down stifling gender and age hierarchies.

The bleak truth is that the relationship between communities of Muslim culture and dominant cultures in Canada and other countries in the West has changed. This needs to be acknowledged. But even more urgent is the need to abandon the fixation on 'Islam' as the most important factor in defining private and public behaviour, social expectations, and aspirations, for this results in a narrowing of perception and leads, inevitably, to an unbalanced focus on differences between nominally 'Muslim' and non-Muslim citizens and migrants. It also obscures the dynamics that reside within each community of Muslim origin, ignoring the factors that accentuate division. Undoubtedly, there are practices among populations of Muslim background that are explicitly faith-based and robust in their effects. Cross-national movements such as the annual hajj to Mecca, communications within the Sufi orders, and the massive and enterprising South Asian movement, Tablighi Jama'at, have a strong influence, with Tablighi appealing particularly to youth (Cherribi, 2003; Sardar, 1995; Bowen, 2004; Afshar, Aitken, and Franks, 2006).

Also undeniable are the strong and, in some cases, aggressive attempts by leaders of mosques and various Muslim associations to extend their control over the migrant populations from Muslim majority countries. Their efforts include exhortations regarding public exhibition of religious observance and demands for 'accommodation' regarding dress and dietary codes, the importing of conservative imams and the exporting of radical recruits to conflict zones in the Middle East and South Asia. Some of these practices make the presence of Muslims more visible in Canada, as elsewhere throughout the West. They also spread fear among non-Muslims everywhere, posing challenges to policies of integration and assimilation. But what escapes attention is that there are even larger sections in the diaspora that are secular and *not* religious – not practising Islamic ritual or following dietary laws, or not believing, or simply not having the time, the means, or the desire to maintain a religious identity in their new country. The majority, for personal or political reasons, are silent observers of the activities of the first group that bargains with the state for concessions and religious accommodation that the majority often oppose. The silence of this group, as Akeel Bilgram (2003) argues, relates to a long history of colonial subjugation and to condescending attitudes by the West, which have created a deep-seated 'moral psychology' that homogenizing ideologies and policies and discriminatory practices only reinforce. It is this psychology of resentment that sometimes helps to mobilize even secular or moderate Muslims against the larger society.

Moreover, although the conservative agenda for the 'Islamification' of social life in the diaspora and the influence of Islam as a potent symbol of political protest can no longer be overlooked, Western governments have been prepared to accommodate the demands of the conservative Muslim elite, thereby exaggerating the distinctiveness of Muslim religious and cultural practices rather than addressing the serious, long-standing concerns expressed by the majority. Their interest, lavished on Muslim cultural practices, speaks to their reluctance to understand and honestly redress the genuine grievances of Muslim populations relating to discrimination in the job market, housing, and access to social services or to take seriously the signs of marginalization of these populations reflected in the growth of self-contained religious spaces and networks, Muslim associations, and mosques and religious schools. They prefer not to see that many of these institutions, as repositories of punishing age and sex hierarchies, deepen the burdens and physical vulnerability of women and girls, thus further isolating Muslim diaspora from the larger society. Media reports about outbreaks of senseless violence among migrant youth in Germany and France, cases involving the gruesome murder of young women at the hands of male relatives in Sweden and Germany, a recent tragic case in

Toronto, and terrifying reports of the rape of young girls in Parisian North African-Arab neighbourhoods may reflect rare exceptions.[1] But these are uncomfortable symptoms of the way in which a chilly and tormenting reception by the larger society can push some members of a migrant community to torment their own in turn, turning the sharp points of frustration and anger against young women and girls accused of turning their backs on their cultural heritage by trespassing its male-defined and male-protective moral boundaries.

On the Methodology of This Research

To conduct this research, we used a comparative method employed within a systemic framework. The use of a systemic framework meant that instances were examined as parts of an integrated whole and not in isolation. This allowed for the comprehensive study of the totality of parameters affecting the status and behaviour of individuals and communities.

The focus in this study is on the four communities living in Canada, and an effort is made to point clearly to the ways in which the Canadian setting shapes the possibilities for integration of communities from Muslim-majority societies in a special way. We start from the premise that the experience of immigrants has many dimensions, and that it cannot be reduced to a single element, such as religion. Also, the Canadian case is distinctive, given the variety of national and ethnic backgrounds of this population, and the fact that (apart from exceptions noted in chapter 5) almost all of the young people in our sample arrived in this country with their families and the great majority of them still live with their parents and siblings. As noted below, the majority of questionnaires, the principal investigative instrument, were administered in Canada.

Starting from the singularities exhibited in Canada, however, selective comparisons with communities of Muslim-majority origin in other countries allows us to sharpen and nuance our understanding. The comparative method provides us with the tool to record similarities and differences in the experience of immigrant and refugee communities in different countries. Among areas of focus in the comparison have been changes in gender and family relations and the situation of youth, as well as changes in cultural affiliation and ethnic and religious identity. Another focus has been on the political and policy consequences of these changes.

Figure 1.1   The interrelated dimensions of the research

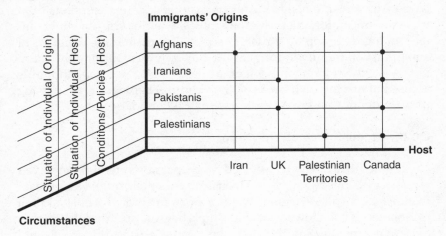

The four communities – Afghans, Iranians, Pakistanis and Palestinians – that participated in this research were each studied in Canada and in one other setting: Afghans in Iran; Iranians and Pakistanis in the United Kingdom; and Palestinians in the Israeli-occupied territories. This framework is depicted in figure 1.1, which helps us understand similarities and differences in the experiences of the four communities in different receiving countries.

As shown in the model, each community was examined in relation to the 'circumstances' or conditions that affect the behaviour of individuals. These circumstances were divided into three groups. The first two sets relate to characteristics of individuals who participated in the study: (1) the 'situation of the individual in the country of origin,' involving variables at home such as social background and family status, urban or rural origin, level of education, type of occupation, and income; and (2) the 'situation of the individual in the receiving country,' involving variables in the new setting such as type of occupation, education, and income. These characteristics were considered in relation to demographic variables such as gender and age. In addition to 'hard,' demographic and socio-economic data, 'soft' factors such as individual attitudes, perceptions and beliefs were also taken into consideration. Finally, these economic and demographic variables and the individual beliefs, attitudes, and perceptions accompanying them were considered in relation to a third set of variables, (3) the 'conditions and policies of the receiving country,' including main trends in the country's socio-economic development and its refugee, immigration, and settlement policies.

In figure 1.1, these three classes of characteristics are shown, together with the four cases treated in Canada and the comparator cases for each community in Iran, the United Kingdom, and the Palestinian Territories. Thus, conditions in the sending country, conditions in the receiving country, and the policy and developmental environment in the receiving country provide us with the main framework for the study.

A word should be added on the role of the comparator cases. As noted, the main focus in this study is on Canada and on the comparison, within Canada, of the four cases. But the comparison of experiences in each of the four Canadian communities with those in parallel communities in other countries also provides us with the opportunity to assess the impact on members of diaspora groups of strategic cultural and socio-economic developmental factors, and differences in policy. The sites selected encompass pronounced differences as well as similarities with regard to level of socio-economic development, political systems, cultural norms, and settlement and integration policies. For example, Britain, like Canada, receives a large migrant population, a sizable part of which comes from Muslim-majority countries. In both countries, relations between various ethno-racial groups are regulated through official multicultural policies, and both countries are also comparable in terms of their levels of social, economic, and political development. However, Canada and the UK are quite different in terms of the configuration of their Muslim populations, the level of these Muslim populations' ethno-cultural diversity, their class backgrounds and histories of settlement. As compared with Canada, Muslims in the UK have lived in the country longer, are more homogeneous, and are more working class.

General sentiments towards Muslim populations are also different in each country. Compared to Canada and the UK, Iran and the Palestinian territories – while different in terms of level of socio-economic development – present cultural settings that are similar in terms of the relatively homogeneous religious and language settings encountered by refugee and migrant communities. The task, theoretically, was to separate the effects of cultural factors from the material conditions arising from minoritizing circumstances encountered by diaspora in each of the receiving countries or, in the Palestinian case, to sort out the cultural from the material effects of dislocation and disfranchisement in the homeland.

These factors are considered further in chapter 7. Here it is noted, for example, that while persons of Muslim background have been subjected to a willful and systematic process of cultural essentialism throughout the West, the incidence of hate crimes in Canada directed against them has been relatively smaller than in the United Kingdom. As well, a comparison of Afghans in Canada with the substantial body of Afghan refugees in Iran also sheds light on the question of whether living in a country which is culturally, religiously, and linguistically similar to one's own (as is the case for Afghans in Iran) will lead to stronger integration, or whether other factors – for example, the economic wealth of the receiving country, the level of international support for receiving refugees, or the presence or absence of a tradition of ethnic tolerance – will be more determining. These comparisons help clarify the distinctiveness of the Canadian case.

Each community in this study was considered as a *system*, a relatively integrated whole with some degree of cohesion and with a set of interrelated *subsystems* that operate within a larger environment, or *suprasystem*. The subsystems for each community include families and individuals as well as institutions such as religious organizations, workplaces, community media, and schools. Within these subsystems and in the community as a whole, individuals were differentiated on the basis of factors such as gender, age, and class, as well as level of education and occupation. Finally, at a higher level, the supra-system included the culture and social norms of the receiving society, the economic situation, and government policies. Open in structure, each system was considered as interacting with its subsystems and supra-systems, affected by them, and, in turn, influencing them.

The data were collected using several research instruments, including administered questionnaires, oral interviews, and focus groups organized with select community members, social workers, and informed individuals in the community. Content analysis of community publications, study of organizations within the communities, and census data analysis were also part of the study. Since we could not base our work on a 'list' of Muslims from which to randomly choose respondents (no such list exists!) and because community members, under pressure, were also quite unlikely to respond to a random call, we could not rely on probability sampling. Instead, we sought to construct a representative sample using traditional 'snowball' methods and within that, through quota sampling, to make sure that we had an appropriate representation of respondents based on age, gender, and class. Our sample frame started by defining individuals in diaspora as those who had moved from the originating country to the new country (Canada, the United Kingdom, Iran, Jordan, or the West Bank and Gaza) no less than two years earlier, either directly or via a second country. Our samples included individuals aged fifteen years or older, born of Muslim parent(s), whether practising or not, and declaring themselves to be of Muslim background (as contrasted, for example, with Palestinian Christians). A separate youth questionnaire was prepared for unmarried individuals fifteen to twenty-two years old. Both men and women, in equal numbers, were participants in the research. All conjugal categories – married, single, common-law status, cohabiting, separated, divorced, and widowed – were included in our sample. The category of 'social class' in the sample frame reflected the respondents' varying social backgrounds, although it relied on the report concerning level of income.

All together, 2,350 questionnaires were administered by trained interviewers from winter 2001 through spring 2004, and were regularly spot-checked to insure reliability. The vast majority of the samples for the quantitative analysis were from Canada, which was the focus of the analysis, and most of those were from Toronto and Montreal, where the overwhelming majority of Canadian Muslims live, along with smaller numbers from Vancouver. In other settings, 94 questionnaires were filled out for Iranians in the UK, 97 for Pakistanis in the UK, 133 for Afghans in Iran, and 149 for Palestinians in the Occupied Territories and in Jordan. As for in-depth interviews, 60 were carried out in Canada, and about 10 for each of other settings. Also 10 focus groups, each comprising at least 8 participants, were organized. Most interviews were in English, but questionnaires were also available and administered in Farsi, Farsi-Dari, Arabic, and Urdu. To avoid the lapse into essentialism, emphasis was given throughout to the differentiated and complex web of class, ethnic, gender, religious, and regional factors that help define relations in the diaspora. The geographical spread of the study and its comparative scope meant that a developed organizational structure was required and that workshops were needed to establish ethical guidelines and provide training for interviewers. Community members and graduate students involved in the project participated in the design of the questionnaire, and coordinators from each community were appointed to oversee data collection in each area. The questionnaire was pretested in each community within Canada and in the comparator countries. Channels for communication and feedback on the research instruments and conduct of the work were established early and maintained throughout the study. Once we eliminated spoiled questionnaires, we were left with 2,229 questionnaires, which were entered into our database. The modal age for male and female respondents falls within the interval, thirty to thirty-nine years old; the great majority of adult respondents were married (about 70 to 85 per cent, depending on the group); most (over 67 per cent) reported having children; and most of those reporting income earned in the range of $20,000–$39,999, although substantial numbers of Afghans (particularly females) reported individual and household incomes under $20,000.

Community-focused research has its challenges and its rewards. It can be enjoyable and enriching as well as emotionally and mentally exhausting. Getting to the stage of writing this book means that we managed to survive the inevitable or needless stresses involved in conducting our research. In the end, what will remain with us will be the enormous reward of feeling that the research has been a tool for analysing and exposing interactive factors and power relations that keep people from realizing their full humanity. It is our hope that over time this knowledge, in association with similar studies, will help dismantle disempowering factors and relations.

We live in a climate of deep emotional turbulence and psychological challenge, where religious doctrine and enthusiasms seem to provide an escape from the disturbing qualities of the prevailing political climate. Whether imaginary or real, many individuals of Muslim cultural background in the West today feel threatened by a climate of fear, suspicion, disdain, and hostility in their new countries. It is also clear that these issues, at the most personal level, are experienced particularly within the domain of the family and in intimate relations, both between spouses and between parents and children. These family relations are often emotionally intense.

The family in diaspora provides a crucible and often serves as a critical point of condensation. It can offer comfort and personal support that helps people endure a difficult situation in the new country, providing them with strength to cope with new challenges. But families can also sustain retrogressive and patriarchal values, reinforcing a sense of separateness and a punishing isolation from the larger society. Like other institutions, the family can serve as a site for contradictory impulses. It can simultaneously encourage integration in the larger society while at the same time encouraging feelings of psychological apprehension and unease. These concerns are discussed in chapter 3. But it is clear that the family will play a crucial role in how one remembers the homeland and anticipates life in the new country and thus powerfully affects one's readiness to adapt new cultural and religious values, or to hold onto and even deepen a commitment to old ones, including values hostile to gender justice and equality between the sexes.

Another crucial pivot is the relation between life within the diaspora community and the larger state and society. The question that automatically comes to mind is whether a qualitative change in the relationship between Muslim diaspora and this larger world is attainable. Perhaps it is, but it will depend on a reconsideration of public policies that regulate and manage minority communities, pushing them into designated professions and mini-Tehrans, Karachis, Kabuls, and Cairos on the outskirts of Western metropolises – and then taking pride in having provided these communities with 'their own neighbourhoods' for cultural and religious practices. Generally, such policies do not foster integration but rather tend to cordon off areas, demarcating boundaries. They can also encourage a sense of fearful self-exclusion. Rather than establishing understanding, mutual respect, co-existence, and fruitful cooperation, such policies can reinforce a potentially embittering division of labour between the groups who drive, serve tables, and clean up after others, and the groups who enjoy upper-class professional life, social recognition, and wealth.

Perhaps the most fruitful way of thinking about such populations in any Western society would be to shift the focus away from the ways and means of integrating or assimilating Muslims to the ways and means of recognizing, accepting, and profiting, economically and culturally, from the presence of all minority populations, including communities with Muslim cultural backgrounds. The receiving societies need to realize that Muslim cultural practices and traditions, along with demands for public recognition and respect as equal citizens, do not comprise the much feared threat to the lifestyle and cherished values of liberal democracies in Canada, Europe, and elsewhere that some believe. The real threat comes when religious practices and traditions are followed self-consciously and resentfully and are used as political statements against the values and practices of the new society. This is when they can be skilfully manipulated for larger political goals by absolutists or fundamentalists from within these communities, with unpredictable consequences. To avert such threats, there is a need to 'de-essentialize' Islam and Muslims, as Talal Asad would have it, and to seriously and continuously interrogate the institutions and relations that attack peoples' sense of self-worth, agency, and dignity. To that end, there is a need for adoption of serious and forcefully implemented anti-racist multicultural policies that can address inequalities and erase the residue of colonial mentality that engenders the treatment of Muslims locally and globally in crucial areas of economic, political, and social lives. That is to say, there is an urgent need for Western states to come up with something better for their growing Muslim populations than legal documents granting residency, citizenship, and work permits or, for that matter, the adoption of official multicultural policies. They should also put aside their short-sighted policies, for the sake of gaining votes, of giving concessions to the conservative minority religious leaders who claim to represent the 'Muslim community.'

There is a need to strike a better balance between integration policies that protect religious freedom and the rights of ethnic and religious minorities to their cultural practices while making sure those public policies do not undermine principles of universality in defining citizens' rights and of equality before the law and in the law. Members of diaspora also have their part to play. As Iranian novelist Nasim Khaksar writes, the process of migration or seeking asylum often represents a sort of rebirth – a terribly slow and painful rebirth that is accompanied by an internal resistance and by an unbearable loss of identity. This sense of loss is particularly acute for migrants or refugees from the Third World, writes Khaksar (1999), as their identity often finds reality in the eyes of the recipient country only through the names of dictators and autocrats from whom they have escaped. In such environments, the dislocated individual may feel that his or her existence is being ignored. She or he has been thrown into 'the globe,' but still stubbornly refuses to be globalist, clinging to an identity that is local and thus remaining an Iranian, an Afghan, a Chilean, or a Colombian. The road to finding or accepting and living with the new identity, Khaksar suggests, passes through accepting the reality of the change, getting to know the new world to which one is reborn, and being fed by it and trying to feed it in return.

2 Community Profiles, Social Origins, and Status

This chapter presents data related to the social and economic status of the four populations in Canada and in other settings, providing a general background for the four communities surveyed – Afghans, Iranians, Pakistanis, and Palestinians. For Canada, in addition to the data of our own samples, we have used social indicators drawn from the 2001 Census (the last census to provide data on ethnicities) that include the size and demographic characteristics of each community, levels of education, and immigration trends.[1] Economic indicators cover rates of labour-force participation, employment, and levels of income, including income composition and the incidence of low income.

It is important to note that the Canadian census data provide information on ethnic communities based on their country of origin and not on their religious affiliations. In any case, not all members of the four communities are Muslims; therefore, adherents of other religions, including Christians, Jews, and Bahais – as well as a large number of secular non-religious individuals – are included in the census figures. This is particularly noticeable in the case of Palestinians in Canada, a significant number of which are Christian. Our samples in the present study, however, cover only individuals who originate from Muslim families in these communities.

It should also be noted that the Palestinian population in Canada is, in fact, larger than the number provided in the 2001 Census, as many Palestinians in the past were designated only as 'Arabs' migrating to Canada from a second country and thus not counted as Palestinians.

Figure 2.1   Size of the immigrant population of the four communities and periods of immigration

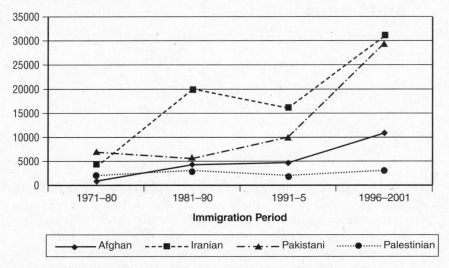

Immigration Period

```
———◆——— Afghan    – – –■– – – Iranian    — · –▲· — Pakistani    ·······●······· Palestinian
```

Source: Statistics Canada, Census 2001, Data Matrix 97f0010xcb01040.

The Four Communities in Canada –
Afghans, Iranians, Pakistanis, and Palestinians

Census Data

In the first section we look at data drawn from the Canadian census and compare them with related items in our study in order to establish the representativity of the study.

SIZE AND PERIODS OF IMMIGRATION

Iranians form the largest group among the four communities (88,225), followed by Pakistanis (74,010), Afghans (25,230), and Palestinians (14,680). The largest number of the four groups came to Canada in the 1996–2001 period: over 73 per cent of Afghans, about 66 per cent of Pakistanis, and 54 per cent of Iranians. Only Palestinians show a lower level of immigration (28.2 per cent) in the same period, as shown in figure 2.1.

Our samples in the four communities show more or less the same trend in immigration. A significant number of surveyed community members (about 42 per cent of Afghans, 50 per cent of Iranians, and 41 per cent of Pakistanis) arrived in Canada in the 1990s. The figure is lower (about 19 per cent) for the surveyed Palestinians. The 1980s were particularly significant for Afghans, 51 per cent of whom arrived in Canada during that time.

In terms of legal status in Canada, the vast majority of the surveyed communities are citizens. Over 74 per cent of Afghans, about 69 per cent of Iranians, over 57 per cent of Pakistanis, and 86 per cent of Palestinians fall into this category. Smaller percentages are landed immigrants: 22.4 per cent of Afghans, 28.4 per cent of Iranians, 38.8 of Pakistanis, and 11.7 of Palestinians are in this category. A very small number of Afghans, Iranians, and Pakistanis are convention refugees (1.54, 1.18, and 1.19 per cent, respectively). It should, of course, be noted that a much larger number of them came as refugee claimants to Canada, and even few among the Afghans and Pakistanis surveyed have illegal status in Canada.

Age and Gender. There are more males than females in each of the four communities (this was also the case for the 1996 Census data). The Palestinian community has the largest gender gap, with 8.9 per cent more males (7,995 males versus 6,685 females), while the Afghan community has the smallest gap, with 2.5 per cent more males (12,930 males versus 12,300 females).

Compared to the Afghan community, the gender gaps for all age groups are more pronounced for the Iranian, Pakistani, and Palestinian communities. The age groups 15–24, 25–44, and 45–64 show larger gender gaps in each of the communities.

All four communities are relatively young. In 2001, the populations in each community predominantly comprised those between 25 and 44, more or less similar to the 1996 Census. The Iranian and Pakistani communities have relatively higher numbers of people in this age group: 32,445 for Iranians and 24,820 for Pakistanis, compared to 7,940 and 4,380, respectively, for Afghans and Palestinians. The second most populous age group for Pakistanis and Palestinians is 0–14, while for the Iranians it is 45–64. The Afghan community's most populous age group is 0–14, followed by 25–44. Overall, 50 per cent of the individuals in each of the four communities are aged between 15 and 44.

Our samples in the four communities show more or less the same gender and age structure. Of our samples in Toronto and Montreal, about 52 per cent are male and 48 per cent female. The majority of those surveyed are 20–39 years of age; over 57 per cent of Afghans, 47 per cent of Iranians, 54 per cent of Pakistanis, and 53 per cent of Palestinians surveyed fall into this age group. Only small percentages of each community (14 per cent of the Afghans, 17 per cent of the Iranians, 15 per cent of the Pakistanis, and 18 per cent of the Palestinians) are above the age of fifty.

Marital Status. The most noticeable trend, indicated in the 2001 Census, is that the majority of the population fifteen years and older in each of the four communities is married. At 63 per cent, the Pakistani community has the highest proportion, followed by Afghans with 57 per cent and Iranians with 54 per cent. Palestinians have the lowest proportion (52 per cent) of married people. By comparison, the 1996 Census data indicated that the majority of members in the four communities were single (56 per cent of Afghans and Palestinians and 52 per cent of Iranians and Pakistanis). Five years later, however, the statistics indicate a shift from majority single to majority married. This shift is likely due both to the marriage of the then young single population (those in 1995 who were in the 15–19 and 20–39 age groups) and to the arrival of more married immigrants to Canada in the 1996–2001 period; the shift also reflects the increasing financial stability of the four communities.

The proportion of divorced individuals among the four communities is well below the Canadian average of 9 per cent. The Iranian community has the highest rate of divorce (5 per cent), while Afghans have the lowest (1 per cent). The percentages for separated, divorced, and widowed in each community are about the same in both the 1996 and 2001 censuses, with women more than men represented in the separated and divorced categories in both data sets. We also see more married men than women in all four communities. For example, according to the 2001 Census, there were 19,780 married males and 18,085 married females in the Iranian community. If we were to assume that people tend to marry within their own communities, then in this example, there is a 'surplus' of at least 1,695 Iranian males who either married outside the community or left their spouses behind in their country of origin.

The marital status of the samples in our study also reflects a very high percentage of married people and a very low percentage of divorcees and separated respondents. Of the 1,313 adult surveyed in Toronto and Montreal, about 76 per cent of Afghans, over 73 per cent of Iranians, over 86 per cent of Pakistanis, and over 76 per cent of

Figure 2.2   Education levels of the four communities in Canada, percentages

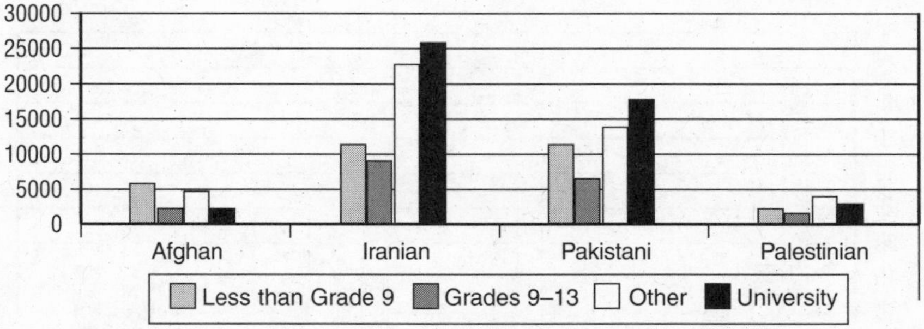

Source: Statistics Canada, Census 2001, Data Matrix 97f0010xcb01041.

Palestinians are married. The percentages of divorcees are very similar to the census data, with Iranians having the highest (6.5 per cent) and Afghans the lowest (less than 1 per cent). The percentage of separated individuals is higher among Afghans (4.5 per cent) and lower among Pakistanis (less than 1 per cent). Also, over 78 per cent of Afghans, 74 per cent of Iranians, over 80 per cent of Pakistanis, and about 76 per cent of Palestinians have children. Afghans have the largest family size, with 18 per cent having three children, over 10 per cent having four, and 12 per cent with five or more. The surveyed Iranians have the smallest family size, followed by the Palestinians and Pakistanis.

Education. The Canadian census provides data for the educational levels of the population fifteen years of age and above. As shown in figure 2.2, the four communities surveyed have a relatively high level of post-secondary education. Iranians have the highest level of university education (37 per cent of the community), followed by Pakistanis (36 per cent), Palestinians (32 per cent), and Afghans (16 per cent).

Men generally have higher levels of university education than women. The gender gap in the educational profile of the communities also existed in 1996. Iranian males are the most educated and Afghan females are the least educated among the four communities. As shown in figure 2.3, the most educated women are the Iranians, followed by the Pakistanis.

Since education data covers people aged fifteen and over, we can use the 'less than Grade 9 level' figures as a proxy for the population's lack

Figure 2.3   Education levels of the females of the four communities in Canada, percentages

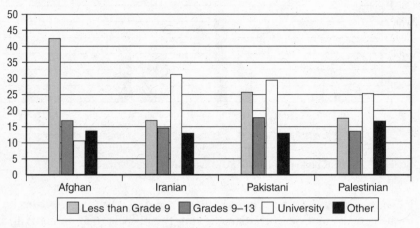

Source: Statistics Canada, Census 2001, Data Matrix 97f0010xcb01041.

of access to adequate education. For example, 15 per cent of Iranian men have a 'less than Grade 9 level' of education, compared to 17 per cent of Iranian women. Also, 16 per cent of Palestinian men have a 'less than Grade 9' level of education, compared to 18 per cent of Palestinian women. The data also indicate that 18 per cent of Pakistani males and 26 per cent of Pakistani females, along with 33 per cent of Afghan males and 43 per cent of Afghan females, did not have access to adequate education.

As will be discussed shortly, our samples also have a relatively high level of education, but this varies by community.

Employment. Figure 2.4 shows the *participation rate* (ratio of labour force to the population and the indicator of those legally eligible to work), the *employment rate* (ratio of the employed to the population), and the *unemployment rate* (ratio of unemployed to the labour force) in percentage terms.

The employment indicators show that among the four communities, Afghans have both the lowest participation rate (52.6 per cent) and the lowest employment rate (43.7 per cent). This could be a consequence of the previously observed lower education levels of the community. On the other hand, the Iranian community has the highest employ-

Figure 2.4   Employment indicators for the four communities in Canada, percentages

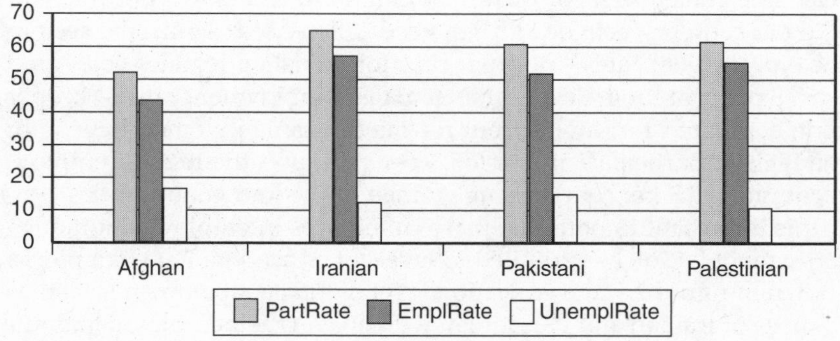

Source: Statistics Canada, Census 2001, Data Matrix 97f0010xcb01040.

ment indicators, with a participation rate of 65.7 per cent and an employment rate of 57.4 per cent, possibly a reflection of the previously noted high levels of education. The participation rate of the Pakistani and Palestinian communities is 61.2 per cent and 62.1 per cent, respectively, while their employment rates are 52.3 per cent and 55.5 per cent.

The average unemployment rate shown in the census for the four communities, however, is quite high, at about 13 per cent, as compared with the Canadian unemployment rate of 7.4 per cent. Yet the unemployment rates for the four communities under study are lower than the average unemployment rate for Muslims in Canada, which is 14.3 per cent. (Diaspora, Islam, and Gender Project, 2005: 4, 11). The exception is the 17 per cent unemployment rate for Afghans.

The employment indicators bring out the gender bias previously noted in education. Women in the four communities have much lower participation rates and much lower employment rates. For example, among males, Pakistanis have the highest participation rate (75.3 per cent), and among females, Iranians have the highest participation rate (57.3 per cent). Females of the four communities show higher unemployment rates than men, except for Palestinian females (10.2 per cent for females versus 11.2 per cent for males). Conversely, Afghan women, at 21.4 per cent, have the highest unemployment rate. The male–female difference in employment indicators is most obvious when considering the Afghan and Pakistani communities, whose women have the lowest indicators. The participation rate of Pakistani females is 44.8 per cent and that of Afghan women is 40.9 per cent, while the percentages for their male counterparts are 75.3 per cent and 63.6 per cent, respectively. Pronounced differences can also be seen in the employment rates – 36.8 per cent for Pakistani females compared to 65.8 per cent for males. Afghan females' employment rate is 32.1 per cent, compared to 54.6 per cent for males. Iranian women have both the highest participation rate (57.3 per cent) and the highest employment rate (48.3 per cent) among women of the four communities.

It is important to note that these differences in employment indicators cannot be solely attributed to levels of education. For example, as shown in figure 2.3, the education level of Pakistani women is similar to those of Iranian and Palestinian women, yet their employment indicators are much lower. This means that internal factors, such as religious and marital attitudes within the community, as well as external factors, such as racial biases in the larger society, influence the lower rates of employment for Pakistani women.

The census also provides data on types of occupation on the basis of industry classification (NAIC), and the occupational classification (NOC), both of which more or less show horizontal specializations such as manufacturing, construction, retail trade, or business, health, social sciences, the arts, and so on. On this basis, the dominant occupation category for all four communities in Toronto, where most of these communities reside, is sales and service occupations (38 per cent for Afghans, about 27.8 per cent for Iranians, 25.3 per cent for Palestinians, and 22.3 per cent for Pakistanis). Other occupational categories prevalent among the four communities are management, business (such as financial auditors, financial and investment analysts, specialists in human resources, and professional occupations in business services), and trades (see figure 2.5). Smaller numbers are involved in health and social sciences, which also include government services. In the processing occupations, mostly blue collar, there is more involvement of the Afghans (10.8 per cent) and Pakistanis (11.4 per cent), compared with Iranians (4.1 per cent) and Palestinians (4.2 per cent). The distribution in the corresponding data from the cities of Montreal and Vancouver are very similar.[2]

The proportion of the population within each community that does not have any specialization that would place them in the category of skilled worker is quite noticeable. This is measured through the 'unskilled labour index' (in each community, the population aged

Figure 2.5   Occupations of the four communities in Toronto, both sexes, percentages

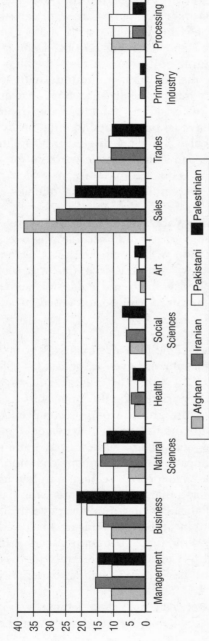

Source: Statistics Canada, Census 2001, Data Matrix 97f0010xcb01042–3.

fifteen and above with 'no education' or 'some high school education,' calculated as a percentage of the total population aged fifteen and above). Compared to the other three communities – with 71.3 per cent of its population aged fifteen and above having no post-secondary qualifications – the Afghan community in Toronto displays the highest value for this index, followed by the Pakistani community with 45.2 per cent. The community with the most specialized labour force, and therefore the lowest proportion of 'unskilled' labour, is the Iranian community, where 43.6 per cent have no post-secondary qualification. The unskilled labour proportions also show a clear gender bias, illustrated by the higher proportion of unskilled female workers for all communities. The exception is the Iranian community, in which the proportions of unskilled labour force among males and females are roughly the same.

Despite the fact that the numerical values of the index are relatively high for the four communities, the figures are lower than the overall average of the 'unskilled' population of the major cities of Toronto (52.3 per cent), Montreal (54 per cent), and Vancouver (50.9 per cent). The exceptions are Afghan men and women and Pakistani women. The occupation of the samples surveyed will be discussed in later chapters.

Income. The average employment income for Palestinians, Pakistanis, and Iranians is above $37,000 – Palestinians have the highest ($43,988) and Afghans have the lowest ($24,340).[3] The higher Palestinian incomes may be due to several factors, including the longer history in Canada of a larger percentage of the group. Compositional effects must also be considered – Palestinians have a higher percentage of males than other communities, and males tend to have higher incomes. The lower levels of education of the Afghan community could be a contributing factor to their lower average employment incomes. However, it should be noted that the Palestinians, who have a lower level of education than Pakistanis and Iranians, nevertheless have a higher average employment income. Again, this may be due, in part, to the fact that (as shown earlier in fig. 2.1) larger numbers of Iranians and Pakistanis immigrated to Canada more recently (between 1991 and 2001), and because they have less 'Canadian experience,' they typically earn lower incomes.

In terms of the discrepancy between male and female average employment incomes, figure 2.6 shows that the males in all four com-

Figure 2.6   Average employment income levels by gender for the four communities in Canada, in CDN dollars

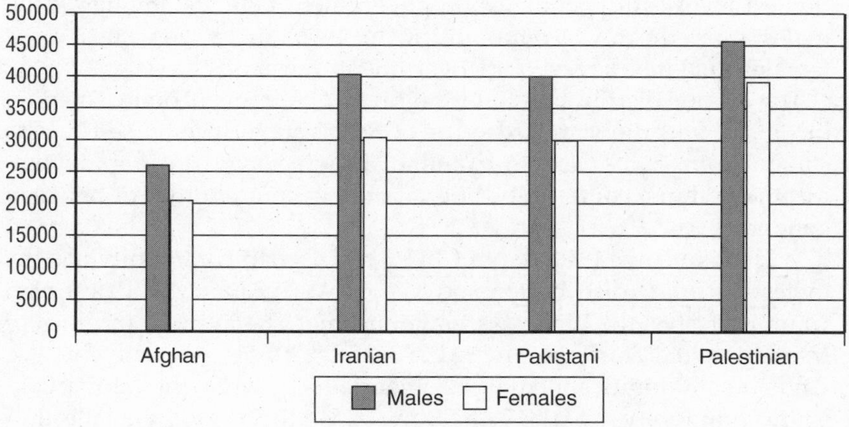

Source: Statistics Canada, Census 2001, Data Matrix 97f0010xcb01043.

munities have higher average employment incomes than the females, with the difference being most pronounced in the Iranian and Pakistani communities, at $9,779 and $9,912, respectively. Here again, the gender gap in average employment incomes cannot be completely attributed to differences in levels of education, as the differences in education between males and females of the Iranian and Pakistani communities are similar to those of the Palestinian community, which has a smaller income gap ($6,922) between males and females.

Individual incomes could be entirely from employment, government benefits or other sources. The majority of the population in each of the communities earns its income from employment sources. Low levels of education and employment rates for a community can translate into greater reliance on government benefits. The Afghan community has the highest level of dependence on government benefits at almost 21 per cent. The reliance of other communities on government benefits is lower, averaging at 8 per cent.[4]

Women of all communities receive a higher proportion of government benefits. Over 36 per cent of Afghan females and 23 per cent of Pakistani females receive government benefits, compared with 21 per cent of Afghan males and 8 per cent of Pakistani males. The percentage of Iranian females on government benefits is 15.4, compared to 7.7

per cent of males, while the percentage for Palestinian females is 12.7 per cent, compared to 7.7 per cent of males. Afghan males have the highest levels of dependence on government benefits among all the males from the four communities. In 1996, there were also more females than males receiving government transfers.

The income distribution figures represent average incomes,[5] median incomes,[6] and the standard error of the average income series. The standard error[7] is used to examine the dispersion in employment income within a community, but not among communities or between genders.

With an average income of $13,196, the Afghan community has the lowest income[8] distribution indicators. At $23,078, the Palestinian community has the highest average income. The average incomes of Iranians and Pakistanis are $21,238 and $20,156, respectively. The Afghan community's median income is $9,637, while that of the Pakistani community is $11,847, the Iranians is $12,733, and the Palestinians is $12,848. One observation to note is that the Afghan community, with the least difference between its average and median income, has more income equality than any of the others.

Females in all of the communities have lower average and median incomes than males. Additional data could help explain these inequalities, apart from the already mentioned differences in education levels. Again, Afghan females have the lowest average income ($10,240), followed by the Pakistani females ($13,211), the Iranians ($15,953), and the Palestinians ($17,559). Among males, Palestinians have the highest average income ($27,181) followed by Pakistanis ($25,611). The average incomes of Iranian and Afghan males are $25,430 and $15,725, respectively. The Pakistani community has the greatest difference in average income between males and females, with the average gender gap in income amounting to $12,400.

In terms of 'low-income incidence,' which is defined as the proportion or percentage of economic families[9] or unattached individuals in a given classification below the 'low-income cut-offs,'[10] the Afghan community has 61.5 per cent of its population below this level. They are followed by the Pakistani community at 41 per cent and the Palestinian community at 35.5 per cent. The Iranian community is better off than the others according to this data, with only 34.7 per cent of its population living below the low-income cut-off (Diaspora, Islam, and Gender Project, 2005: 14–15).

The low-income incidence between males and females is similar for

Table 2.1 Household income of the respondents

Income	Afghans	Iranians	Pakistanis	Palestinians
Under $20,000	19.38	9.17	11.64	0.63
$20,000–$29,999	18.46	12.13	14.03	3.17
$30,000–$39,999	15.69	14.2	14.03	6.67
$40,000–$49,999	10.46	13.91	15.22	17.78
$50,000–$59,999	4.62	8.58	7.76	9.21
$60,000–$69,999	4.0	5.92	5.07	5.08
$70,000+	1.54	17.16	11.94	8.89
Not applicable	5.54	5.03	1.19	0.95
No answer	20.62	14.5	19.1	47.62

all communities. The only community in which the low-income incidence of females is lower than males (meaning that there are more
males below the income cut-offs than females) is the Palestinian, in
which there are 35.3 per cent females and 35.5 per cent males below the
low-income cut-off.

The household income data collected from our own sample (table
2.1) also reveals that sizeable percentages of the respondents' incomes
fall below the low-income cut-offs. The very low percentage of the
Palestinians is due to the fact that over 47 per cent of respondents in
that community did not answer the income-related question. In terms
of higher income categories, Iranians have the largest percentage of
individuals earning incomes of $70,000 or more (17.16 per cent), fol-
lowed by Pakistanis (11.9 per cent).

Overall, the census data and our samples show similar characteristics for the four population groups under study. The population of the
four communities, most of whom immigrated to Canada during the
1990s, is young, with the majority aged between twenty and thirty-
nine, with more males than females, and with the majority married
with children. All four communities have a relatively high level of
post-secondary education – much higher than the national average –
with females being less educated than males. There also exists a high
rate of unemployment, also much higher than the national average,
with a noticeable gender bias, as women's participation and employment rates are lower than those of men. In terms of income, all of the
communities derive their income predominantly from employment,
and there is less reliance on government benefits.

Data of the Surveyed Communities in Canada

This section deals with the general profile of the samples in our study, including rural/urban origin, family background, and social status before leaving their native country, as well as changes that have taken place in their social status. As in other chapters, the data focuses on Toronto and Montreal, where the vast majority of the immigrants in Canada live.

URBAN/RURAL ORIGIN

The members of the surveyed communities mostly originate from urban areas, even though there are differences among the communities, perhaps partly related to different degrees of urbanization in the originating countries. For example, according to 2004 United Nations data, over 34 per cent of the 157.3 million people living in Pakistan resided in urban areas, whereas about 67 per cent of Iran's population of 69.3 million was composed of urban residents. In Afghanistan, with a population of 24.9 million in mid-2004, 24 per cent lived in urban areas.[11]

Over 98 per cent of Iranian males and females in our study come from cities, followed by Palestinians (78 per cent male and 76 per cent female), Pakistanis (over 70 per cent male and 80 per cent female), and Afghans (67 per cent male and 81 per cent female). Overall, Afghan and Pakistani men have a larger proportion (about 23 percent) who immigrated originating from rural areas. The average figures for both men and women of Afghan and Pakistani origins are, however, lower (about 16 and 15 percents, respectively).

These figures are different for the younger immigrants (fifteen to twenty-two years of age). Young Afghan males, in particular, have a much higher percentage of individuals originating from rural areas (over 26 per cent, as compared to 8.5 per cent for young Pakistani males, 2.3 per cent young Palestinian males, and zero per cent for Iranian males). The reason for this is that the war in Afghanistan, the Soviet occupation, the subsequent period of Mujahedeen and Taliban rule and, eventually, the American-led invasion, seriously disturbed rural areas of Afghanistan.

The overwhelming majority of the adults studied in these communities were born in their homeland. The exception are adults in the Palestinian community. As a result of dispersions after the establishment of the State of Israel, a sizeable percentage of Palestinians were born in other countries. Among the older respondents, about 72 per cent of Palestinian men and 47 per cent of Palestinian women were born in their original homeland, and the rest were born in Jordan, Lebanon, and other Middle East countries, as well as in the United States and Canada. Over 92 per cent of Pakistanis, 98 per cent of Afghans, and almost 100 per cent of Iranians were born in their country of origin.

The vast majority of the adults in each of the four communities grew up and were socialized in their place of birth (over 92 per cent of males and over 88 per cent of females). A larger number among the younger members of these communities grew up in other places, including Canada. For example, 50 per cent of young Afghan males and over 65 per cent of young Afghan females grew up in a place other than their city of birth.

FAMILY BACKGROUND

There are similarities and differences among adult respondents in the four communities surveyed with regards to their parents' levels of education and types of occupation and their family backgrounds. The majority of the respondents come from urban, middle-class backgrounds. Their fathers have mostly 'medium' or 'high' levels of education, ranging from a high school diploma, a college certificate, to university baccalaureates and graduate degrees. About 23 per cent of the Afghan respondents' fathers have a 'high' education level (i.e., having completed university). The figures for the Iranian and Palestinian respondents are over 26 and 25 per cent, respectively. The Pakistani figure seems unusually high, with about 51 per cent of the respondents' fathers reported by their children to have attained a university-level education. The figure for the female Pakistani respondents is even higher (about 65 per cent). Over 40 per cent of respondents' fathers in other communities have a 'low' educational background (no education, elementary, or some high school education). Again, by exception, 17.6 per cent of Pakistanis fall in this category.

The mothers' educational levels, however, are 'low' for all four communities, with about 80 per cent of the mothers of the Afghan respondents, about 60 per cent of those of the Palestinians and Iranians, and over 55 per cent of Pakistani mothers not having a high school diploma, having only elementary schooling, or no education at all.

As for the occupation of the parents, the majority of the respondents' fathers come from the new urban middle-class (the *salariat*) in

Figure 2.7   Fathers' occupations in the country of origin, percentages

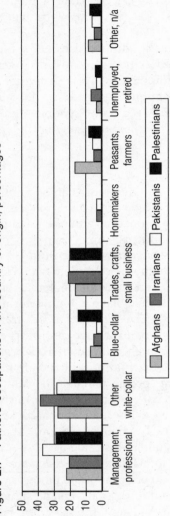

their countries of origin. Over 51 per cent of Afghan, about 60 per cent of Iranian, 65 per cent of Pakistani, and 48 per cent of Palestinian fathers are reported by their children to have had managerial, professional, and other white-collar occupations, ranging from doctors and lawyers to civil servants, military personnel, teachers, and technicians. Next to these occupations, the largest percentages came from trades, crafts, and small businesses. Over 16 per cent of Afghan, over 21 per cent of Iranian, and about 20 per cent of Pakistani and Palestinian fathers were in these professions. Much smaller percentages of the fathers of the four communities had blue-collar occupations, and even smaller numbers were peasants and farmers. Afghan fathers had the largest percentage of peasants and farmers (over 17 percent). Figure 2.7 depicts the distribution of the fathers' occupations in the four communities.

The occupation of the vast majority of mothers is identified as homemaker; over 73 per cent of Afghan, 69 per cent of Iranian, 79 per cent of Pakistani, and 77 per cent of Palestinian mothers fall into this category. The next largest categories, particularly for Iranian mothers (21 per cent), are managerial, professional, and other white-collar jobs. The percentages in these categories are 7 per cent for Afghan, about 11 per cent for Pakistani, and over 13 per cent for Palestinian mothers.

Figure 2.8   Respondents' education level before leaving their country of origin, percentages

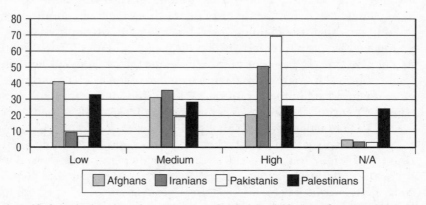

Low: No formal education, elementary, some high school; Medium: Completed high school, certificate or diploma, uncompleted BA; High: BA, uncompleted post-BA, graduate degree; N/A: Not available.

STATUS IN THE COUNTRY OF ORIGIN

More or less in line with the social status of their parents (fathers in particular), the majority of the respondents come from the urban middle classes, with medium to high levels of education and the occupational backgrounds of the *salariat*.

As shown in figure 2.8, more than 70 per cent of the Pakistanis and about 51 per cent of the Iranians left their respective countries with a BA degree or with some post-graduate education or degree. These figures are lower for the Afghan and Palestinian respondents (about 22 and 13 per cent, respectively, have a university education). The very low figure for Palestinians relates to the fact that about 24 per cent of the respondents did not answer this question.

The same trend is more or less observable for the level of education of spouses in the country of origin. That is, about 50 per cent of the Pakistani and 38 per cent of Iranian respondents' spouses report having a university education. The figures are much lower for Palestinian (15 per cent) and Afghan (10 per cent) respondents.

As for the occupational status of respondents in the country of origin, figure 2.9 shows that sizeable percentages (over 58 per cent of Iranians, and 53 per cent of Pakistanis, as opposed to over 39 of Afghans and over 18 per cent of Palestinians) come from managerial, professional, and other white-collar occupations. Generally, smaller percentages of the respondents are in blue-collar occupations. The same is true for trades, crafts, and small businesses. Given that the respondents are predominantly from urban areas, the percentages of those with peasant and farmer backgrounds are also very limited.

A relatively large number of respondents from the four communities fall into the category of student, which is related to these populations' young age. This is particularly true of Afghans and Palestinians, about 32 per cent and 44 per cent of whom, respectively, were students in their countries of origin. A smaller percentage of the four communities were unemployed in their countries of origin: about 8 per cent of Pakistanis, 5 per cent of Afghans, 3 per cent of Iranians, and less than 1 per cent of Palestinians surveyed fall into this category.

We can also see a similarity in the spouses' occupations in their country of origin, to varying degrees. A sizeable percentage worked in the white-collar occupations – about 50 per cent of Iranian and 46 per cent of Pakistani spouses, and 29 percent of Afghan and 15 percent of Palestinian spouses. Homemakers constituted the second-largest occupational category for spouses, with over 17 per cent of Pakistani, 11 per

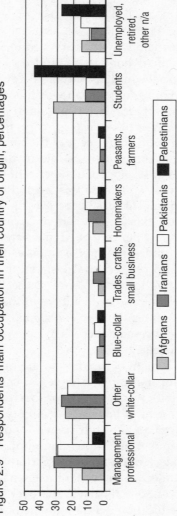

Figure 2.9   Respondents' main occupation in their country of origin, percentages

cent of Afghan, 8 per cent of Iranian, and 3 per cent of Palestinian spouses falling into this category.

Some respondents from the four communities reported having had a second job – about 12 per cent of Afghans, 13 per cent of Iranians, 12 per cent of Palestinians, and 5 per cent of Pakistanis.

WHY THEY LEFT THEIR ORIGINAL HOMELAND

A variety of reasons explain why the surveyed individuals in the four communities had left their homelands, and it is hard to single out which of the factors was the most important. Because of different political and economic conditions in the originating countries, the responses vary significantly for each community.

Escaping political persecution was a very important factor for Afghans and Iranians, with 40 per cent of the first group and over 32 per cent of the second choosing it as one of the main reasons for leaving their countries of origin; about 8 per cent of Pakistanis and 22 per cent of Palestinians also mention this factor. Religious persecution seems to be a less significant reason for leaving – 8 to 9 per cent of Afghans, Iranians, and Pakistanis and about 2 per cent of Palestinians mention this factor. Over 4 per cent of Afghans and 8 per cent of Iranians identified gender and sexual persecution as the main reason for leaving, while less than 1 per cent of Pakistanis and close to 1 per cent of Palestinians cited this factor. Violence in the family was another reason for smaller percentages of members in the four communities, ranging from about 4 per cent for the Pakistanis, almost 3 per cent for Iranians, and about 1 per cent and less than 1 per cent, respectively, for Afghans and Palestinians.

War, civil war, and foreign occupations were major factors for emigration, particularly for the Afghans (over 83 per cent) and the Palestinians (over 51 per cent); war was a factor for over 10 per cent of Iranians and about 3 per cent of Pakistanis. Military service was a main reason for close to 20 per cent of Afghans and for over 5 per cent of Iranians. A significant number in all four communities left their country of origin because of a lack of economic opportunities. This was one of the main factors for almost 24 per cent of Afghans, over 36 per cent of Iranians, over 47 per cent of Pakistanis, and over 64 per cent of Palestinians. Pursuing an education was a main factor for over 11 per cent of Afghans, over 30 per cent of Iranians and Pakistanis, and over 32 per cent of Palestinians. A better future for their children was also an important factor for over 24 per cent of Afghans, over 54 per cent of

Iranians, about 50 per cent of Pakistanis, and about 35 per cent of Palestinians.

The majority of those surveyed had come to Canada as landed immigrants. Close to 50 per cent of Afghans, 64 per cent of Iranians, 67 per cent of Pakistanis, and 67 per cent of Palestinians fall into this category. Many, particularly among Afghans and Iranians, had come as refugees. About 25 per cent of Afghan men, 23.8 per cent of Afghan women, 14.2 per cent of Iranian men, and 15.2 per cent of Iranian women entered as convention refugees. These percentages are smaller for Pakistani men and women (5.03 and 3.9 per cent, respectively), and for Palestinian men and women (5.1 and 5.2 per cent, respectively). Smaller percentages in all of the communities had come to Canada sponsored by their spouses or parents.

THE REASONS FOR COMING TO CANADA

The reasons the surveyed populations chose to come to Canada are multiple and vary from one community to another, and again it is hard to single out which factor or factors was the most important. A significant number of respondents (over 44 per cent of Afghans, over 63 per cent of Iranians, over 59 per cent of Pakistanis, and over 68 per cent of Palestinians) said they had heard good things about Canada. More or less equal numbers had chosen Canada for better living standards and job prospects. Many came to Canada because they had relatives in this country – over 48 per cent of Afghans, about 40 per cent of Iranians, over 36 per cent of Pakistanis, and 50 per cent of Palestinians.

An easier immigration process compared to other countries was another reason given by the respondents. Over 40 per cent of Afghans, Iranians and Pakistanis, and over 59 per cent of Palestinians, gave this reason for choosing Canada as their new country of residence.

Smaller percentages had come to Canada as a result of arranged marriages. This factor is more varied for the four communities and for men and women; over 13 per cent of Afghans and over 14 per cent of Palestinians, as opposed to 4 per cent of Iranians and 8 per cent of Pakistanis gave this reason, with a higher percentage of women (except for Palestinians) than men falling into this category. A very small number of respondents, with the exception of Afghans, came to Canada as students and chose it as their new country of residence upon completion of their studies. Among the other reasons given, some mentioned that they had no other option.

Data from Settings outside Canada

The selected four communities outside Canada are different in terms of size and length of time of their formation. Pakistanis in the UK represent a youthful, growing, and economically disadvantaged community. The 1991 UK Census was the first to include a question specifically regarding the ethnic origin of individuals. The total population in England and Wales in 1991 was 50.88 million. Of these, some 469,000 individuals (about 0.9 per cent) said they were Pakistani. In the 2001 census, the total population had increased to 52.04 million. The number of Pakistanis had nearly doubled to 714,800 (about 1.4 per cent) (ONS 2005a: 42, table 17).[12]

These numbers convey an impression of the rapid growth of the Pakistani population in the UK but understate the visibility of the group; Pakistanis are densely concentrated in the Manchester, West Yorkshire, West Midlands, and Greater London areas. In 2001, for example, some 74,885 persons self-identifying as Pakistanis lived in the Greater Manchester Urban area, including 5,811 in Bolton, 23,169 in Manchester, and 12,864 in Oldham; 111,949 in West Yorkshire (58,801 in Bradford); 131,844 in West Midlands (103,573 in Birmingham, some 6.9 per cent of the local population); and 153,479 in Greater London (20,644 in Newham, 5.9 per cent of the local population) (ONS 2004a[13]: table KS06).

The experience of the Pakistani population lags behind the UK economy, taken as a whole. In the UK the percentage of households whose income fell below 60 per cent of median disposable income gradually climbed from about 13 per cent in 1961 to a high in 1991 of just over 21 per cent, and then tapered off in 2003–4 to 17 per cent (ONS, 2004b: 79, fig. 5.17).[14] For Pakistanis and Bangladeshis, however, 63 per cent of households received incomes less than 60 per cent of the median disposable income in 1995–6, and this figure still stood at 58 per cent in 2000–1. The Pakistani/Bangladeshi low-income rate more than doubled the low-income rates for black populations, Caribbean and non-Caribbean (ONS, 2001c: table 5.22). In 2001–2, only 4.4 per cent of employed Pakistanis were in the higher managerial and professional group (about the same percentage as Caribbean blacks and only about a third of the rate for 'Other Asians') (ONS, 2001d: fig. 4.14); by contrast, 16.1 per cent of Pakistanis (as against 4.7 per cent of whites) were unemployed in 2001–2, a percentage which rose to 24.9 per cent for individuals aged 16–24 (ONS, 2001e: fig. 4.20).[15]

Reflecting concern over the Muslim and Pakistani populations' size and economic vulnerability, the British Home Secretary announced in an official visit to Pakistan in 2008 that the UK Muslim population now numbered about 2 million (up from the 1.6 million in the 2001 Census); that more than one third were dependents, under age 16; and that 43 per cent of Muslims outside London were Pakistani (Travis, 2008).

As for Iranians in the UK, the census does not provide separate data and classifies Iranians in the 'other-other' category, which is made up of a number of ethnic groups, including North Africans and Arabs. In 1991, there were 32.2 thousands Iranians, excluding the 'children born to Iranian parents' and 'those whose immigration status was unclear.' According to Spellman (2004: 38), the 2001 Census recorded that 40,767 Iranians lived in England and Wales.

At the time of the survey, there were 2.3 million Afghan refugees in Iran. The majority, or 1.4 million, were male, and over 43 per cent were under the age of seventeen.[16]

The Palestinian refugees in the Occupied Territories provide a uniquely different example. Palestinian refugees in the West Bank, Gaza, and Jordan, like other Palestinian refugees in other camps, are part of several flows of displaced populations resulting from the Arab–Israeli wars of 1948 and 1967 and subsequent conflicts and confrontations. The vast majority of Palestinian refugees in the region are under the auspices of the United Nations Relief and Works Agency (UNRWA), which was created to deal with massive Palestinian refugee problems.[17] There are also 'unofficial' camps recognized by UNRWA. The 1951 Convention Relating to the Status of Refugees does not cover Palestinians under UNRWA's protection, with the exception of those who were expelled from their lands after 1967 and who are covered directly by the UNHCR (Elsayed-Ali, 2006). In some countries, such as Lebanon, there is another category of Palestinian refugees, known as 'non-ID' refugees who live in the worst possible conditions.

Many Palestinian refugees were dislocated more than once, particularly from the West Bank to Jordan. Since the West Bank was under Jordanian occupation after the 1948 war and until 1967 when Israel occupied it, the new population of Palestinian refugees from the West Bank included hundreds of thousands of the so-called displaced persons. Samples for the present survey were taken from West Bank, Gaza, and Jordan, and from among the camps, villages, and cities. A smaller number was also taken from inside Israel's Shaab Palestinian-Israeli village, where a major proportion of the population consists of refugees.

For the four communities studied in these settings, the sample frames chosen were similar to those in Canada in terms of demographic characteristics such as gender, age, and marital status. Over 64 per cent of Afghans surveyed in Iran are between twenty and thirty-nine years of age. Over 42 per cent of Iranians and 45 per cent of Pakistanis in the UK also belong to this age group. For the Palestinians surveyed in the Palestinian Territories, this age category is much lower (about 11 per cent). Overall, the Palestinian sample focuses on older Palestinians living in refugee camps who were dislocated between 1948 and 1967. Their average age is thus much higher than for other groups in the study.

As for marital status, comparable to the situation in Canada, the vast majority of the respondents are married (over 91 per cent of Afghans in Iran, and 86 per cent of Pakistanis in UK). These percentages are lower for Iranians in the UK (about 60 per cent) and Palestinians in the Occupied Territories (69 per cent). The majority of Afghans and Pakistanis, similar to the communities in Canada, were married in their countries of origin. The percentages for divorced and separated respondents are very low across the four communities.

One important difference between communities surveyed in and outside of Canada relates to the urban/rural origins and social status of the respondents. That is, the percentages of those coming from rural areas are higher elsewhere compared with their counterparts in Canada. Over 26 per cent of Afghans surveyed in Iran, as compared with about 16 per cent in Canada, come from rural areas. This is also the case for Pakistanis in the UK, over 20 per cent of whom have rural origins, as compared with 11 per cent in Canada. However, similar to Iranians in Canada, none of the Iranians surveyed in the UK have rural origins.

As for the social origins of their families, with the exception of Iranians in the UK, the vast majority of the other communities have traditional middle-class, peasant, and trades and crafts origins. This is different from their counterparts surveyed in Canada, the majority of whom come from new middle-class (*salariat*) families. Over 37 per cent of Iran-based Afghan respondents' fathers were peasants, compared to 17 per cent of Afghans in Canada. This is the case more clearly of Palestinians in the Occupied Territories, over 51 per cent of whose fathers were peasants, compared to 7.9 per cent of the Palestinian respondents in Canada.

The percentages of fathers with blue-collar professions are also much higher compared with those in Canada, particularly for Afghans in Iran and Pakistanis in the UK: over 14 and 24 per cent, respectively, as compared with about 6 and 2 per cent, respectively, of their counterparts in Canada. As for the mothers' occupations – with the exception of Iranians and Pakistanis in the UK, about 14 and 15 per cent of whom, respectively, said their mothers were in professional and other white-collar occupations – the vast majority in the four communities were homemakers. The parents' levels of education are also lower compared to the analogous figures for Canada. This is particularly true of Afghans in Iran and Pakistanis in the UK. Overall, the four communities surveyed outside Canada, to varying degrees and with some exceptions, come from less privileged classes.

Social Status in the Country of Origin

Similar to the social status of their parents, individuals from the four populations outside Canada had lower levels of education in their countries of origin; larger percentages of them were engaged in traditional middle-class occupations, with higher percentages being peasants. This is particularly the case for Palestinians in the Occupied Territories and Afghans in Iran (over 20 per cent and 8 per cent, respectively, as compared to 1.3 and 1.9 per cent for their counterparts in Canada). As well, the percentages for managerial and new middle-class (*salariat*) professionals and other white-collar workers are much lower for respondents outside Canada. For example, as shown in figure 2.10, while over 39 per cent of Afghans, over 58 per cent of Pakistanis, over 52 per cent of Iranians, and over 18 per cent of Palestinians in Canada were in managerial, professional, and other white-collar occupations in their countries of origin, the percentages for their counterparts in each community surveyed outside Canada are about 20, 37, 22, and 2 per cent, respectively.

We also see a big difference in the level of education achieved in the countries of origin between the communities in Canada and in other settings, as the four populations in Canada had much higher levels of education before leaving their countries of origin compared with their counterparts elsewhere. For example, over 68 per cent of Afghans in Iran had a 'low' (less than high school diploma) level of education before coming to Iran, as compared to about 42 per cent of Afghans landing in Canada. The differences are much bigger for Pakistanis and Iranians. The percentages of those with 'low' levels of education in the

Figure 2.10   Managerial, professional, and other white-collar occupations in Canada and other settings, percentages

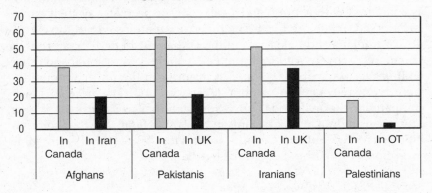

Figure 2.11   'High' levels of education in Canada and other settings, percentages

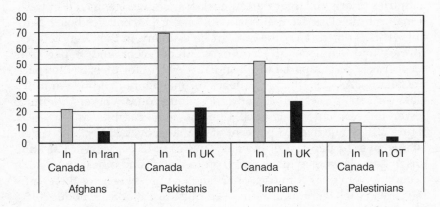

two communities in the UK are over 30 and 25 per cent, respectively; the comparable figures for Canada are about 6 and 9 per cent, respectively.

Also, a much smaller percentage of the four communities outside Canada have a 'high' (university) level of education. That is, at the time of this study, 7.6 per cent of Afghans in Iran and less than 1 per cent of Palestinians in the Occupied Territories had 'high' levels of education. The figures for Pakistanis and Iranians in the UK are higher (22.5 and 26 per cent, respectively), which is still way below the percentages of their counterparts in Canada, which are about 51 and 70

per cent, respectively. For a comparison of the 'high' levels of education in the countries of origin of the respondents in Canada and in
other settings, see figure 2.11.

Education and Employment

Like their counterparts in Canada, the surveyed communities outside
Canada strive hard to adapt to new conditions. All four communities,
to different degrees, have pursued further education in their new
countries of residence. Over 30 per cent of Afghan men and over 46
per cent of Afghan women in Iran pursued education at different
levels. As for Pakistanis in Britain, over 45 per cent of men and over
67 per cent of women furthered their education. These figures are
lower for Iranians in Britain (over 29 per cent men and over 35 per
cent women), partly because on average they already had a higher
level of education in their country of origin. The figures are also lower
for Palestinians in the Occupied Territories (over 38 per cent for men
and over 19 per cent for women), partly because of the age difference
in the samples taken from Palestinian refugees who, as explained
earlier, were older.

The community members pursued their educations at different
levels. Data varies significantly from one community to another,
between genders, and in comparison to their counterparts in Canada.
For example, 16.6 per cent of Afghan men surveyed in Iran cited university-level education, and about 5 per cent cited graduate-level. The
number of Afghan women in Iran who entered university was much
lower (6.9 per cent), with a much smaller number entering graduate
level (1.3 per cent).

The figures for Pakistanis and Iranians in the UK who have pursued
university-level education are much higher, particularly for Iranians.
Over 44 per cent of Iranian women and about 36 per cent of Iranian
men surveyed in the UK continued their education at this level, many
of them completing graduate degrees (over 18 per cent of the men and
over 17 per cent of the women). Over 20 per cent of Pakistani men and
23 per cent of Pakistani women surveyed in the UK also furthered
their education at the university level. As for Palestinians in the Occupied Territories, over 16 per cent of men and 3.9 per cent of women
surveyed continued their education at this level.

Comparatively, the percentages of those pursuing their education
in Canada compared with their counterparts in other settings are
lower for both men and women across the four communities, with the

exception of Palestinians: respectively, 8.6 and 4.3 per cent for Afghan men and women; 28.3 and 13 per cent for Iranian men and women; and 18.7 and 10.2 per cent for Pakistani men and women. The figures for Palestinians are 29 and 25.2 per cent, respectively, for men and women. This is partly because members of these communities in Canada already had a higher percentage with university education in their home country. However, the figures for those seeking certificates and diplomas at the college level were much higher for both men and women in Canada for all the four communities. Compare, for example, the 18.8 per cent of Afghan men and 17.4 per cent of Afghan women in Canada to the 1.3 per cent of men and 5.5 per cent of women in Iran. This might reflect a tendency in Canada to secure some sort of technical and practical training in order to enhance one's chances in the job market. Another explanation is that opportunities for attaining such training are more readily available in Canada than in Iran. Besides, the Iranian government's resettlement policy has been a paternalistic protection of a population whose stay in the country is considered as temporary. Hence, it provided only the basic survival needs for Afghan refugees; in Canada, however, the presence of Afghan refugees and migrants was not considered temporary either by the government or by the Afghans themselves. The attempt to acquire education and technical training was, therefore, geared towards opportunities in the job market and towards building a new life in the adopted country.

More or less similar to the situation of their counterparts in Canada, the levels of education and types of occupation in the original countries, along with whether or not further education has been achieved in the new country of residence, have had an impact on the type of profession individuals could enter. Generally, compared to Canada, a smaller percentage of people surveyed in the other areas came from managerial, professional, landowner, and business backgrounds. For example, none of the Afghans in Iran came from managerial, landowner, and business occupations in their country of origin, and only 6.9 per cent of Afghan men came from professional backgrounds (doctors, lawyers, engineers, etc.). The percentage for professional Afghan women was even lower (2.7 per cent). The comparable figures for Afghans with professional backgrounds in Canada were 16.4 and 5.8 per cent, respectively, for men and women. Also, none of the Palestinians surveyed in the Occupied Territories came from managerial, landowning, business, and professional backgrounds; about 2.9 per cent of Pakistani men and no Pakistani women in the UK were from managerial backgrounds, and about 20 per cent of Pakistani men (and no Pakistani women) had professional backgrounds. Canadian Pakistanis surveyed, however, had much higher percentages in these categories: 12.6 per cent of men and 3.4 per cent of women had managerial backgrounds, and 27.6 per cent of men and 11.3 per cent of women came from professional backgrounds. The percentages for managerial and professional backgrounds for Iranians in the UK were relatively higher and more similar to their counterparts in Canada. That is, about 10 per cent of men and 3.8 per cent of women were in managerial positions, and about 15 per cent of men and 11.5 per cent of women were in professional categories.

The percentages for 'other white-collar' occupations (civil servants, military personnel, teachers, technicians, etc.) were also relatively lower for the communities surveyed outside Canada. About 1.3 per cent of Palestinian men and 2.6 per cent of Palestinian women in the Occupied Territories, along with 13.8 per cent of Afghan men and 18 per cent of Afghan women in Iran, came from these categories. The percentages for Pakistanis in the UK were 8.7 for men and 12.8 per cent for women. These percentages, at 21.7 and 15.3 per cent, respectively, were higher for Iranian men and women in the UK.

The percentages of those with peasant or small farmer background were noticeably high among Palestinians, Afghans, and Pakistanis surveyed outside Canada; 28.7 per cent of Palestinian men and 11.8 per cent of Palestinian women and 12.5 per cent of Afghan men and over 4 per cent of Afghan women were peasants before displacement. The figure for Pakistani men was 11.7 per cent. Also, a much smaller percentage of those surveyed in the four communities outside Canada came from blue-collar backgrounds. The same is also true of trades, crafts, and small businesses, which will be discussed below.

In their new countries of residence, the small percentage of those with 'managerial, professional and business occupations' have done relatively well and could continue to work in more or less similar occupations. For 'other white-collar workers,' as shown in figure 2.12, smaller percentages of Afghans and Iranian men with such occupational backgrounds have found jobs in the same categories. Iranian and Pakistani women and Palestinian men and women have increased their percentages in this category.

In a situation similar to their counterparts in Canada, however, a larger number of those surveyed in other settings moved to blue-collar

Figure 2.12   Other white-collar workers in country of origin and in new country of residence, in other settings, percentages

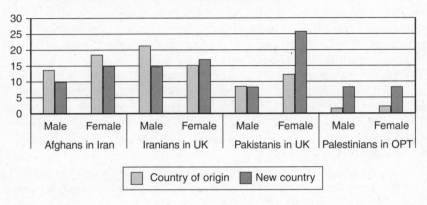

Figure 2.13   Blue-collar occupation in country of origin and in new country of residence, in other settings, percentages

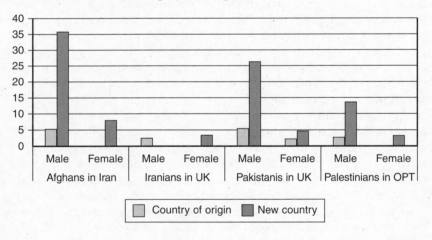

occupations. This is particularly true of Afghans in Iran and Pakistani men in the UK. The same is true of trades, crafts, and small businesses, and a higher percentage of those surveyed moved into these occupational categories (see figs. 2.13 and 2.14.).

In many cases, community members who had high levels of education and came from middle-class backgrounds had moved into blue-collar jobs. Typical of the sexual division of labour, the percentages of

Figure 2.14   Trades, crafts, small businesses in country of origin and in new country of residence, in other settings, percentages

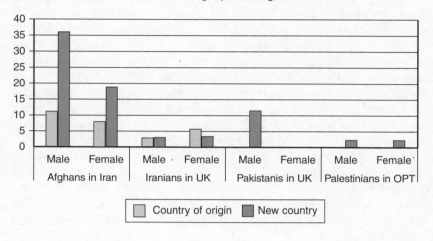

Figure 2.15   Homemakers in country of origin and in new country of resi-dence, in other settings, percentages

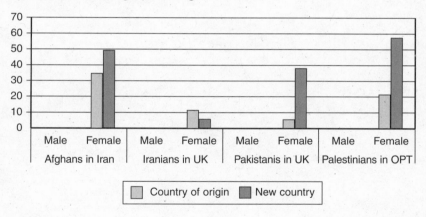

homemakers, as shown in figure 2.15, also grew for all women of the communities surveyed, except Iranian women in the UK.

Comparing the profiles of the four diasporic groups in Canada and elsewhere, the Canadian sample clearly represents more people with higher levels of education in their countries of origin and a larger number of people with professional and other white-collar occupations compared with their counterpart communities surveyed in other countries. It may be argued that some sort of pecking order could be at work in the 'choice' of which country to go to. That is to say, those who are better off have a better chance of moving to a more prosperous place. The most obvious case relates to Afghans in Iran and in Canada. The more educated and financially secure had better chances of moving to Europe and North America, while those with lesser means did not have much choice other than moving to neighbouring Iran and Pakistan. At the same time, the different class composition of the four communities in Canada compared with their counterparts in other settings, as reflected in levels of education and types of work at the point of departure, might explain the better opportunities and stronger sense of contentment and belonging that we observed among the four populations in Canada (which will be discussed in subsequent chapters).

3 Family and Spousal Relations in Diaspora

Family, whether it is the main domain of cultural norms, values, and practices or a protected space that insulates the immigrant or exile from public watch and interference, is nonetheless affected by changes in life circumstances. How the changes are processed and absorbed or made the subject of a continuing internal contestation differs for individual families, depending on social and economic conditions and other interactive factors that negatively or positively influence the process of adjustment. Many migrants or refugees, and particularly younger individuals, while valuing aspects of their formative cultural practices and mores, gradually become as selective in engaging with their ethnic communities and identifying with their ancestral cultures as they are in dealing with the social and cultural practices of the larger society. Some who find a liberatory quality in separation from the old culture begin to reassess the social relations, cultural values, and practices of their home country through newly detached and dispassionate eyes. Yet, for many others, the sense of eternal loss not only does not recede with the passage of time but also may even intensify as hopes fade for building a new home, making new friends, and enjoying a satisfying life in the new country.

There is a more or less common response to the changing circumstances among those who have left a productive and rewarding life behind and who are unable to pick up from where they left off or start a different but equally satisfying life in the new country. This response is a permanent nostalgia and resentment, and a psychological need to set up a new frame of reference by connecting to a community or to past or revaluated cultural beliefs and practices – as if this new frame constructs a sense of belonging and reconnects them to the imaginary 'lost paradise' in their homeland. The role of family and the quality of family relations are central to this process. Family can represent either a comfort zone or a conflict zone to the individuals involved. Studies of various migrant communities point to the negative impact that social isolation and loneliness in the new environment has on spousal relations. Many have suggested that men and women process the experience of migration and resettlement differently and that these differences become a continuous source of tension within the diasporic family (Grmela, 1991; Nassehi-Behnam, 1991; Kocturk, 1992; Afshar, 1994; Eastmond, 1993; Buijs, 1993; Moghissi, 1999; Moghissi and Goodman, 1999; Ashrafi and Moghissi, 2002; Husain and O'Brien, 2000). With displacement and cultural change often comes an attempt to reassert traditional values and escalating conflict within the family, particularly if men feel they are losing control. Generally, women are suggested to be more likely than men to find migration to be a 'catalyst for change' in their search for independence and sense of identity. Once the reality of exile and the need to adjust to new conditions have been established, they may welcome the change from strictly controlled gender roles within the family and the reduced pressures coming from the extended family and from society at large. In a study of Iranians in the United States, for example, 'oppressive constraints in traditional societies' is mentioned as the reason that Iranian women are 'more eager than men to depart from traditional norms.' If this eagerness is not shared by men, or at least not accepted at a similar pace, researchers argue, it can jeopardize the dynamics of mate selection and conjugal relationships (Hojat, Shapurian, Foroughi, et. al., 2000).

A major task in the process of this research was to examine whether men from the communities of Muslim cultural backgrounds in this study – Afghans, Iranians, Pakistanis, and Palestinians – are indeed more predisposed than women to be stuck in nostalgia for their known and familiar culture, with its clear-cut gender roles and sex and age hierarchies, and, if so, whether religion plays a disproportionate role in supplying energy to these conservative attitudes. As well, we hoped to identify the social, economic, and cultural pressures that may lead individuals to barricade themselves behind ideas of 'cultural difference' and 'Islamic traditions,' resisting the changes, particularly in gender roles, which the new setting demands.

We must emphasize that we are aware of the limitations of trying to research the 'truth' about family relations. This is a caution for all research projects attempting to enter the intimate and vehemently guarded labyrinths of personal lives. In particular, one has to be aware of the important roles played by interviewer and respondent in attaching meaning to the words used in questionnaires – especially phrases like 'happy marriage.' Even when two individuals share a common cultural and linguistic background and a strong relationship of trust has been established in the interview situation, the method of framing these meanings is not always transparent (see Mishler, 1986, 1995; Harvey, 2000). As suggested later in our example of the religious couple who report themselves to be 'happy,' we need to probe these formal designations in seeking explanations for the patterns observed.

The central assumption in this study has been that forces that determine gender perceptions and gender roles within diasporic communities are not independent causal factors. One's national origin and cultural traditions, religion, and pre-dislocation socio-economic status to a large extent define gender perceptions and gender roles. The new country's social meanings of gender, its political culture and legal practices, as well as its specific settlement and integration policies, also press on relations between men and women in the diaspora. Gendered cultural expectations and structures can survive or can lose their saliency, depending on the conditions of life in the new country.

This means that family relations can change in a variety of directions in diaspora. Decline in the family's socio-economic status or cultural pressure from the outside can become sources of tension at home, or these changes can lead, by contrast, to more bonding and internal dependence and even to strongly defensive solidarity within the family. Either path of change reflects the fact that the conjugal unit in any society is not isolated but always feels the effects of external forces, even if, for analytical purposes, we sometimes treat it as a world of its own. And among migrant populations, even within the family unit, women's and men's attitudes can be quite different in dealing with the stresses of the migration and resettlement process. However, it is generally the case that normative expectations in the new country, as well as legal practices and social services that appear to favour women, can change gender dynamics and assumed harmony within the family.

The statements of men and women from the four communities that were the focus of our study in Canada and in other settings illustrate the significant diversity in their perspectives and social values, even though they all originated in countries dominated by Islamic laws and religious practices. That is, challenges to older ideas are processed differently by women and men in different communities and in different settings. However, the apparent similarities among Muslim societies in the application, to varying degrees, of principles of sharia often cloud fundamental differences among people of Muslim cultural back-grounds in terms of the rigidity of adherence to religious prescriptions applied to spousal relations.

The point is that these differences may reflect the influence of exter-nal factors that help frame people's image of proper gender relations and gender roles. It then follows that efforts to return to a pre-given culture, with an associated social conservatism that is often justified through religion, are not the inherited values of Muslim men. More generally, one cannot assume that more religiously committed men are more (or less) abusive than other men. A study of the influences of reli-gion and church attendance on spousal violence in Canada, for example, found a weak correlation between religious commitment and spousal violence and that, in fact, conservative Christian women appear to be more abusive towards their partners than conservative Christian men (Brinkerhoff, Grandin, and Lupri, 1992). This is despite the fact that conservative religious men, usually more than other men, tend to believe in the 'God-ordained' authority of men over women and in women's responsibility to men as the family caregivers. More-over, changing gender dynamics alone do not always lead to spousal conflict. It would be more reasonable to argue that displacement only brings to the surface pre-existing conflicts and tensions, particularly if we expand the concept of spousal violence to include verbal abuse and put-downs, emotional harassment and forced sex.

All of this directs us to the assumption that if it is, indeed, mostly men who justify the sexist content of their culture of origin, trying to blunt the demands of their new circumstances by resorting to 'cultural heritage' and using religion as an excuse to avoid any change in gender roles, they might be reacting, at least partially, to the greater difficulty they have in adjusting to a new society or new conditions of life. That is, the difficulty of finding satisfying jobs in the new country and the pressures arising from normative expectations regarding gender roles are stressors that take away men's sense of masculine authority and power within the family, disrupting the clear-cut gender roles that are assumed to be part of the 'Muslim culture.' In other words, relations within the family are affected by a complex web of class, ethnic, gender, religious, and regional factors, and are not simply determined by pre-existing cultural values and gendered religious beliefs imported from originating countries. That is to say, conservatism in the family reflects not only the ways females and males traditionally relate to each other in their original cultures but also stems from the ways in which the host country makes – or refuses to make – room for immigrant women and men.

A few examples from oral interviews and focus groups conducted in various settings illustrate the diversity of views and their underlying reasons.

[I]n my opinion, women can adjust and adapt to the society when they immigrate better than men. I think that men try to avoid adjusting and they cannot cope to the changes in the society and environment. I believe the unsuccessful marriages of immigrants all have their roots in the past and back home. For example in Iran, because of the social situation, women put up with a lot of things. This is either because of their children or because of the financial dependence on their husbands. However, the Canadian government supports single mothers. Other than this, some women fall for the superficial freedom that they see in the Western world. These are the women who were too limited and felt too much pressure in their family in Iran. (Iranian female in Toronto)

Here are other quite diverse views:

With my husband, thank God, it is a special relation. My husband is a very understanding person. But life in Canada is totally different than our life back home. There are no changes in our relationships since we moved to Canada, but there are many things that we need to get used to. I believe that we even get closer to each other in Canada, as we only have each other here. Our relation with our children is also fine. (Palestinian female in Toronto)

My husband did not support me to bring up the children in a Muslim household. He would say never mind all of this, we don't live in a Muslim country here and you don't find any one hard-pressed to follow religious traditions these days ... [When he was studying], all our lives rotated around his studies. We had to be quiet when he had exams; we had to sympathize with him and with the pressure he was under to finish, and at times he would make me feel that I knew nothing about what he was going through. He would spend most of his time studying and the rest of the time surfing the Internet. He became purely hooked on the Net and I really do not know what he did with that, but I know our relationship as a husband and wife changed drastically. (Palestinian female in Montreal)

I met my husband in Afghanistan. He always felt good here despite the women's freedom. Compared to some other Afghan men, he is very open and wise. I once asked him, if Afghanistan went back to a normal, stable and peaceful country, would he go to settle there with his family? He replied that returning to one's homeland was very desirable but the womenfolk would never accept to return after living in Canada, and returning to traditional women's roles after getting the taste of a modern women's lifestyle, such as getting access to disposable diapers for a baby and such other luxuries. (Afghan female in Montreal)

I met [my wife] in the first term of our graduate studies in Tehran (we were classmates) ... I think I should not have married at all because I am a very selfish person; I have a high self-esteem and this is not good for marital relationships. In marriage, both should step back a bit. But she is very tolerant and generally is a person who sacrifices a lot for her family [sisters and brothers] as well as for me. I expect things to be taken care of at home. I know she goes out at the same time as I do and comes back with me, but cooking, for instance, must be done every day; I don't eat leftovers. Some guys eat whatever is ready to eat. Not me ... I know this is hard for her, and she is as tired as I am, but this is something I had told her from day one. I have tried to be good, and I have changed a lot, I think. I no longer expect one hundred per cent of her; but I do expect fifty to sixty per cent. (Iranian male in Montreal)

My husband, deep down inside, is very traditional, even though on the surface he seems very integrated [into Canadian society]. If he had been more Westernized, I would have had to adjust to that too. My husband says that before, when he was a student, he was not that much middle-ground. He was a lot more Westernized. [*Her husband did his undergraduate study in the U.S. before he moved to Canada.*] He says that he's older now, so his thinking has changed ... We try not to be influenced by outside things. The society here is very different from our [Pakistani] values. We try to keep our values, because we want to raise our children in a Pakistani atmosphere. (Pakistani female in Montreal)

Participants in a focus group discussion for Afghans in Iran and Iranians in the UK provided the following wisdom in response to a question on possible changes in marriage and family relations:

My parents met and decided to get married twenty-five years ago; I didn't have any problem in choosing my husband. But for my [younger] sister, it was according to traditions and through a matchmaker. (Afghan female refugee in Iran)

In Iran, the girl can see the boy, and her family asks her if she wants to get married to him ... I am more comfortable with the culture in Iran. When I returned to Afghanistan, my husband's family told me to go out with a chador, do this or don't do that. The custom required that we first visited the elders in the family. Afghan women have more freedom in Iran, they can go shopping, attend school meetings, talk to the teachers, and change their way of thinking. I went to school in Iran and have Iranian friends. I have learned Iranian customs and I follow them. Afghan men who were brought up in Iran are kind and understand their wives better. Afghan men in Iran help their wives, but it is possible that when they return and see the other men, they change. (Afghan female refugee in Iran)

It is the Iranian culture, and it impacts on people. I mean unfair discrimination which leads to humiliation of the other person has diminished. Family life has become more important, there is some kind of fair judgment towards both sexes. (Afghan male refugee in Iran)

The new country's gender politics and social and cultural norms can also strengthen or weaken the gender roles that prevailed before migration to a new country. The two statements below by female respondents in the UK reflect this reality.

A major problem for Iranian women in England is divorce. They get the civil divorce, but the husband refuses the Iranian (sharia-based) divorce for which they should go to the Iranian embassy. Some men refuse to do that and this causes much problem for the woman, as she cannot travel to Iran because for coming out, according to the Iranian law, the husband's permission is required. (Iranian female social worker in the UK)

I had heard so much about 'women's rights' in Europe when I lived in Iran. Coming to the UK ten years ago, I realized that there is some truth to it ... The Islamic regime has increased the Iranian men's selfishness and expectations [and] has made stronger their dominance [over] the family and on women's life. In Iran we thought, well, that's the way it is and we have to put up with it, particularly when you have kids. But when I came out of Iran, I realized that it is better for me and for my children to end the unbearable relationship. (Iranian female in the UK)

The differences of opinion within the same community are also reflected in the responses of Afghan females and males in a focus group conducted in Iran.

This [polygamy] is not done in all parts of Afghanistan. But the norm is two to three wives. If the wife does not give birth to a son, the husband marries again to have a son. (Afghan male in Iran)

If I don't have a son, I will agree to my husband marrying again to have a son. But if I have a son, I don't agree to it. (Afghan female in Iran)

I don't agree to this at all. (Second Afghan female in Iran)

I think one should ask for divorce and leave. (Third Afghan female in Iran)

In Afghanistan a woman has no legal right; she is not supported by her family to be able to get a divorce. (Fourth Afghan female in Iran)

A Palestinian male youth in a refugee camp in the West Bank reflected on the same subject using his own personal experience:

My parents are divorced. My father married a second wife and my mother asked for [a] divorce. My father lives with his new wife, and my mother is living with us ... My relations with my father are very formal, but before the divorce it was better. The divorce affected me badly. It is very hard; besides the shame that this caused us, I had to take care of my mother. I stopped going out with my friends as I had to take care of two houses. (Young Palestinian male in the Occupied Territories)

In analysing the changing dynamics of family and spousal relationships, several key questions related to levels of education, job satisfaction, and the extent of religious commitment have been treated as important for their possible impacts on the experiences of women and men in diaspora.

Gender Relations Pre- and Post-Migration

As mentioned in chapter 2, the majority of those surveyed had married in the country of origin. In all four communities in Canada and else-where, the number of married women is much higher than that of men. A small number of men and women in each of the communities in Canada (about 3 per cent of Afghans, Pakistanis, and Palestinians, and over 6 per cent of Iranians) were married more than once. In this category, we have similar data for their counterparts in other settings (about 3 per cent of Iranian males and females, and over 5 and 2 per cent, respectively, of Pakistani males and females in the UK, as com-pared with about 6 and 1 per cent, respectively, of Afghan males and females, in Iran and about 5 per cent of Palestinian males in the West Bank and Gaza).

Those who had married prior to migration mostly married between the ages of twenty and twenty-nine. No male respondent in Canada or in the other settings had married below the age of sixteen, and the number of female respondents from all communities in this category is also below 1 per cent, except for Afghan females (5.16 per cent). The percentages are slightly higher in other settings (22 per cent for Afghan females in Iran, 3.85 per cent of Iranian women, and 7.69 per cent of Pakistani women in the UK).

Sharp differences among the communities are apparent in relation to the question, 'Who decided whom you should marry?' Amongst Ira-nians in Canada, over 55 per cent had chosen their partners them-selves. The figure was much lower for the other communities studied in Canada (about 13 per cent of Afghans, 9 per cent of Pakistanis, and over 21 per cent of Palestinians). Only about 6 per cent of Iranian men and 15 per cent of Iranian women in the UK sample, as opposed to almost 2 per cent of Iranian males and over 3 per cent of Iranian females in Canada, named their father as making the choice of mar-riage for them. The percentages were slightly higher for Palestinians in the West Bank (about 11 per cent for men and less than 16 per cent for women, respectively) as opposed to their counterparts in Canada, about 3 per cent and 5 per cent for males and females, respectively. The percentages for Afghan male and females in Iran in this category (about 14 and 49 per cent) were also much higher that their counter-parts in Canada (about 4 per cent and 13 per cent for Afghan males and females, respectively.) The highest percentages were those of the Pak-istani males (about 41 per cent) and females (about 51 per cent) in the

Table 3.1   Quality of spousal relations, percentages

Responses	Afghans		Iranians		Pakistanis		Palestinians	
	Male	Female	Male	Female	Male	Female	Male	Female
NA	17	22	28	21	14	11	16	20
Low	15	26	16	22	9	15	14	15
Medium	51	36	39	41	45	48	32	39
High	17	15	17	16	31	26	38	26
Total	100	100	100	100	100	100	100	100

UK; again, this is much higher than for Pakistani males (about 6 per cent) and females (about 15 per cent) in Canada.

In our samples, gender and national origin seem to powerfully affect respondents' perceptions, attitudes, and behaviour with regard to their experiences of family life and spousal relations, as well as in their willingness to give testimony about intimate relationships. These differences may also be explained by differences in class composition of these populations in different settings, respondents' levels of education or degrees of job satisfaction.

To help summarize the data on quality of spousal relations, an index was calculated based on four questions: (1) In your relationship with your spouse, how often do you think that things are going really well? (2) At the other extreme, have you ever considered separating from your spouse? (3) Overall, how happy has your marriage been since coming to Canada? (4) Has your relationship with your spouse become better, stayed the same, or become worse? Table 3.1 presents the distribution of summary scores for each of the gender–community segments in Canada.

Declaring the existence of stress or violence within the family, or admitting to a 'low' quality of spousal relationship (reporting 'unhappy feelings,' feeling 'on the verge of separation,' or feeling that 'things are getting worse'), varies among the four communities, and particularly between males and females. This may be related to real differences in the experience of spousal relations across communities between males and females, or to differences in the willingness to declare openly a stressful relationship. Thus, males in each group are less likely than females to report a 'low' quality of relationship; in each of the communities, comparing percentages for males with those for females shows the existence of a substantial gender gap. As an example, a 'low' quality of relationship is reported by 26 per cent of Afghan females, but only by about 15 per cent of Afghan males, by 22 per cent of Iranian females, but only 16 per cent of Iranian males, and by 15 per cent of Pakistani females, but only 9 per cent of Pakistani males. Apart from these gender differences, in comparing data for both males and females across communities, differences by ethnicity are also substantial. Pakistanis and Palestinians are consistently more positive than Afghans and Iranians about their marriages.

To give a more detailed view of the specific tensions that develop within spousal relationships, an index was developed for which respondents were asked about six aspects of their marriage: (1) how often they argued with their partner; (2) the difficulty with which partners 'solve problems when they arise'; (3) whether arguments had 'ever resulted in actual physical violence'; (4) whether the arguments had ever made her or him 'frightened' by what the partner 'says or does'; (5) whether the respondent had ever been 'insulted' by the spouse, and; (6) whether the spouse had ever 'made fun' of their 'actions or opinions.'

Males and females in the four communities in Canada report increased tension as compared with the tension they experienced in their countries of origin. Tension between spouses also varies among the four communities within Canada. Generally, Iranians, male and female, report a higher level of tension in Canada, followed by Pakistanis and Palestinians. But equally important, tension estimated by males is always less than tension reported by females in the community, fitting with the greater tendency of males to report a 'high' quality spousal relationship. Figure 3.1 shows the levels of tension in the countries of origin and in Canada. Looking at these data across the migration process, about 15 per cent of Afghan males remembered 'much' or 'some' tension in the home country, compared with 29 per cent who report this in Canada; likewise, for Palestinian males, the figures have gone up rapidly from 22 per cent to 46 per cent. Among the groups reporting smaller differences, figures have gone from 31 to 38 per cent for Afghan females; from 32 to 46 per cent for Palestinian females; from 44 to 55 per cent for Pakistani females; from 49 to 57 per cent for Iranian males; and from 63 to 65 per cent for Iranian females.

Although, as we see, the ascent is less dramatic for some groups than for others, tension always increases after the move to the new country. None of these groups has found family life less stressful in

Figure 3.1   'Much' or 'some' tension in spousal relations, in the country of origin and in Canada, percentages

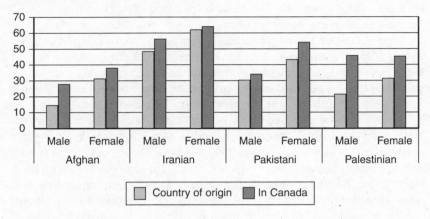

Canada – at least, no group is prepared to testify to stress levels at home that match what they have experienced in the new country. Still, a large number of respondents say they have 'never considered separating from their spouses.' Again, the highest percentages, respectively, expressing this view are for Pakistani males and females (78 and 73 per cent) and the lowest are for Iranian males and females (51 and 43 per cent), with Palestinian males and females (72 per cent and 63 per cent) and Afghan males and females (72 per cent and 59 per cent) falling between.

Comparing the experiences of family tensions in Canada and in other settings, it seems that family tension is experienced more intensely in Canada or, at least, is more freely reported by the four groups there than in other settings. For example, only about 5 per cent of Palestinian males and about 9 per cent of Palestinian females in the West Bank reported experiencing some tension with their spouse, compared with 46 per cent of Palestinian males and females in Canada. Afghan men and women in Canada also score a bit higher in this area than their counterparts in Iran (respectively, 29 and 38 per cent of Afghan men and women in Canada, compared to over 26 per cent of Afghan men and almost 32 per cent of Afghan women in Iran). The comparative percentages are about 21 and 34 per cent, respectively, for Iranian males and females in the UK, compared to 57 and 65 per cent of Iranian males and females in Canada. We see a more significant gender difference in the report of family tension among Pakistani males and females in Canada (32 and 55 per cent for men and women, respectively), which are, in any case, higher for Pakistani females than males in the UK (about 38 and 28 per cent).

The difference between the surveyed communities in Canada and in other settings in experiencing (or reporting) marital tension can be explained in several ways. It can be attributed, perhaps, to greater inhibition in the other countries, given that there is much more public discussion in Canada about family tension and violence; or, it may reflect the reality of a more pressured and stressful way of life in Canada as compared with the UK and with Iran. Alternatively, one may conclude that concern with more practical or material life issues in other settings does not allow spouses to just 'sit back' and think about the quality of their marital life, unless actual physical violence is involved. In any case, nostalgia and changing perceptions about gender roles certainly play a role. Given that a much larger percentage of individuals in all communities come from a more educated, middle-class background, there is the possibility that in Canada the higher expectations for gender equality and greater emphasis on individual autonomy may stimulate greater sensitivity to problems within the family, and thus tend to increase reported feelings of tension.

The last interpretation is supported by the following statements by Pakistani males:

... Then she had the opportunity to work at a women's centre, and they are mostly feminists there. So, to be in the midst of these feminists, and then to have that background [of staying at home and raising children], I think her attitude changed. For example, take the issue of changing my daughter's diapers when she was a baby. It would feel odd to me to do this; this is not what men do. But my wife would say, 'Why won't you do this? You're her father. You should do it. Everyone does it here.' In traditional [Pakistani] culture, a man can take care of his son, but not his daughter. For the daughter, the mother is there; she'll take care of these things. This used to be very difficult for me to deal with. I was thinking, where have I come [to, here in Canada]? What kind of country is this? Everything has totally changed. So that is how there has been a change. (Pakistani male in Toronto)

With regard to how we live together, yeah, we are equals ... [From my wife's perspective], it is like, my world is separate from your world. I will respect your world, and you respect mine. If I feel like it, I will respect it, if I don't, then I won't. Because I am a different person, you can't impose anything on me. If you like something, it doesn't necessarily mean that I like it, too. This was very difficult for me to digest, because how could I like something and she not like it? It was just assumed that the things I like, she will like them, too, wherever I go, she will go with me; she is my wife, she is part of me ... This is where we have clashes. That concept of oneness that we have [in Pakistan], it disappears here. Here they have more of a concept of individuality. (Pakistani male in Montreal)

Yet, at the same time, the Pakistani male in Toronto was critical of the slow pace of change in his community:

But I don't think we have progressed as much [in the community here], in terms of the equality of women, understanding women, generally speaking. We lag behind. The girls [our daughters] ask questions of us, about women being treated equally in the mosque, about women going to the graveyards, generally questioning women's roles in religion, society, and culture. These issues come up more here. Because here, other [non-Muslim] women have equal rights, and [my girls] don't have them. I think the non-Muslim Pakistanis have progressed more.

Nonetheless, there are significant differences in terms of gender and national origin in reporting actual physical violence across all communities in Canada and in other settings. Our samples show more experience – or more reporting – of spousal violence in other settings than in Canada for the surveyed communities. For example, 14 per cent of Pakistani males and 10 per cent of Pakistani women in the UK reported the occurrence of spousal violence, compared with less than 1 per cent and about 2 per cent of Pakistani males and females in Canada. Also, while the same percentage of Afghan males in Iran and in Canada reported the existence of violence in their spousal relations, a larger percentage of Afghan females in Iran (12 per cent) responded positively to the same question compared to their counterparts in Canada (9 per cent). As well, the incidence of spousal violence seems higher for Palestinians in the West Bank and Jordan (close to 7 and 8 per cent, respectively, of males and females) than their counterparts in Canada, who reflected the lowest percentages among the four communities (about 1 per cent of males and less than 1 per cent of females).

The only exception is the Iranian respondents, with zero per cent of Iranian males and close to 4 per cent of Iranian females in the UK, compared with about 2 per cent of males and 8 per cent of females in Canada reporting physical violence in their spousal relationships.

How should one understand the substantial differences in tension reported among respondents from the four communities in Canada, and between them and their counterparts in other settings? For example, with the exception of Iranians, the males in each community are more likely than females to report 'low' spousal tension on the cumulative index, and females (except for Palestinians) are more likely to report 'high' tension in the relationship. This may reflect differences among males and females in terms of what constitutes tension or violence – something not specific to these communities. Also, a very rosy view of the spousal relationship is given by Pakistani and Afghan males. Commenting on their experience in the variety of behaviours provided in the six questions cited above, only 2 per cent of Pakistani and 5 per cent of Afghan men think their relationships with their partners is very tense, the lowest estimates among males. The factor of nostalgia and of wanting to protect an idealized image of one's personal life seems to be at stake here.

Should we conclude that where tension exists in the country of origin, it continues or perhaps increases as a result of dislocation and relocation, but that if relations were relatively amicable, they survive the pressures of migration? In other words, is it likely that the root of the problem may have already existed in the home country and is only amplified in the new country?

A female Iranian social worker in London offers the following assessment of the situation:

> Living in diaspora (*ghorbat*) reveals or accentuates the pre-existing problems between husband and wife, simply because the restrictions women feel and [that] force them to endure aggression and violence, such as the woman's financial dependence, or her fear of losing her children's custody, are lifted outside Iran. Many couples are astonished that their old problems get to the crisis point with relocation. I have had men who have told me: '[My wife and I] lived together in Iran for many years. We would argue and fight but in the end we would always make up and continue with our life. I never believed that she would call the police on me. If I knew [what would await me] I would never come to this country.'

The three following statements suggest that new stresses in Canada may help crystallize a difficult situation and the push for a resolution, or perhaps also that the changed legal environment makes a resolution possible:

> Physical violence continued even after [our] arrival to Canada ... When we were both working it became harder and harder to live together. My husband did not want to take care of the house or his family. I only called the police once and that was when he wanted to return home after being away for two weeks. He wanted the key of our car, but I refused to give it to him and asked him to go. He forced himself in and wanted to beat me. I called the police and explained the situation [and they] in turn asked him to go away and leave me [alone]. That was the only time. (Afghan female in Montreal)

> He was twelve years older than me. We didn't have a good relationship with each other. Tension, fighting, and beatings started immediately after the marriage. I knew that he had relationships with other women ... After a while, I planned to come to Canada somehow and get [a] divorce ... I got the Canadian divorce, not the sharia one. (Iranian female in Toronto)

> My fiancé moved to Canada a few months before me because his paperwork was ready sooner. During this time, I got the chance to think about my future and about my decision to marry this guy. I realized that he was not the right guy for me, and when I came to Canada, after a series of long fights and arguments, we finally broke up and went separate ways. (Another Iranian female in Toronto)

The statements below, taken from oral interviews with Iranian respondents in the UK and Palestinians in the West Bank, may confirm these assessments:

> Once in Britain, we had to change our lifestyle and become responsible adults, find a job, a proper residence, and build a family. We were no longer young political activists with family supports. I found a job, gave birth to a child, and was expecting my husband to follow and act responsibly. But he went on living a student life, free schedule, free love, and no family responsibilities. But he did not approve of such behaviour from me ... Our relations as husband and wife changed completely. I had to take care of my child and do the house chores and the rest ... The Euro-

pean environment also had its effect. I think [the] male–female relation-ship is less egalitarian in Europe than in the U.S. [where I had studied, met my husband and married]. (Iranian female in the UK)

My wife and I were separated several years ago. I don't know if problems were pre-existing or started after migration. The point is that the change occurred in the quality of the relationship. My wife settled quickly, was integrated, learned English sooner than I did, found a job. But for me it is the political activity that is the number one priority. I wanted to help other refugees ... These were my priorities, I would come home at two or four in the morning. In any case, we did not have an understanding among us; our paths were different. (Iranian male in the UK)

The Arab society views women and marginalizes them ... men control women. The man's opinion is imposed on the woman even if he is younger than her. Lots of rules are imposed on women, in marriage and engagement. Parents watch their daughter's behaviour before and after marriage. A woman, according to them, should be oppressed ... no freedom. Everything is prohibited, prohibited, prohibited. [These are] the negative traits that we got from our parents. (Palestinian female in the West Bank)

I do not feel that my relationship with people is deep; I wish I could talk with them more. I feel that my relatives my age have limitation in talking; we talk only for a few minutes, and that's it. Outside the refugee camps girls talk with boys for hours; here in the camp girls talk with girls and boys with boys. It has to do with the traditions. In the past, fathers con-trolled their daughters, preventing them from playing with the boys, also in cities they raise girls like this. At a certain age girls should not play with boys. And we who are in a refugee camp and come from peasant origins keep those traditions. (Young Palestinian female in a refugee camp in the West Bank)

Q: Do you have any conflicts with your wife?
A: Sometimes, when I come back home late, or when she wants to go out and I do not want to, but these are small fights. There aren't any real fights, it is normal between couples.
Q: How is your relation with your daughter?
A: She is my life.
(Palestinian male in a refugee camp in the West Bank)

Noting differences among female responses from each community in reports of a 'happy' marriage, the experience of spousal tension, and claims about sharing in decision-making, can we assume that in some communities more than in others there is a tendency to cover up difficulties or to keep silent about abuse or even ordinary troubles? Or should we assume that the differences observed among the communities in reporting the quality of spousal relations are related to differences in social class, level of education, and strength of religious identification, this last factor itself reflective of the level of an individual's reliance on the community for her or his sense of belonging? For example, for a religious person from a tightly knit community, to admit to failure in marriage may be seen as somehow admitting to a failure to follow an emotionally inscribed religious obligation or guideline establishing patriarchal responsibility, or even, eventually, to an incipient breakdown of authority.

This difficulty in interpretation is especially of concern when assessing reports of the incidence of violent, threatening, or demeaning behaviour in the conjugal unit, where it is complicated by the tendency (by no means unique to the groups that are the focus of this study) to deny or not acknowledge the existence of such problems. Perhaps there is too much at stake in relations of intimacy to admit, even to oneself, that one is in a difficult or unhappy situation. Again, this is not a phenomenon unique to immigrants or to people from the Middle East. But given the political situation, the denial may be more stubbornly internalized as a protective shield as the couple, deprived of larger family ties, draws together because it feels socially isolated and vulnerable.

The following testimonies are instructive in this regard:

> I believe that [my husband and I] even get closer to each other in Canada as we only have each other here ... We both believe that it is really hard to raise children in this country, as they have too much freedom. We do not want our children to sink in the Canadian culture. (Palestinian female in Toronto)

> Our relationship is good. Since we are alone here and there are no other relatives around us, we lean on each other and we are much closer than before. (Iranian female in Toronto)

It is also possible that the refusal to acknowledge or report the existence of violence is motivated by fear of how authorities will use the information or treat the abuser (Flynn and Crawford, 1998). Other times, it is felt that the community's 'honour' is at stake. The perception of both men and women may be that by making a 'private' matter public, they expose the whole community to more abusive perceptions and stereotypes. This, of course, is a result of power relations between majority and minority communities, since when it comes to the cultural hang-ups and values that promote gender violence, the dominant Anglo-European culture is as flawed as any minority culture. But for the minority culture, defending the community's reputation at all costs is much more important, especially in the face of the upsurge in anti-Muslim feelings.

Often men know and take advantage of women's hesitance to report violent or other abusive acts, as described by a female respondent who was repeatedly physically abused:

> He was under the impression that I would call the police, so he would threaten me about how the family and the community would view the situation, the gossip that would take place, and [how] the family's name would be tarnished due to my complaints. So I hoped that things would change with time, but they got worse, and it became too much for me to bear. So my husband left home and I did not stop him from leaving. (Afghan female in Montreal)

In fact, the need for community approval may affect many aspects of a woman's life, as reflected in this comment by another respondent:

> I would never accept my mother to marry again. She is young, but there are many other young Afghan women that are widows, separated, or in the same conditions as my mother, that are not remarried. And even if she is special, I can't accept it. I have already given a thought about it. Deeply, I would like her to remarry, but all my community will laugh at me and at us. My culture, my society does not allow it. (Afghan youth in Montreal)

Education, Job Satisfaction, and Spousal Relations

It is not unusual among ethnic minorities of different cultural backgrounds for a man to make a living in the new country at a job unbefitting his educational qualifications, and with fewer rewards. This economic decline, together with a loss of friends and social status, provokes a deep emotional vulnerability, because he must rely more on family members and, particularly, on his wife. In such a situation, the wife is expected to provide the previously expected domestic services, along with, possibly, holding down a job herself and catering to the man's wounded ego (Moghissi and Goodman, 1999).

Focusing on the four communities surveyed in Canada, the estimate of educational attainment is complicated in this study by the fact that the achievement of respondents must be assessed in both the country of origin *and* in Canada, and that educational patterns vary widely by community and by gender. As was mentioned in chapter 1, not only were the respondents' levels of education in respective countries of origin different but so were the levels of education they obtained in the new country. That is, as will be shown in chapter 6, some individuals did not augment their education in the new country, while others pursued post-secondary degrees at a college or university.

In an attempt to capture different educational patterns for Canadian respondents, the respondents were divided into four 'educational types' based on the completion of a BA (or higher) in one's country of origin and in Canada: Type A, a BA or higher at home, plus a BA or higher in Canada; Type B, no BA at home but a BA or higher in Canada; Type C, a BA or higher at home but no BA in Canada; and Type D, no BA at home and no BA in Canada.

Levels of education seem to have an impact on the quality of spousal relations. For example, Iranian men and women with BA degree or higher in Canada report a 'high' quality of relationship, and the same is also true for the small number of Afghan males with Canadian degrees. Those with more education also tend to claim less tension at home, whatever is, in fact, the reality of the situation. This is the case for Afghan, Iranian, and Pakistani men and women, amongst whom those with degrees are consistently less likely to report 'high' tension than those without degrees. As well, there seems to be a correlation between obtaining a degree in one's country of origin and claims of a 'high' level of sharing in decision-making and household responsibilities.

Perhaps the most plausible explanation for this educational advantage is that those with degrees are more likely to obtain better jobs and a better economic status, and this in turn may contribute to a better spousal relationship, reducing tension and helping to foster equality in decision-making. However, such respondents represent a more privileged section of their communities, since the percentages obtaining a university degree in Canada are relatively small. Even those with degrees from their home countries may encounter difficulties when their credentials are not formally recognized, and thus have a hard time finding a good job.

That is why, as discussed in chapter 2, despite high levels of post-secondary educational accomplishment (almost double the national average), Muslims in Canada generally have a high rate of unemployment. This sobering situation raises the possibility that dissatisfaction in the workplace or the problem of finding work may produce a general feeling of unhappiness that is echoed or reinforced by circumstances at home.

As might be expected, males in the four communities who felt that their job made good use of their education brought a more positive and less insecure tone to the reports. As well, Iranian, Pakistani, and Palestinian females who were satisfied with the pay-off of education for work were also more likely to find their home situation to be of 'high' quality. The effect is particularly strong for Palestinians, where 48 per cent of males and 28 per cent of females who feel their current job is 'much better' or 'better' than the one in the old country record a 'high' quality spousal relationship, as compared to only about 8 and 10 per cent, respectively, among males and females whose job is judged to be 'worse' or 'much worse' than in the country of origin. For other groups, the corresponding estimates for a 'high' quality of spousal relationship are similarly tied to job satisfaction: 37 per cent for Afghan males who feel their current job is 'much better' or 'better,' as compared to 9 per cent who report their job is 'worse' or 'much worse' (a 28 per cent difference); 39 per cent for Pakistani males who feel their current job is 'much better' or 'better,' as compared to 26 per cent who report their job is 'worse' or 'much worse' (a 13 per cent difference); and 35 per cent for Pakistani females who feel their current job is 'much better' or 'better,' as compared to the 20 per cent who report their job is 'worse' or 'much worse' (a 15 per cent difference).

The tendency of respondents to report equal sharing in power and household responsibilities is also more apparent for those among most of our groups who feel they have been 'treated fairly' on the job. For example, among Iranian females, 21 per cent of those who feel they have been treated fairly on the job score 'high' on spousal sharing of decision-making and duties, compared to 4 per cent who feel they have not been fairly treated, a difference of about 18 per cent. Among Afghan males, 49 per cent of those who feel they have been treated fairly on the job score 'high' on spousal sharing of decision-making, compared to 38 per cent who feel they have not been fairly treated, a difference of about 11 per cent. As well, claims to sharing in decision-making are more evident among those who feel they have a 'much better' or 'better' job in Canada in relation to their job at home. The strongest effect is noted for Afghan males, where we also see a link between claims about sharing in decision-making and the perception that one has a job which 'makes good use of one's education,' reinforcing connections for them between a positive job experience, a 'high' quality of spousal relations, and 'low' tension at home. For this group in particular, who left a deprived and often dangerous situation, the move to Canada appears to have become a shared family project for social ascent; we observed similar patterns for the Palestinians in our study. Other factors can also play a part in shaping relations between spouses. For example, among Iranians and especially Iranian males who have suffered losses in economic status in making the move to the new country, educational achievement by itself seems to be important in its effects on the experience at home, while the 'gender gap' between males and females in their perceptions of fairness in decision-making is relatively small. This more 'modern' profile may be linked to the community's strong secular orientation, as shown earlier.

Religion and Spousal Relations

The effects of religion on family life can be assessed by examining claims about the quality of spousal relations, tension at home, and equality in decision-making in relation to the four religious types we have defined – the 'strongly committed' (relatively high on both religious identification and on religious practice), 'ritual practitioners' (high on practice but not high on identification), 'virtually religious' (high on identification but not on practice), and 'secular' (low on both identification and on practice). In doing so, we should keep in mind that we rely on respondents' claims about marital experience, not on direct observations of their behaviour.

Generally, the Canadian samples show that high scores on religious identification and religious practice are connected to the tendency to claim a 'high' quality spousal relationship, and this claim is always stronger for males than for females. Thus, for each of the four communities and for both males and females, those 'strongly committed' to their faith are more likely to claim a 'high' quality relationship than those tending to be 'secular' (see table 3.2).

For example, 37 per cent of 'strongly committed' Afghan males report a 'high' quality relationship as compared to 10 per cent of those with a more 'secular' orientation, and 63 per cent of committed Palestinian males report a 'high' quality relationship as compared to 24 per cent of those tending to be 'secular.' However, the frequent incidence of reports of a 'high' quality relationship for the more religious groups must be considered in the context of data showing an increase in spousal tension in Canada across all communities in the study. Thus, using the definitions for religious types developed in chapter 5: the 'strongly committed,' (high in religious identity and practice), 'ritual practitioners,' (low in religious identity and high in practice), and 'virtual religious' (high in identity and low in practice) among Pakistanis, as well as 'strongly committed' Afghans, are more likely than the 'secular' (low in identity and practice) to report a 'high' quality spousal relationship at the same time that members of these communities, generally, report more spousal tension in Canada than in their home countries.

These data can be read in several ways, beginning with the recognition that communities of Muslim cultural background are remarkably different in their identification with religion. For example, it is possible that the 'happy' religious couple, fulfilling family duties they conceive of devoutly as religious prescriptions, may feel genuinely happier in their marriage, even though they experience more spousal tension in Canada than they did at home. For the 'strongly committed' man, the desired state would be one in which he feels secure, even if under pressure, while for the woman, it would mean accepting traditional ways without criticism. In a more active version reflecting such an attitude, the couple would go beyond the mere performance of ritual, trying to find in their beliefs and practices some degree of compensation for the demanding pace and ordinary troubles of life in the new country. This would mean 'working at' and nourishing the family relationship (or some ideological notion of it) which, for them, is seamlessly bound to religious devotion. However, it is also possible that they are not happy at all, but feel compelled to hide the truth about their relationship from themselves and from everyone else, denying tensions and major or even minor resentments. To do otherwise, in their minds, would be an act of disloyalty to the faith and to the community of believers, and would stain their reputation. For them, the commitment to attend religious events and to display, for example, an appropriate modesty in dress also stands as a constant reminder of what is expected at home.

Table 3.2 Percentages reporting 'high' quality spousal relationship by religious types

	Strongly committed	Ritual practitioners	Virtual religious	Tending to the secular
	Very high or high religious identity and very high or high religious practice	Low or medium religious identity and very high or high religious practice	Very high or high religious identity and low or medium religious practice	Low or medium religious identity and low or medium religious practice
Afghan males	37	10	17	10
Afghan females	21	16	21	12
Iranian males	_a	–	–	17
Iranian females	–	–	–	16
Pakistani males	30	38	40	25
Pakistani females	29	32	27	15
Palestinian males	63	53	35	24
Palestinian females	21	41	45	15

a Very small N.

The general conclusion is that claims to 'happiness,' subjective as they may be, can be interpreted in a variety of ways, keeping in mind the complexity of measuring 'happiness' in any case, given that the term is generally an overused and vague concept, and that it tends to be based on context. Claims about one's 'happiness' can be closely bound to ideas and ideals concerning class, gender, and culture. So, we have approached the notion of 'happiness' cautiously in this study. We can assume, however, that to admit to having a troubled relationship is more acceptable among those who have a smaller stake in protecting their standing as Muslims in the community. Even so, this does happen – indeed, with substantial frequency – but more among religiously committed females (including Pakistani women) than among males. By contrast, secular respondents, both male and female, are not subject to these religious obligations, and thus are freer to describe what they feel regarding problems in their marriages. For them, home, religious piety, and personal respectability are not so firmly fused.

The picture is a bit mixed regarding the effects of religious commitments on declarations of spousal sharing in decision-making. For example, the majority of female respondents (47 per cent of Iranians, 50 per cent Afghans, 76 per cent of Pakistanis, and 61 per cent of Palestinians) said that the sharing of decision-making and the division of household responsibilities with their spouses were reasonable. Only a small minority answered in the negative: about 20 per cent of Iranian women, compared to only 4 per cent of Palestinian women, and 8 and 9 per cent, respectively, of Pakistani and Afghan females (percentages do not add up to 100 because a respondent could also indicate that the question was not applicable or decline to answer). Generally, Afghan males are much more likely than Afghan females in each religious group to make the case for a 'high' level of sharing decision-making between the couples at home; but these gendered differences melt away for some groups (for example, among Pakistanis) and are even reversed for those tending to the 'secular.' As well, the pattern in sharing decision-making relating to children does not differ very much from the pattern observed in other matters, such as financial decisions, suggesting that these ideas have a strong ideological grip and persist regardless of topic. The pattern is complicated and is powerfully inflected by religious thinking, by cultural ideas specific to particular communities, and, even though the effects are not uniform, by level of education and job satisfaction in each community.

The data on spousal relations confirm our concerns about the flaws of essentializing perceptions when it comes to people of Muslim cultural background. Individuals in the four communities with whom we worked show a remarkable lack of homogeneity in their self-identification and in their perceptions about their positions within the society and in the family. Indeed, as we argued in chapter 1, the differences we uncover among the four communities in Canada challenge the appropriateness of the notion of a homogeneous 'Muslim' diaspora, pressing upon us the need to interrogate carefully the political import of the term and to ask why, how, and under what circumstances these particular diasporic groups are formed in the West.

The findings also support the claim that external socio-economic factors are significant in shaping perceptions of one's place in the world. However, the research does not fully support the idea that it is mostly or uniquely men who act against the pressures of social integration and adjustment by resorting to religious rituals and values. While there are substantial differences among the communities in terms of religious identification, the differences between men and women usually are smaller. *how much smaller?*

It is important to emphasize, however, that we never assumed that women were less religious than men. Indeed, women worldwide continue to be devoted followers of religions in their great variety, and often there is no discernible difference between them and men in their attachment to misogynist rituals and dogma. Our assumption was narrower. We suggested that in a situation where they encounter a chilly reception in the host state, migrant men are more inclined and certainly have the greater opportunity to use religious excuses to curb change in gender roles in their community and thus to block women's efforts towards greater individual autonomy and equity in the workplace and at home. Our findings do not prove this assumption to be wrong.

What needs to be emphasized, however, is that women, without departing from formal adherence to established religious beliefs and rituals, often present a different understanding of religious prescriptions in the area of women's rights and obligations to the family and to society. Moreover, the data also seem to suggest that the idea that there would be greater opportunities for women in the West has not proved itself to be the case for a significant number of our female respondents. Disappointment on this score may have had a powerful impact on their readiness to confront existing structures and relations that are familiar and thus more secure than the unknown and challenging conditions associated with change. It also militates inevitably against women's self-perception and independent thinking. A study of South Asian immigrant women in Canada, for example, pointed out that women with stronger patriarchal beliefs are not only less likely to support the provision of assistance to battered women but also may not even 'perceive a situation as wife abuse when they witness it. This inevitably leads to delay in seeking help' (Ahmad, Riaz, Barata, and Stewart, 2004). In any case, the fact that respondents in our survey who report tension and unhappiness in their marriage still avoid divorce is quite instructive here.

We wanted to demonstrate the heterogeneity of peoples from 'Muslim societies,' suggesting that it is a mistake to relate their experience entirely to Islam – as if religion could shape every aspect of one's life – ignoring differences in political attitude and the profound effects of ethnic, regional, and class divisions. Our data confirm this. They show that national origin, culture, ethnicity, gender, and class status divide migrants and citizens from majority-Muslim societies and that, despite its claims, religious attachment does not unite them into a single, homogenous bloc formed around a confession of belief or rigid adherence to a single set of practices. This evident heterogeneity has important effects on the conduct and subjective experience of ultimate relations among spouses at the core of family groups.

4 Religious Identities and Identification

An underlying concern in this study has been that, given the diversity of populations of Muslim cultural background in the West, wrapping them in a single religious cloak tends to cloud crucial differences among various groups and divert attention away from their most pressing practical needs. As has been discussed in chapter 1, Muslims, particularly in Canada, are quite diverse; their numbers include peoples from culturally and linguistically distinct societies in the Middle East, South and South-east Asia, and Africa who vary in ethnicity and culture as well as religious affiliation. By one account, Muslims in Canada originate from more than eighty-five nations and comprise dozens of ethno-racial and linguistic groups (*Globe and Mail*, 27 October 2004: 25). As also discussed in chapter 1, the Canadian Muslims' triple identity, based on old and new national and religious affiliations, makes analytically inadequate the commentaries, debates, and policies that tend to privilege religion in discussing Muslim diaspora and their concerns.

The tendency to treat Muslims as a homogeneous group dominated by a single religious ideology inevitably aggravates the already tense relations between Muslim populations and their new societies. What makes this one-sided, essentializing approach even more difficult to bear is that, unlike in the past, evidence of an expanding divide within the West's populations from Muslim-majority countries is readily observable. Aside from the gap between the religious and secular sections of these communities, there exist ever-expanding and seemingly unbridgeable divides over theological and political issues separating factions within the religious camps. The antagonistic rivalry between Saudi Wahhabies and Iranian Shi'as, a clearer manifestation of which is unfolding on Iraqi soil today, has caused internal clashes between absolutist and moderate Muslims, not to mention clashes within each group. These confrontations have led some scholars to speak of the existence of clashes *within* the only nominally singular 'Muslim civilization,' expanding on Huntington's infamous exegesis on clashes between civilizations (Bilgrami, 2003). A case in point in Canada are the divisions within the Shi'a population – such as manifested in Toronto's Shi'a associations and mosques, including Mahdiyeh and the Imam Ali and Vali Asr centres – resulting from opposing political stands, individual power struggles, and overseas funding. Some of these organizations operate in line with the politics of Iran's Islamic Republic, as opposed to others representing Lebanese, Iraqi, and Pakistani Shi'as (Soltanpour, 2005). Also, it is perhaps reasonable to assume that ethnic and linguistic bonding can be more unifying than religion. Or, as Bassam Tibi argues, '[e]thnic conflicts within the Islamic civilization bring to expression the politicization of differences among local cultures' (Tibi, 2001: 219).

The varying national origins, ethnic compositions, and religious and political divisions and concerns of the populations classified under the term 'Muslim' are not entirely lost on policy- and decision-makers. For example, the influential 1997 report on Islamophobia in Britain (Runnymede Trust, 1997) aimed at confronting prejudice against Muslims and the depiction of Islam as being of a monolithic, 'essentialist' nature, and the 2005 report produced by the Congressional Research Service in the United States, are instances where these points of difference are underlined as part of the policy agenda. Yet, oddly, Muslims are the only diaspora population in which character, behaviour, attitudes, inclinations, and normative conduct still continue to be defined by religion alone. This is not the case for other migrant populations, whether they be Argentine or Russian Jews in Tel Aviv, or Salvadorian, Puerto Rican, or Haitian Catholics who have recently made their way to Latino communities in Queens, Brooklyn, or the Bronx or, for that matter, African-Jamaican Protestants who have settled in Scarborough or in the Jane-Finch community in Toronto. In these communities, too, religion plays a role, one that is sometimes supportive and integrative within the dominant community and sometimes contradictory to it. But it is understood that religion in these communities plays only one role among many, and it does not draw as much attention on the part of social commentators.

The conflicting discourses and debates are also observed by scholars focusing on the Muslim diaspora in the West. Referring to sectarian differences and other divisions that characterize Muslims in Britain, Iftikhar Malik (2004), for example, argues that the issues involved are both 'mundane and spiritual.' Aiming 'to evolve strategies to cope with serious socio-economic challenges,' these divisions, says Malik, involve 'the problematic of old and new identities' and 'the relationship with the old and the new home.' Class divisions must also be added to this list. 'While there are genuine worries among the lower strata regarding job opportunities, educational facilities for the younger generation, and secure housing, the elite is concerned about the institutional depiction of Islam and the overall place of the community within a multicultural setting' (93). Ruba Salih also points to various divisions among Italian Muslims, notably among Italian converts who aim to affirm a European or, rather, culturally based *Italian* Islamic identity free from the intrusion of 'foreign, fundamentalist' ideologies. Drawing on its European character, this identity is distinguished from the mostly Arab-based Islamic ideas put forward by the so-called embassy mosques financed by Muslim countries, and particularly by Saudi Arabia, which claims to be the only legitimate body to represent Muslims (Salih, 2004: 1001–2).

Divisions also exist within Muslim populations in the United States, reflecting contrasting historical, political, and ethno-national trajectories among African Americans, Arabs, and South Asians, as well as among other groups with varying socio-economic profiles and political goals (Esposito, 1998; Saeed, 2002; Leonard, 2003). But across these communities, argues Karen Leonard, specifically religious divisions are also widening, and at the same time, alliances are shifting in favour of more moderate, liberal tendencies (2003: 151–2), or what Muqtedar Khan (2003) calls 'Muslim democrats' (in opposition to militant ideologies or the fundamentalist expression of conservative co-believers). A vivid example of such a 'moderate' tendency is expressed in the statement made by Abu Laith Luqman Ahmad, a member of the North American Imams Federation and imam at the United Muslim Masjid in Philadelphia. Ahmad goes so far in his disagreement with the defensive tendencies lodged within the Muslim population that he denies the existence of Islamophobia, arguing, instead, that what exists is 'Islamophobia-phobia' (fear of Islamophobia), an exaggerated concern used manipulatively by Islamic radicals and their supporters.

In Canada, Muslims are divided over several major issues, notably the matter of funding from Saudi Arabia to certain Muslim associa-

tions, and particularly the role of religion in public life, which has
come into the open since the split between those campaigning for and
against the application of sharia to family and inheritance disputes
under Ontario's *Arbitration Act*. This political initiative, launched by
the Canadian Society of Muslims and pursued by the newly founded
Islamic Institute of Civil Justice (Dar-ul-Qada), was vehemently
opposed by the Muslim Canadian Congress (MCC) and the Canadian
Council of Muslim Women, as well as by individuals who are either
openly secular or only nominally Muslim.

Simply put, the *persona* of the new immigrant is multifaceted and
cannot be reduced to a single element. Apart from religion, we need to
be mindful of the influences of other realities at national and international levels that help kindle the formation of new identities and their
possible impact on individuals' readiness for or resistance to social
and cultural integration. Within this context, we argued in chapter 1
that the increasing commitment to religious identity among Muslims
in the West may be a way in which deeply rooted frustrations and
resentments against the policies and practices of the receiving countries are expressed – policies and practices which are seen as denying
these groups an equitable share in productive, satisfying work and its
rewards, and a dignified sense of selfhood, equality, and respect.
General dissatisfaction is also fuelled by political frustration and anger
at what is seen as continued colonial intervention and aggression in
Muslim countries, exemplified in the West's unfair and unfettered
material and vocal support for Israel, and the invasions of Afghanistan
and Iraq. Ironically, this exasperation over global politics appears to be
particularly powerful among the younger, more economically and
socially adjusted and successful segments of the population, those
who have deeper roots in Canada, the United States, and Europe, and
so have a firmer sense of entitlement as citizens. For them, opting for
religious identification is a means of expressing political solidarity and
standing by 'their' people. As well, adherence to religion is perhaps a
way of rejecting the normative expectations of the receiving country
without being labelled antisocial. But, ironically, these relatively privileged younger individuals take a political position by stressing the
very differences in religious dress, attitudes, or behaviour that provide
the basis for the unjust and stereotyped treatment of Muslims, both
locally and globally.

The receiving society, unaware of or uninterested in looking at the
root causes of Muslim discontent and resentment, acts upon those dif-

ferences in injudicious and defensive ways. That is, it allows and even encourages the existence of isolated, self-sufficient communities, and tolerates practices that are not legally or socially acceptable in the county at large, rather than probing into the structures and institutions that marginalize and discriminate against Muslims in important areas such as the job market, housing, and access to social services. A major goal in this study has been to contribute to a better understanding of the institutions and relations that promote a nagging consciousness about marginality and being treated as an 'outsider' among the culturally, linguistically, ethnically, and politically diverse populations of Islamic cultural background in Canada and elsewhere.

Religious Type, Religious Identity, and Religious Practice

Statistics Canada's 2001 General Social Survey reports that attendance at religious services has fallen across the country in the last fifteen years. In 1986, 28 per cent of individuals aged fifteen and over said they attended religious services on a weekly basis; in 2001, the percentage had declined to 20 per cent. As well, in 2001, 43 per cent of those surveyed reported that they had not attended religious services in the previous twelve months, as compared to 26 per cent in 1986. However, Statistics Canada's series on religions in Canada, released in 2003, records a reverse trend for non-Judeo-Christian religions, including Islam, Hinduism, Sikhism, and Buddhism. The highest propensity to declare a religious affiliation (regardless of whether or not the respondents actually practised this religion) is that recorded for Muslims. In fact, 76 per cent of Canadian Muslims surveyed ranked religion as being important to them, and 65 per cent reported individual religious activity at least once a week (Janhevich and Ibrahim, 2004). Granted that relatively high birth rates within some segments of Muslim communities and immigration patterns are the main reasons for growth in the share of Muslims in these statistics, the fact nonetheless is that the Canadian religious landscape is undeniably changing, as it has in Europe and the U.S. In a sense, self-identified and practising Muslims, rather than being influenced by the secular values of the new country, may influence it to become more religion-conscious and compel it to give the appearance of espousing religious values in public life. The impact of Muslim votes on Canada's Liberal Party leadership convention in 2006 is a case in point. According to some accounts, the victory of the party's new leader, Stéphane Dion, and the defeat of Bob Rae, came in part through the manipulation of issues of race and religion (*Globe and Mail*, 6 December 2006). The mass email sent by the Canadian Islamic Congress to its members, its active mobilization of Muslim delegates to the convention, and letters sent to the country's mosques asking Muslims to vote en masse for one candidate, as well as the mass email sent to Muslim delegates by the president of the Canadian Arab Federation accusing one of the candidates of supporting 'Israeli Apartheid,' are all believed to have influenced the outcome of the leadership race.

Generally, the question of maintaining religious involvement, behaviour, and belief, as opposed to adopting a new national identity, is of central concern to both Muslims and their adopted countries. But we need to make a distinction between *religious identity* (a subjective state) and *religious practice* (a complex expression of public and/or private ritual performance). In the literature on religious identity and identification, a distinction is generally made between religious commitment, understood as devotion to a 'meaning-endowing framework' (a 'confession' of a personally held *belief*) as contrasted with a feeling of being bound to a religious *community* through 'social convention.'

For example, in an early article on the subject, Allport and Ross (1967) distinguish between 'intrinsic' and 'extrinsic' religious orientations, the first representing a personal commitment and the second denoting ritual conformity driven by group pressure. Querying the distinction, Cohen et al. (2005) suggest that linking 'intrinsic' motivation to 'personal' or 'individual' experience reflects a cultural bias characteristic of American Protestantism, which sees 'extrinsic' religious practices (centred on the community) as being of lesser moral value or as being characteristic of efforts to escape from practical problems through ritual (Smith, McCullough, and Poll, 2003). The distinction between *religion* and *religious practice* is also discussed by Anne S. Roald (2002) in a study of Muslims in Sweden. Roald argues that Swedish society is built on a secular world view, and religion has no part to play in public life. The right of an individual to freely practise his or her religion, however, is protected in the Swedish *Law of Religious Freedom*, provided the practice is confined to the private domain. Given the 'privatization' of religion, Roald asks, how far one can practise one's religion before it is regarded as causing public offence? She also posits that the law may be supporting freedom *from* religion, rather than freedom *of* religion.

Overall, the consensus among scholars seems to be that the treatment of Islamic civilization in the West is an important factor in defining Muslims' attitudes to their adopted countries (Khan, 2000). Other factors, such as economic security or insecurity, are also mentioned as influencing new identity formation or making particular aspects of one's identity more salient than others (Goldwasser, 1998). In any case, it may be that preserving one's religious identity is, as Yvonne Haddad (1998: 25) suggests, 'the mother of all issues' for most Muslims.

In a study among second-generation Muslim immigrants in the U.S., Lori Peek (2005) points to three stages of religious identity formation: (1) religion as *ascribed identity*; (2) religion as *chosen identity*; and (3) religion as *declared identity, in response to a crisis*. Political events can be crucial in producing identities of the third kind. Peek found, for example, that religion was only 'one of the many aspects that defined [for participants] who they were during their formative years,' but that many had moved to the third stage (religious identity declared 'in response to a crisis') as a result of the events and aftermath of 11 September 2001. In particular, the unprecedented rash of anti-Muslim incidents was a factor that prompted many to stress their Muslim identity and to adopt Islamic symbols, including the Muslim dress code (Peek, 2005: 233). Referring to a survey in Britain that had found 90 per cent of South Asians in that country used religion to self-identify, Husain and O'Brien also suggest that the signifier 'Muslim' has grown out of social exclusion and political disenchantment (Husain and O'Brien, 2000: 4). Exclusivity and isolation are also assumed to set Muslims in Canada on a confrontational course with the host culture (Shakeri, 1998:162). This can stimulate or reinforce anti-Muslim prejudice and discrimination, thus prompting individuals to draw even further away from a 'national' identity and social integration.

The following excerpts from focus-group discussions conducted in Canada with Afghan, Palestinian, and Pakistani participants in this study suggest support for these hypotheses, highlighting links between feelings of isolation and religious involvement, a heightened sensitivity to issues of appearance and how others perceive them, and feelings of being under political scrutiny:

People become more religious in Canada. There are no relatives or old friends here, so religious feeling here is real, not as [it was] back home where people wanted to prove to others that they were religious. (Palestinian female, Group Discussion 2)

Most of my friends started covering themselves here, and I learned about religion here ... Here we pray. Back home they taught us how to pray, but they didn't tell us to pray ... Now I am teaching this to my children. (Palestinian female, Group Discussion 1)

My religion became stronger here, since there is a lot of stress in this society. Also, our religion is a guideline for us, in order to raise our children. It is always better to answer our children's concerns and questions through religion. (Palestinian male, Group Discussion 1)

I started praying in Canada. I also attend some Islamic classes. (Palestinian female, Group Discussion 4)

In Pakistan, [people] don't even care. In these countries [in the West], you become more conscious. (Pakistani female, Group Discussion 3)

We are conscious of our appearances as Muslims and how people see us. We also have more time here. In Pakistan there are weddings, visiting relatives, you don't even have time for other stuff. (Pakistani female, Group Discussion 2)

I am not sure if I am a Muslim ... But as H. said, I would defend Islam when I feel it is required. (Iranian female, Group Discussion 2)

[Whether or not I identify myself as a Muslim] depends to whom I want to introduce myself. If I feel that their reaction is negative, I'll introduce myself as a Muslim very strongly. It's more cultural because I am not a religious person. I defend Islam not because I agree with it one hundred per cent, but because I feel people react to it without having enough knowledge about it. (Iranian female, Group Discussion 2)

When we got separated, [my husband] started going to the mosque ... He was not a religious person [before]. When he was in Germany, he used to drink a lot. We had relationships with lots of Iranians and drinking was some kind of tradition in these communities. But it happens rarely here. When he came to Canada, he became religious-minded. He became a Muslim here. (Afghan female, Group Discussion 1)

These statements very clearly show that religion, at least for these individuals, helps to make up for the loss of a sense of identity that other people take for granted in the known and familiar environment of a homeland. The absence of the larger networks of family and friends in diaspora creates a void and generates the need for a self-affirming connection to a group. The members of this group may not share the same national origin and cultural heritage, but they share the feelings of being outsiders and intruders who have somehow been judged unfit. Religion can fill that void for some individuals, and it can be especially important in this regard in a big city, where spatial dispersion and a more anonymous public life disrupt the sense of connection.

In any case, while we need to differentiate between religious belief and religious practice as two important aspects of religious identity, we make no assumptions about the moral worth of the 'intrinsic' and 'extrinsic' aspects of religious orientations or experience. Although correlated, religious belief and religious practice are distinct ways of accepting religious direction and discipline. Certainly, religious practice, as defined in this study, has a stronger relationship to public performance and a more overt social component exemplified by such measures as attending mosque and following Islamic dress code. It should be clear, however, that even to declare one's 'identity' as a Muslim, particularly after the events of 11 September, may motivate a pattern of behaviour that has public effects – if it leads, for example, to a determination to send one's children to Islamic schools or to make sure that one's children marry within the faith. These are contingencies that can reflect the effects of religious identity at a high level; with a performative aspect that is more evident, it can produce strong reactions from the larger community. At the same time, we should remember that for some respondents in this study, a 'Muslim identity' may not be so intense and may convey more of a desire to maintain cultural continuity rather than adhere to a set of binding religious beliefs. Or the beliefs may stand apart, without a behavioural counterpart, producing the 'virtual' religious stance noted below. Yet another group comprises 'ritual practitioners' who exhibit religious behaviour but do not express strong religious beliefs. Finally, there are individuals who are resolutely secular in both belief and practice, despite pressures within their communities to conform.

Cross-tabulating the two dimensions of religious identity and religious practice and dividing each dimension into a scale of 'very high' and 'high' as contrasted with 'low' and 'medium' yields a *four-fold typology*, defined as follows:

- *Strongly Committed* ('very high' or 'high' in religious identity *and* 'very high' or 'high' in religious practice)
- *Ritual Practitioners* ('low' or 'medium' in religious identity *and* 'very high' or 'high' in religious practice)
- *Virtual Religious* ('very high' or 'high' in religious identity *and* 'low' or 'medium' in religious practice)
- *Those tending to the Secular* ('low' or 'medium' in religious identity *and* 'low' or 'medium' in religious practice)

As shown in figure 4.1, the four communities in this study are very different from each other in terms of the distribution of religious types within them. Again, contrary to stereotypes that all peoples of Muslim background are very religious and that their communities are similar in terms of the strength of religious belief and practice, we see that the Afghan, Iranian, Pakistani, and Palestinian communities are quite different from one another, and that within each community, individuals show different degrees and kinds of religious affiliation. Indeed, with the exception of Pakistanis, a substantial segment of those surveyed are less religious, 'tending to the secular' (scoring 'low' or 'medium' on both religious identity and religious practice). About 31 per cent of Afghans, 89 per cent of Iranians, and 43 per cent of Palestinians fall into this category. Even among Pakistanis, 18 per cent claim 'low' or 'medium' on the scales of both religious identity and religious practice. By contrast, 57 per cent of Pakistanis, 29 per cent of Afghans, and 27 per cent of Palestinians are 'strongly committed' ('high' or 'very high' on both religious identity and religious practice). The extreme groups in this comparison are Iranians (89 per cent 'tending to the secular') and Pakistanis (57 per cent 'strongly committed' to religious identity and practice, with substantial additional numbers either registering as 'ritual practitioners' or 'virtual religious').

To explore the strength and consolidation of religious identity, respondents were asked whether they considered themselves to be 'Muslim.' Responses to this first identification question demonstrate the difference among communities involved in the study. About 85 per cent of Pakistani males and 88 per cent of Pakistani females identify themselves 'very strongly' as Muslims, followed by Afghan males and females (71 and 77 per cent, respectively), and Palestinian males and females (54 per cent and 56 per cent, respectively). By contrast, only 14 per cent of Iranian males and about 21 per cent of Iranian females iden-

Figure 4.1   Religious types by community

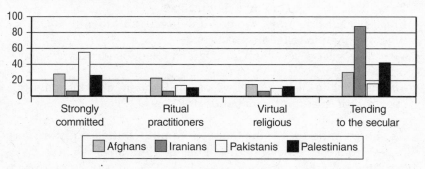

tify themselves as Muslims 'very strongly,' while 28 per cent of Iranian males and 17 per cent of Iranian females respond to the question about Muslim identity by saying 'not at all' (fig. 4.2).

Extended interviews with selected participants confirm the existence of this pattern, which separates members of each of the four communities in their sense of identity as a Muslim. In response to the question as to whether or not they consider themselves to be Muslim, two Afghan participants responded:

> I am a religious person and I try to follow my religion, although it's not easy. I pray almost five times a day even when I am at work or at school. I wear hijab and I eat only halal food. I fast in the month of Ramadan. I go to mosque only for Eid prayers. I consider that I am a modest Muslim. Although people have religious freedom to some extent, in general one finds it hard to freely practise religion in Toronto. (Afghan female)

> I am giving elementary religious knowledge to my children, but in the future I will send them to attend the mosque for religious learning. In Canada, there is freedom of religion and culture but still Islamic hijab is not welcomed by some people. On Fridays, which is a religious holiday in Islamic countries, unfortunately in Canada an employee cannot leave the job to practise his or her prayers. Therefore, I usually miss my prayers. I cannot take time off from work for my prayers, so I pray during my short breaks. (Afghan male)

Two Pakistani respondents identified themselves similarly:

Figure 4.2 Self-identification as Muslim, percentages

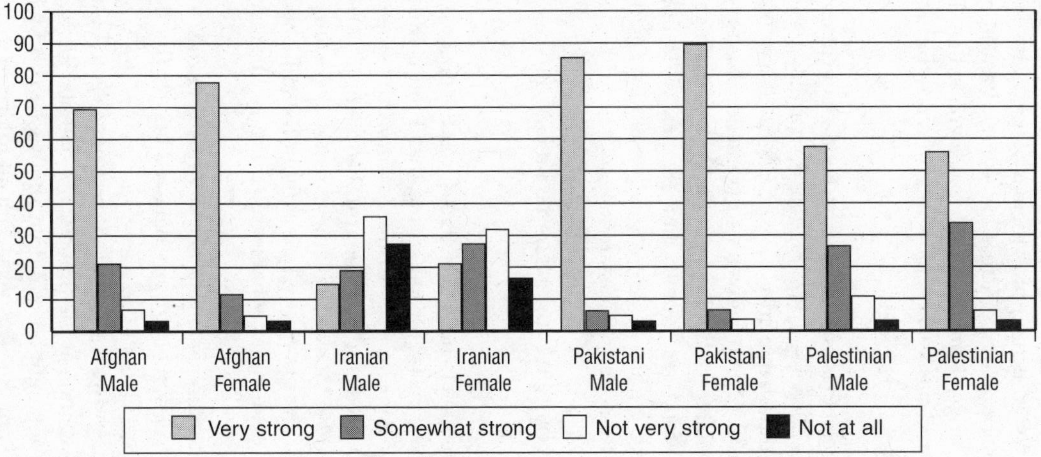

I do identify as a Muslim. I pray regularly. I do not wear hijab, but I also do not wear short skirts, or dress indecently; I am in between. I attend religious meetings, Koran lessons, et cetera. when I can manage it between jobs and classes. I eat halal food and fast during Ramadan. (Pakistani female)

I have never been to Islamic school in Canada, but I attend religious meetings and Koran lessons. I pray regularly; so do my parents and siblings. We all follow the Islamic dress code but, again, it hasn't been enforced on us, and again, Canada has given us the freedom to carry it out. At home I always eat halal food, but living in the West you can't always stay away from the fast-food restaurants that are here. I fast during Ramadan because I need to grow as a religious person. I do actually want to fast when it's not Ramadan. (Pakistani male)

The statements by two Iranians and a Palestinian respondent show the contrast:

What motivated me to become active is that the majority of people living here in the West insist on telling me that I am a Muslim. I am not a Muslim! I have come from a Muslim country, but I am not a Muslim. I am an atheist and I feel strongly about it. People in the West think that out there everybody is Muslim; well they are not, there are people there who are living their lives perfectly fine without [Islam], and there are people there who are challenging what is called Islam over there. (Iranian male)

I grew up in a religious family, and my husband did, too. I have lost all my beliefs now. I don't have any religious beliefs. (Iranian female)

My family was not very religious. It was not easy to be a Palestinian and a Muslim in Lebanon at the time for my parents. We had quite a secular upbringing. We taught our children about Islam and we practised in an open way. In France, it was very difficult to fit; we were openly discriminated against. It is a lot easier in Quebec; we have the choice to be who we are. My children have been taught the humanistic values of Islam. (Palestinian male)

Recognizing that for some individuals, subscribing to this identity can represent more of a cultural attachment than a religious one, respondents were also asked to identify the nature of the connection and whether their 'religious beliefs, faith or religious identity' had become stronger, stayed the same, or become weaker in Canada compared with how they remembered these aspects of their lives in their country of origin. Responses varied from members of one community to the next. The following are some typical responses:

> My religious feelings have not changed at all. In fact, we are getting more attached to our religion, as it is our special identity that we do not want to lose. We miss being home, especially during special occasions such as Ramadan and Eid, as not all of us can take time off to be with each other. (Palestinian male)

> Religious beliefs are [part of] the process of growth of every child in Iran. So I cannot say that I did not have any, but it was weak. My father drank alcohol but he fasted at Ramadan; many people were like my father. We were not a very religious family. After [the Islamic] revolution, I put aside those religious beliefs and started to work with the left-wing people. My beliefs are the same as before I came here. (Iranian female)

> Well, having a belief [in God] is really important ... God's will is behind everything ... I learnt [this] from my father and I have taught it to [my wife] Roya as well, that it is not the physical practice that matters. I mean, the idea of *namaz* [prayer] is that you remember God and think about God [so] many times per day. This is what you should be doing ... Now, if you think about God in ways besides *namaz*, you are still doing the same job. Here, during the weekdays we don't get to scratch our heads. But every Sunday when the church bells toll, we have our ritual ... Roya goes in front of the open window and I, from inside or along with her, we thank God for having this house now, for being better off than we were last year, for our education, financial, and other improvements that we have had. So, no, it does not matter that it is a church bell; they are all the same. The sound has become a symbol for us to be reminded of God. (Iranian male)

In table 4.1 on 'religious identity,' a higher score is assigned to those who replied that their identification with Islam is of a 'religious' nature, with lower scores assigned to those who answered that it is a 'cultural identity' only, or a 'combination' of religious and cultural elements. The tallied scores on the three questions for religious identity are shown.

Table 4.1   Religious identity, percentages

Responses	Afghans		Iranians		Pakistanis		Palestinians	
	Males	Females	Males	Females	Males	Females	Males	Females
N/A	1.76	3.87	32.47	20.11	2.52	0.57	3.0	1.74
Low	7.06	3.23	36.36	35.87	3.14	5.11	15.5	13.04
Medium	52.94	59.35	27.92	38.04	37.74	35.23	55.5	55.65
High	32.35	27.10	3.25	5.43	35.22	38.07	22.0	21.74
Very high	5.88	6.45	0.00	0.54	21.38	21.02	4.0	7.83
Total	100	100	100	100	100	100	100	100

Table 4.2   Religious practice, percentages

Responses	Afghans		Iranians		Pakistanis		Palestinians	
	Males	Females	Males	Females	Males	Females	Males	Females
N/A	1.18	2.58	4.55	4.35	1.26	1.70	0.50	0.00
Low	5.29	10.97	75.97	69.57	6.92	4.55	14.50	11.30
Medium	44.71	52.26	14.94	20.11	29.56	29.55	47.50	57.39
High	25.29	14.19	1.95	3.80	15.72	22.73	11.50	6.09
Very high	23.53	20.00	2.60	2.17	46.54	41.48	26.00	25.22
Total	100	100	100	100	100	100	100	100

The answers to specific questions that contribute to this measure of religious identity are often striking. For example, about one-third of Iranian respondents who indicate a Muslim identity say this identity is 'more of a cultural one.' At the other extreme, only slightly more than 1 per cent of Afghan males and females answer 'not at all' to the religious identification question, while *not one* of the Pakistani females takes this view. Likewise, about 38 per cent of Pakistani males and 36 per cent of Pakistani females say that their religious feelings are 'much stronger now' than they were in the home country.

Turning to questions of religious practice (table 4.2), each respondent was asked whether she or he attended mosque or Friday prayers, Qur'an readings or other religious ceremonies; whether they ate halal food; whether they fasted on Ramadan only, on other days as well, or not at all; how often they prayed; and whether they followed Islamic dress on a 'regular' basis. Scores were tallied for each element.

As with religious identity, there are striking differences among the four communities in terms of religious practice. As shown in table 4.2, over 46 per cent of Pakistani males and over 41 per cent of Pakistani females scored 'very high' on this measure while, at the other extreme, over 75 per cent of Iranian males and over 69 per cent of Iranian females scored 'low.'

If we combine those who scored 'very high' or 'high,' we can rank the four groups as follows, in descending order: Pakistanis (64 per cent female and 62 per cent males) on religious practice; Afghan males (49 per cent); Afghan females (34 per cent); Palestinian males (38 per cent); Palestinian females (31 per cent); and Iranians (6 per cent females and 5 per cent males).

The high scores on religious identity and religious practice for Pakistanis, in contrast to Iranians (as well as to other participants in this study) may be attributed in part to the distinctive political history of this community. Islam was used as an ideological tool to legitimize the formation of the state of Pakistan. Subsequently, this had an impact on the psyche of Pakistanis in the home country that continues to rub off on Pakistani respondents who have moved to Canada, and for whom the project of affirming Pakistani nationality continues to be fused with a commitment to Muslim identity and the duty to conform to Islamic practice.

The following statements by two Pakistani respondents, male and female, are instructive in this regard:

In my family, the way I was raised, my parents were very open-minded. They told us about Islam, but then they let us have our freedom to do what we wanted. They told us, 'We won't impose anything on you.' But when we went out to university or to school, people would ask us [during Ramadan], 'Are you fasting?' And then if we said, 'No, we aren't,' we would be considered odd ... Over there, religion is a cultural imposition. You don't know it at the time, but it is true. Everybody does the same thing, so you have to do it, too. If you don't do it, then you'll stand out and appear odd. I was not among those who disagreed, who stood out. Culturally, you become part of that machinery. If everyone is going to the mosque to pray on Fridays, you go with them, too. If some mullah comes to speak, you go to hear him, too. My brother and I, we would go. We understood the rituals, but we didn't do them with our heart. We just did them automatically, without thinking. And this is how you're raised. (Pakistani male)

It's important for me that my son looks up to the religion [when he grows up]. He should be proud of his identity. He shouldn't deny it. He should be proud to be a Pakistani Muslim, not just a Muslim. Both identities go together. [It] is important to emphasize Pakistani. To be a Pakistani is to be a Muslim. (Pakistani female)

Gender and Religious Identity

In a study conducted in the early 1990s in Holland among second-generation Turkish migrants, the researchers found gendered attitudinal differences as '[t]ensed acceptance, sepsis and even rejection of the religious tradition,' noting that this was more apparent among females than males (Van der Lans and Rooijackers, 1992: 62–3). Our study, however, produced contrasting results, as very small differences were observed between males and females within each community in religious self-identification, particularly at the extremes of 'very high' and 'low.'

In the typology of religious types (fig. 4.1), Pakistanis generally show a high percentage of persons who are 'strongly committed,' while Iranians show a high percentage of persons who 'tend to the secular.' This is also reflected in the data for religious self-identification. The percentage spread between Pakistani males and females scoring 'very high' and between Iranian males and females scoring 'low' is less than 1 per cent for each pair. As well, less than 1 per cent separates Palestinian males and females scoring 'high,' and only about 5 per cent separates Afghan males and females scoring 'high.' This effective erasure of gender difference points to a very strong cohesion within each community in identifying the level of commitment to 'Muslim' religious identity that is deemed appropriate.

The consensus on religiosity appears to overpower differences by gender that one might otherwise expect, reflecting the very sharp practical differences in the experiences of women and men in the country of origin, some of which are still present in Canada; as well, unequal family power relations and spousal tensions in the country of origin may continue in the host country.

Simply put, there appear to be two basic configurations regarding religious commitments and gender distinctions: (1) men and women are about the same: communities where males and females share a strongly similar attachment (or disdain) for attending mosque, eating halal, fasting, praying and wearing Islamic dress – in our study, the Pakistanis and Iranians are at the two extremes; and (2) men are more religious: communities where men exhibit a higher or somewhat higher degree of religious practice than women – in our study, the Afghans and Palestinians, with the Afghans showing a higher commitment to religious practice overall.

Moreover, where there is a tendency towards gender difference, females tend to be higher in *religious identity*, while males tend to be higher in *religious practice*. Perhaps this reflects the traditional pattern observed in many places between women and men in 'being' and 'doing,' buttressed by the gendered assignment of public performance and/or religious leadership in Muslim communities.

As regards specific religious observances, Pakistani females are slightly more likely than Pakistani males to fast (88 per cent of women fast, with 38 per cent fasting on days other than at Ramadan, compared to 84 per cent of males, with 24 per cent fasting on days other than at Ramadan); women are also more likely to 'always' eat halal (78 per cent, compared to 74 per cent of males); and to pray (78 per cent, as compared to 67 per cent of males). These are religious performances that can be completed at home. By contrast, Pakistani males are more likely than Pakistani females to 'always' participate in public religious settings, attending mosque, Friday prayers, or Qur'an readings (40 per cent of males compared to 27 per cent of females).

Among Afghans, males demonstrate an edge, but the differences, again, tend to be ritual-specific, with the male edge more prominent in public performances: 89 per cent of Afghan men fast (including 16 per cent who fast on days other than Ramadan), compared to 83 per cent of Afghan females (including 28 per cent, exceptionally, who fast on days other than Ramadan); about 25 and 26 per cent of Afghan males and females, respectively, follow Islamic dress code. A greater difference shows up in public religious ceremonies, where 52 per cent of Afghan males attend the ceremonies 'always' (20 per cent) or 'often,' compared to 13 per cent of Afghan females (9 per cent of whom 'always' attend).

Palestinians tend to fall in the middle to high end of the religious practice spectrum. About 41 per cent of Palestinian males attend mosque 'always' or 'often,' compared to 73 per cent of Pakistani males and 52 per cent of Afghan males; 89 per cent of Palestinian respondents 'regularly' fast, but mainly at Ramadan; about 75 per cent of Palestinians 'regularly' eat halal; 46 per cent 'regularly' pray, and 27 per cent 'regularly' follow Islamic dress code (a number about equal to that of Afghan males, but much less than Pakistani males).

As expected, Iranian males and females, as groups in the study, exhibit the lowest religious identity and the least fondness for religious practice: 85 per cent of Iranian males 'never' follow Islamic dress code; 71 per cent 'never' pray; 67 per cent 'never' fast, attend mosque or Friday prayers; and 35 per cent 'never' eat halal. The figures for Iranian females are about the same, but with 21 per cent saying that they 'rarely' (rather than 'never') pray and fast, as compared to 12 to 15 per cent of Iranian males.

Maintaining Religious Identity through the Generations

Studies of Muslim populations in various countries in the West note the high priority parents assign to Islamic instructions for their children as a means of strengthening their identity. In Holland and Belgium, Islamic schools are publicly funded, while in other countries, they function as independent institutions (Wagtendonk, 1991; Smith, 2002). Islamic schools are not publicly funded in Canada; religious instruction is an after-school or a weekend affair, often taking place in mosques, community centres or private homes, and it is sometimes combined with 'heritage language' or mother-tongue teaching. Often, Islamic gender-related education is combined with religious education (Bartels, 2000).

To understand and compare the experiences of our respondents in this matter, we asked them if they were sending their children to Islamic schools, how important it was to them that their children marry someone 'within the Islamic faith,' and how important it was to them that their children associate with other Muslim children. The following are samples of responses from our interviews:

> My husband sometimes goes to the mosque for prayers. I strongly feel that my children should have religious knowledge. I don't want to send them to a full-time Islamic school, but I do send them to learn the Qur'an and acquire religious knowledge [at] the nearby *madrasa*. (Afghan female)

> [My religious feelings are] much stronger now, as I am trying to influence my daughters to be more religious. I am trying to be a good role model

for them. I do not want them to get lost in the new world. (Palestinian male)

My husband, like all other Iranians, is not [as much] a 'strong-believer' as Muslims in other countries, and that's because of Shi'a practices. On one hand, there are religious practices, dogmas towards sexual relations outside marriage, low regard for women and all that, and on the other hand there is pleasure-seeking, drinking, and in particular, 'opium' – as it is not forbidden in Shi'a Islam. So, the children could *see* these contradictions in their father and, consequently, none of them grew religious, really, or showed religious tendencies ... Neither me nor my children identify ourselves as 'Muslim.' 'Muslim-born' would be more accurate. (Iranian female)

My daughter knows that her father is very conscious about religion and Islam. She doesn't have an interest in Islam, herself. The way I revolted against my father, my daughters revolt against me now; the same way. I understand that ... When my daughter was four years old, I thought about enrolling her in a Muslim school, so that she [could] learn about her culture and everything. When I went to find out about one school, they told me that the girls here have to wear the hijab ... I don't like the fact that someone imposes one particular type of Islam on someone else ... I think this [should be] a choice, and everyone has a choice, to wear it or not ... So I said no, my daughter will not go to Muslim school. (Pakistani male)

As we see in table 4.3, females are generally more anxious than males (with the exception of Afghan males) about their children's Muslim identity. The issue seems to have a particular salience for women. This may be related to the perception that discipline bound up in a religious commitment can help protect children against what many parents feel is an excessively 'liberal' attitude in the West towards the moral conduct of youth. And, in any case, it is the mother who is often given credit – or blamed – for the moral conduct of children. Thus, although Iranian females, for example, score low in their overall religious identification, as compared to their sisters in other communities, about 42 per cent of them, exceptionally, show a 'high' concern for maintaining their children's religious ties. This is a higher percentage than might be expected in the Iranian community, but at the same time, a very low percentage of Iranian females (and a very

Table 4.3   Efforts to maintain children's religious ties, percentages

Responses	Afghans		Iranians		Pakistanis		Palestinians	
	Males	Females	Males	Females	Males	Females	Males	Females
NA	25.15	27.10	44.81	27.17	30.82	23.30	26.00	27.83
Low	1.75	1.94	1.30	0.54	1.26	1.70	1.00	0.00
Medium	7.02	7.74	24.68	23.91	18.24	12.50	20.00	8.70
High	37.43	35.48	22.73	42.39	33.96	39.20	44.00	44.35
Very high	28.65	27.74	6.49	5.98	15.72	23.30	9.00	19.13
Total	100	100	100	100	100	100	100	100

low percentage of Iranian males) score in the highest category ('very high') on this measure. Here, the sharpest difference is to be found, instead, between Iranians and Pakistanis, and particularly between females in each of those communities, despite the high levels of economic achievement and aspiration they have in common. While about 23 per cent of Pakistani females express a 'very high' commitment to maintaining their children's religious ties, only 6 per cent of Iranian females expressed such views.

The uneven commitment of Iranian females to passing on religious values to their children is shown in two related measures. In the first, respondents were asked to indicate if it was 'very important,' 'somewhat important,' 'not very important,' or 'not at all important' for their daughters and sons to associate with other Muslim children. About 36 per cent of Afghan females and 31 per cent of Pakistani females felt it was 'very important' that their daughters associate with children from Afghan or Pakistani backgrounds, and between 34 and 39 per cent felt that this was 'very important' for their sons. By contrast, only about 3 per cent or less of Iranian males and females felt that it was 'very important' for their sons and daughters to associate with Muslim children. In parallel questions, respondents were asked to assess the importance of their daughters' or sons' marrying someone within the Islamic faith. About 52 per cent of Afghan females and about 57 per cent of Pakistani females felt it was 'very important' for their daughters to marry someone of the Islamic faith, and between 51 and 60 per cent felt that this was 'very important' for their sons. Again, by contrast, only about 7 per cent of Iranian females felt that it was 'very important' for their daughters to marry within the faith, and about 8 per cent of Iranian females felt it was 'very impor-tant' for their sons. Apparently, even the more religiously motivated Iranian females do not translate this concern very often into definite measures to control their children's associations or marriage partners; this is something we find only with impressive frequency among Afghans and Pakistanis, and particularly among Afghan and Pak-istani females.

In table 4.4 we summarize the broad results for religious identity and religious practice within the four communities.

good summary

Table 4.4   Community, religious identity, and religious practice

Community	Religious Identity	Religious Practice
PAKISTANIS	Overall: Very high religious identity, females higher than males	Overall: Very high religious practice, males and females equal
	Modal groups: Virtually no difference between males and females at 'very high' level	
AFGHANS	Overall: High religious identity, males and females equal	Overall: Very high or high religious practice, males higher than females
	Modal groups: Only small difference separating males and females scoring 'high' identity	
PALESTINIANS	Overall: High religious identity, females higher than males	Overall: High religious practice, males higher than females
	Modal groups: Only small difference separating males and females scoring 'high' identity	
IRANIANS	Overall: Very low religious identity, males and females equal	Overall: Very low religious practice, males and females equal
	Modal groups: Virtually no difference between males and females at 'low' level	

The Role of Mosques and Islamic Associations

Since the events of 11 September, the question of a resurgent 'Islamic identity' has become of paramount importance to Western societies. Accordingly, we have seen a shift in the national politics and immigration policies of all Western states, as well as in the practical experience of migrants. The identity markers 'Muslim' and 'Islamic' have been given great prominence and have been persistently assigned to all individuals originating from Muslim societies. This has had a far-reaching, practical consequence for the day-to-day life of the population. Its immediate impact, albeit not obvious to outsiders, has been to promote a feeling of cultural and social exclusion directed against individuals of Muslim background, and to provide an incentive or excuse for public discrimination against them in providing equal access to jobs, housing, and schooling, as well as access to services such as health care. The diminished sense of entitlement to the rights and guarantees taken for granted by other citizens has, inevitably, caused deep resentment and anger, damaging hopes for a dignified sense of selfhood and social belonging, and often energizing a politically charged connection to religious belief and ritual practice that is more rigid and unforgiving than the one experienced or practised in the home country. The strong and sometimes disproportionate reactions of nominally Muslim populations in various European countries to racist provocations by the European majority are quite instructive in this regard.

Within this context, the role of mosques and Islam-based groups, along with Muslim educational or service associations, deserves special attention. Undoubtedly, Muslim institutions provide a sense of community and offer valuable material and psychological support that Muslims need and often can't find in state-funded and state-run institutions. However, by reducing the need for making use of non-Muslim institutions and services, including services provided by the state, the steps taken by the religious bodies may also diminish the possibilities for their constituents to have contact and to interact with others in the larger society, helping solidify the existence of Muslim communities in Canada and elsewhere that tend to be self-sufficient and isolated. The 'easy' solution of using faith-based services undermines the legitimacy of state institutions and weakens the reach of the Canadian government in encouraging social integration. Equally important, the Islam-based institutions have a conservative character, which are given new prominence by the state. By downloading certain crucial services onto these organizations or making them partners in their delivery – and by following the policy of a seemingly benign and neutral 'non-interference' in community-based institutions – the state further strengthens the power and authority of these conservative religious institutions within their respective communities and makes it increasingly difficult for other tendencies in these communities to express their voices. Even without any formal endorsement, the informal partnership tends to give the Islam-based institutions the standing of para-statal authorities.

Our survey of twenty-two Muslim associations and groups in the Toronto area, many of them federally registered and some officially government-sponsored through the Ministry of Citizenship and Immigration, shows that while the function of the more conservative religious institutions is to promote Islamic rituals and values, cautioning believers to purify their body and soul against polytheism (*shirk*), most also provide essential settlement services, such as skill-training and job search assistance, a food bank for the poor and needy, Islamic funeral and burial services, and family and marriage counselling. These services accompany traditional religious activities, such as Islamic study circles, Friday prayers, and hajj conferences. Almost all the institutions have weekend classes for children, Qur'an readings, and religious training classes for women and youth. A few run elementary schools and orphanages.

Generally, in countries with significant Muslim-minority populations, the tendency is towards establishing central authorities or umbrella organizations that claim to incorporate various faith-based groups and associations and to represent the interests of Muslims in negotiations with states concerning official recognition and accommodation. This is something that is preferred and encouraged by the host governments and is perhaps more successful in countries with less ethnically diverse Muslim populations, such as Germany with its large Turkish population and over 2,300 mosques, prayer rooms, and Muslim groups (Soper and Fetzer, 2003), and Britain, with its predominantly South Asian population and over a thousand registered mosques and other Islamic institutions. (Even though France's Muslims are also predominantly from a single – North African – origin, the French system, so far, has not committed itself to adopting policies that accommodate Muslims.) In Germany, about ten umbrella organizations claim to represent the interests of the Turkish Islamic population (Goldberg, 2002: 40–2). Similarly, Britain's Muslim communities, despite divergent ideological and political divisions, including some with foreign links, are represented and mobilized when the need arises by a few umbrella organizations. These include the traditional Council of Mosques and Council of Imams, along with other organizations that now function under the new leadership of the British-born generations, such as the Islamic Society of Britain. Following years of campaigning, British Muslims have finally succeeded in establishing state-funded Islamic schools (Rex, 2002; Osler and Hussain, 2005).

At present, over 250 mosques, Islamic associations, and Islamic centres are active in Canada, excluding numerous prayer rooms. In 2002, forty-two of the total sixty-seven active Canadian mosques were in Ontario. The Coalition of Muslim Organizations of Ontario (COMO), representing about thirty-four Muslim organizations, and the Association of Progressive Muslims of Ontario (PMO), which aims at providing a collective voice for Muslim communities and acts as an interlocutor between Muslim communities and various levels of the government, try to identify and prioritize Canadian Muslim concerns. They also lobby for or assess the impact of legislation on Muslims and attempt to promote better understanding and improve inter-faith dialogue. COMO, for example, assessed and submitted a response to Bill C-36 (the *Anti-Terrorism Act*) and Bill C-17 (the *Public Safety Act*). The country's other influential Muslim organization, the Islamic Society of North America (ISNA), is a conservative organization that, according to its spokesperson, receives substantial funding from Saudi Arabia (*Globe and Mail*, 8 November 2005). The association lobbies actively for the establishment of state-funded Muslim schools in Canada. It spearheads annual Islamic conferences in Toronto that bring together thousands of Muslims from across the country.

How best to accommodate the demands of Muslims for recognition of their rights to retain their cultural heritage and religious practices without the fear of being ostracized, isolated, and discriminated against is a pressing political issue for all liberal democracies. Meeting these demands, however, is not as simple as it might appear. Putting in place well-defined anti-discriminatory policies and institutional forms and mechanisms for their forceful implementation is an urgent issue. But complex strategic questions lurk behind these issues, which must be publicly debated and resolved – most notably, the various meanings of equality, and the tension between group rights and individual rights.

For example, how are we to reconcile the principle of equal treatment of all ethnic and religious groups and guarantee the equality of rights for all citizens in and before the law, and at the same time attend to the special measures and exceptional allowances demanded by some groups? Many Western states are struggling to strike a balance between the two principles, and none seems to have succeeded. Then there is the question of the tension between the rights of groups and the rights of individuals, as well as the duty of the state to protect the rights of all citizens from harm, domination, and exploitation. Some of the demands advocated by conservative elements within the Muslim communities, for example, are not as benign and inconsequential to individuals as these organizations and their supporters want us to believe. Neither do the majority of community members want to see the materialization of these religious demands. The most vivid example is the harm that would be caused to women by the application of sharia in family matters such as marriage, divorce, polygamy, child custody, and inheritance. The same can also be said about the proposal for state-funded religious schools – with their emphasis on religiously ordained gender roles and sexist moral ethics proclaimed as the inalienable group rights of Muslims. Certainly, these potentially harmful 'cultural practices' cannot be put at par with recognition of the rights of Muslim girls to wear head-covers, if they so choose, or the legitimate demand to make space and time available for Muslim prayer at workplaces and schools. The question, then, is whether states can provide official recognition and freedom for religious practices in some areas, but with consistency and integrity deny them in others. Finally, there is the question of who can speak on behalf of an ethno-religious community and negotiate its social and legislative priorities.

These are complex problems for all groups wishing to assert a demand for collective rights, but particularly for diasporic communities of Muslim cultural background, given the highly charged political setting and remarkable national, ethnic, cultural, class, and religious diversity of these communities.

Drawing on our analysis of questionnaires, transcripts of group discussions, and individual interviews, we have highlighted differences in the importance attached to Islamic rituals and Islamic identities – and, indeed, to the role of faith per se – in the lives of individual members of the four communities of Afghans, Iranians, Pakistanis, and Palestinians studied. But we argue that too much emphasis on the role of religion in shaping the experience of diaspora from majority-Muslim countries drastically narrows the psychological horizon available both to policymakers and to members of these communities, effectively reducing the identity of individual members to but one of its constituent parts. As the case of the Pakistanis illustrates, even where a pattern of strong religious involvement seems to exist, one needs to be cautious in identifying the factors driving religious identification. Indeed, excessive preoccupation with the demands of diehard religious minorities within these communities risks diluting or neglecting broad social and economic concerns that are crucial to the majority, reinforcing the efforts made by traditionalists to manipulate the frustration of Muslim diaspora in directions of their choosing; it means neglecting legitimate needs and yielding, instead, to the demands of a radical religious agenda. The result would be the further alienation of moderate Muslims and secular individuals from these communities and the creation of political solidarities reflecting rigid religious views.

5 Youths:
Living between Two Generations and Two Cultures

The issue of youths of Muslim cultural background emerges, in the first instance, because the educational and occupational success of this group and the integration of its members are essential for the development of a genuinely multicultural, inclusive, and affirming society. However, under the pressure of international events, a new wave of racism today presents Islam as a leading danger. This has had a contradictory impact on Muslim youths living in the West, both in terms of life experience and life options. On the one hand, these youths are facing many of the structural barriers that were not expected to impede their progress, as they had that of their parents, towards a productive and dignified life as equal citizens. On the other hand, today's Muslim youths (or a significant proportion thereof) refuse to abandon Islam or its public expression in order to overcome or circumvent those barriers. Indeed, through their deliberate engagement in Islamic symbols and practices, these youths are strenuously claiming their rights as citizens; they are challenging the liberal democratic societies in which they live to respect their democratic right to choose. Depending on one's perspective, this can be understood as giving new meaning to the idea of integration, or it can be taken as the product of integration (or assimilation) imposed by others.

In this sense, religion does not have the same kind of direct functionality for Muslim youth that it had for the older generation, for whom adherence to Islam was a way of preserving identity and connecting with other members of their ethno-religious group. For them, it fell within the sphere of an easy, protective, and affirming sociability, and provided a point of anchorage. This traditional adherence to religion may persist for some young people, but for youth raised and socialized in the West, religiosity can also mark out a sort of reflexive questioning of the secular values of the larger society that, in their view, has become stuck in its colonial mentality. Theirs is perhaps a more political and transgressive form of religiosity, since it challenges dominant perceptions about Islam and Muslims. More generally, it may be a reaction to the West's perceived sense of superiority that looks down on all beliefs, practices, values, mores and morality not generated on its soil. Yet, even in this objection to Western individualism and lack of spirituality, the reaction of Muslim youth in the West sometimes curiously echoes it. Indeed, as Jocelyne Cesari (2003: 259–60) suggests, for young people in Europe, the new forms of religiosity are often characterized by individualism, privatization, secularism, and the new patterns of consumerism, since, 'like buyers, people are increasingly choosing which tenets and rules of their religion they will recognize and which they will ignore.' What we have found in this study is that this is particularly true of young Muslim females and males, who are not as excluded as their parents from the larger society's resources and rewards. Coming generally from a middle-class background and sharing the same competitive impulses, the same drive for material success, and often, the same tastes and values of their generation at large, they are still acutely aware that they are different from the rest of their peers. The responses of the young Canadian Afghans, Iranians, Palestinians, and Pakistanis in this study reflect these new developments, but each community shows them in its own distinctive way.

Demographics

The 'youths' in our samples included unmarried individual members of the four communities aged from fifteen to twenty-two. With the exception of the Palestinians, the majority of the youths were born in their 'country of origin' (97 and 87 per cent of Afghan males and females; 94 and 100 per cent of Iranian males and females; and 76 and 74 per cent of Pakistani males and females, respectively, in each group). By contrast, very few of the Palestinian youths were born in Palestine; rather, they cited 'other Middle East' countries (45–52 per cent), the United States or Canada (33–35 per cent), and Jordan (5–7 per cent). Only 9.5 per cent of Palestinian males and 12.5 per cent of the females in the sample were born in Palestine.

Most of the Iranian and Pakistani youths had left their country of origin in the decade and a half following 1990. The Pakistani males were the most recent arrivals in Canada; some 40 per cent in the sample had left their home country after 2000. Exceptionally, about 33 to 38 per cent of the Afghans had left their home country in the 1980s. A combination of reasons was mentioned for the departure of our youthful respondents from their country of origin. Many – some 70 per cent of Afghan males, 53 per cent of Afghan females, 48 per cent of Palestinian males, and 53 per cent of Palestinian females – listed 'war or civil war' as a main motivator; 13 per cent of Afghan males (as well as 17 per cent of Iranian males) also cited 'military service' as a factor. In addition, some 42 per cent of Iranian males listed 'political persecution' as a reason for leaving their home country. For many, political or security concerns accompanied the desire to pursue their education and other motives. But securing an education was more a concern for Iranians and Pakistanis, and less for Palestinians or Afghans, as only 7 and 9 per cent, respectively, of Palestinians and Afghan females and 17 per cent of Afghan males said they left their countries of origin in order to get an education.

Like the adults in this study and at even a higher level, the vast majority of the younger-generation respondents, with the exception of Afghan males, had origins in urban areas (over 78 per cent of Afghans, 97 per cent of Iranians, 73 per cent of Pakistanis, and 59 per cent of Palestinians). In terms of family background (again, like the adult respondents but at a much higher level), the majority of the youths' parents came from the new middle classes. The higher level of education of their parents resulted from better access to educational opportunities as compared to the parents of the older generation. Of the youths' fathers, over 77 per cent of the Pakistanis, over 76 per cent of the Iranians, over 68 per cent of the Palestinians, and over 38 per cent of the Afghans hold undergraduate and graduate university degrees. The figures for fathers attaining a university degree in the adult sample are 41 per cent for Pakistanis, 27 per cent for Iranians, 24 per cent for Palestinians, and 24 per cent for Afghans. The level of education for the youths' mothers is also quite high compared to the corresponding figures for adults, with over 66 per cent of Iranian mothers and about 60 per cent of Pakistani mothers having attained a 'high' (university) level of education, followed by 42 and 16 per cent for Palestinian and Afghan mothers, respectively.

The data regarding the occupation of the youths' mothers present a somewhat different picture compared to the relevant data of the adults surveyed. In line with the higher level of education mentioned

above, the number of mothers in white-collar and professional occupations is noticeably higher, and the number of those in homemaking
is much lower, than the figures for the adult members of the communities. This may point to the relative improvement of the women's sit-
uations as compared to that of the older generation. About 29 per cent
of the mothers of Afghan youths, along with about 50 per cent of the
mothers of Iranian youths, as well as 28 and 26 per cent of the mothers
of Pakistani and Palestinian youths, respectively, were in white-collar
and professional occupations. The percentages in these occupations
among mothers of adult members of the communities were 7, 21, 11,
and 13 per cent, respectively, for Afghans, Iranians, Pakistanis, and
Palestinians.

About 54 per cent of the fathers of the Afghan youths were in civil
service, military, professional, and managerial occupations, including
doctors, lawyers, and engineers. The figures for the fathers of Iranian,
Pakistani, and Palestinian youths in these categories are about 47 per
cent, 43 per cent, and 38 per cent, respectively. Similar to the related
figures of the adults, the second-largest category of occupations for the
four communities is in trade, crafts, and small business (with about 32
per cent for Palestinians, 28 per cent for Iranians, 18 per cent for Pakistanis, and 17 per cent for Afghans). Smaller percentages of the
youths' fathers worked as blue-collar workers.

The majority of the youths were elementary and high school students when they emigrated – except for Afghans, of whom over 33 per
cent of boys and over 21 per cent of girls in our sample had left
Afghanistan with no education. This was partly due to the fact that
some were very young when they left their home country. Others came
from poor or rural families, and still others were affected by the disastrous educational system imposed during the period of Mujahedeen
and Taliban rule. About 24 per cent of young Afghans had elementary
education, and about 10 per cent had some high school education. As
for the Iranian youths, about 14 per cent had elementary education
and 44 per cent had some high school education before migration. The
figures for Pakistani youths before emigration were about 23 per cent
with elementary and 19 per cent with some high school education.
Very few young Palestinians reported elementary or high school education in their 'country of origin.' Most had not lived in or been educated in the Palestinian territories, as they had grown up in other
places where the parents were refugees. A larger number of Pakistani
youth (about 19 per cent) had completed high school in their home

country. A smaller percentage of youths from the four communities also had certificates or diplomas, or had some years of undergraduate education in their countries of origin.

In Canada, most of the young respondents continue to be students at different levels. Generally, about one-third to one-half of Iranians and Pakistanis with a well-to-do background, both males and females, continued to study for their baccalaureates, while 20 per cent of Iranian males, 14 per cent of Pakistani males, and 15 per cent of Pakistani females had already completed them. Less than 20 per cent of Afghans and Palestinians were in university, and some 25 per cent of Palestinian females had already completed their BAs. Among young Afghan males and females, the largest groups (33 and 36 per cent, respectively) cite 'completed high school' as their highest educational attainment since moving to Canada, and roughly one-quarter list 'some high school.' The situation for young Palestinians is different, as about 17 per cent of females and fully 26 per cent of Palestinian males in our sample have obtained a certificate. Taking all this together, however, the differences between Afghans, on one hand, and Iranians, Pakistanis, and Palestinians, on the other, is quite sharp. Some 52 to 68 per cent of Pakistani, Iranian, and Palestinian youths, males and females, had either completed a BA or were working on it, or had completed a certificate or diploma. For Afghans, the comparable figure was about 32 per cent (females) and 27 per cent (males). Only 7 per cent of Afghan females had completed a BA. No Afghan male at the time of study had completed a bachelor's degree.

Family Relations

Despite differences in dates of departure from countries of origin and arrival in Canada, and smaller differences in age, young respondents in our study share important attributes in their relations with parents and family. Indeed, the great majority of them remain closely tied emotionally to their parents, siblings, and other relatives; they depend on them for support and continue to reflect their values. This is a crucial element, one which firmly establishes the place of youths in these communities.

This phenomenon is partly a result of the migration experience. Because of the war in Afghanistan, about one-quarter of the Afghan males were joined by parents or siblings after they moved to Canada; another quarter had family members who could not emigrate at all.

Also, about 20 per cent of Pakistani males in Canada (typically, some-what younger than those in the other groups) were preceded by the arrival of other family members. These are partial exceptions. Nearly all of the rest of the youths in the study travelled to Canada together with members of their families. Also marking a difference, about one-third of the better-off young Iranian and Pakistani men live outside the parental home, while most of the remainder continue to live with parents or siblings.

Still, despite these gaps in migratory experience and living arrange-ments, the variety of tensions youths encounter in growing up, and, perhaps, the even more challenging difficulties of being implicated in the two cultures of homeland and diaspora, for the young people we interviewed the family remains energetic and robust as a base of soli-darity, affection, and support. Far from tearing them apart, the experi-ence of migration has been a testing and bonding one for these migrant families. Certainly, there are differences of opinion between parents and their children, and real causes for tension, but there is no evidence in the population studied of a 'lost,' stranded or alienated generation.

Indeed, the modal social character of family interaction in the four groups studied is regularly intense. More than 55 per cent of youths interviewed, from among Afghans, Iranians, Palestinians, and Pak-istani females, visit their parents or siblings 'frequently' or 'every day,' with 58 per cent of Afghan females and 48 per cent of Iranian females saying that they visit with their parents daily. Among Pakistanis, by exception, the contrast between males and females in terms of living arrangements (a third of young Pakistani males live apart) is also repeated in sharing time with one's parents. The Pakistani men are less frequent visitors; about half of Pakistani males see their immediate rel-atives only 'sometimes' or 'not at all,' in contrast to the 38 per cent of Pakistani females who dutifully see parents 'every day.' Additionally, besides immediate family, some 31 per cent of the young Pakistani females say they 'frequently' visit aunts, uncles, and cousins.

Still, despite these differences for one group, about 70 per cent of youth respondents for all four communities, male and female, feel their relationship with their parents is going 'really well.' Among those who are still living with their parents, upwards of 55 per cent report that they 'never' or 'seldom' consider living away from home. At least 60 per cent of respondents say their relationship with parents since coming to Canada has been 'happy' or 'very happy.' No more than 10 per cent of respondents say that their relationship with parents has 'gotten worse' since arrival (only 1 per cent of young Pakistani males would admit to that). Indeed, roughly 40 per cent or more of Pakistanis and Palestinians feel that their relations with parents have 'gotten better.'

These family-centred and affirming attitudes are vividly reflected in answers to questions regarding efforts to seek help with personal problems. For these emotionally charged personal issues, almost all of the youths reported that they seek help from 'friends,' or from 'relatives,' or a combination thereof. Virtually no one reports seeking help for personal problems from societal organizations, whether religious or secular. Even more family-centred and protective than the average in the sample, some 37 per cent of Pakistani females and 48 per cent of Palestinians, male and female, seek help from relatives only, even leaving friends aside; this compares with 20 to 22 per cent of Afghans, male and female, and Iranians and Pakistani males who seek help from relatives only. But one should not overdraw the difference between Pakistani, Palestinian, and Afghan females. The Afghan group remains highly traditional; some 74 per cent of Afghan females, like 77 per cent of Palestinian females, are not allowed to stay overnight at the home of a same-sex friend, and from 44 to 47 per cent of young Afghan and Palestinian women report that they must come home immediately after attending school. Iranians and Pakistanis, being from wealthier backgrounds, show a more 'modern' approach to such concerns; among them, it is also more common for young people to 'argue or negotiate' with their parents before reaching a conclusion on decisions important to them.

The strong adhesion to family, however, does not erase gender differences. The gender divide remains important among these youths. Males and females, for example, are quite unlike in their habits of spending 'leisure time' with their parents. Among the females, some 20 per cent of the Iranians, 23 per cent of the Pakistanis, 28 per cent of the Palestinians and 35 per cent of the Afghans report spending 'leisure time' with their fathers 'every day.' This is the pattern for no more than 7 to 17 per cent of their male counterparts. Again, 34 per cent of Iranian, 56 per cent of Afghan, 57 per cent of Pakistani, and 62 per cent of Palestinian females spend 'leisure time' with their mothers 'every day,' as compared to frequencies for the male youths in these groups which never exceed 38 per cent. Only 3 per cent of Iranian males report spending 'leisure time' with their mothers 'every day,' although a relatively high number (28 per cent) report that they do so 'often.' These young Iranian males also restrict their time with their fathers, only 3 per cent reporting that they spend 'leisure time' with them 'every day,' and only 14 per cent saying that they do so 'often.' Like other groups, they visit their parents frequently, but as the most modern, best educated, and least religious group, young Iranian males are also, apparently, the busiest with non-family activities and thus appear to be more distant from their families of origin.

In dealing with financial problems, nearly one-half to three-quarters of Iranians, Pakistanis, and Palestinians rely on relatives only. Again, virtually no one reports seeking financial help from community or religious organizations. But perhaps, in part, because fewer members of their families have been able to immigrate to Canada, relatively more Afghans report that they depend on 'friends' or a combination of 'friends and relatives' for financial help than do the other groups. Again, poorer and less educated than the others, some 13 per cent of Afghan females also find themselves seeking assistance from social service agencies. At 6 per cent, Pakistani females are the only other group in substantial contact with such agencies. This is the only area in which public support is sought; apart from this, it is worth underlining that virtually none of the youth respondents reported seeking help for personal or financial issues from outside agencies or religious organizations, medical personnel, or, in cases of trouble, the police.

Even in finding a job, some 38 per cent of Palestinian males and 25 per cent of Palestinian females seek help with relatives only. The other groups depend mainly on 'friends' only, or on 'friends and relatives.' Again, the one exception is Afghan females, some 11 per cent of whom seek job help from community organizations. No other group depends on such organizations or social service agencies to get a job. Perhaps this is a result of the greater exposure of Afghan females to social service agencies for financial support, itself a result of their greater poverty and their diminished opportunity to pursue a university education. Except for this group, the ability of Canadian state institutions, community or religious organizations to serve as useful supports for Muslim youths when the need arises finds little support in this data.

Our understanding of these issues becomes more nuanced when we turn from statistical results to the testimony of parents and youths offered in the extended, less structured interviews. These can be identified by theme, the enforcement of strict rules at home being a common issue, and probably the area in which conflict over the shift from the old country to the new is sharpest and most clear cut. As an example, in Iran, as one Iranian parent living in Toronto reported:

> Parents of a married man with three children [feel free to] interfere with his life and try to give him advice and make some decisions for him [and] even the children think it's necessary to take advice from their parents. But here, children don't see the need to do so and the parents don't depend on their children as much either.

Along the same lines, a Palestinian mother explained that although their son was only six when they left Jordan, 'here we cannot be too strict with him as all other kids are free.' From the other side, a young Pakistani woman in Montreal revealed:

> You know, sometimes people are really curious, and they want to exper-iment, but I was never like that. I had friends who smoked and had boyfriends, and things like that [but] ... we couldn't go anywhere. It wasn't just an issue of permission, but also logistics ... who would take us there, drop us off.' [Still, they] had fun in Pakistan. [They never felt] suf-focated.

A Toronto Iranian father confessed:

> I was a very strict and dictator parent. However, here in Canada you can't follow the old Iranian tradition and lifestyle to raise our kids. I've had arguments with them, but I am very close with them and I participate in all of their plans.

Men are not always the stricter parent. A Toronto Iranian mother said her husband was 'more lenient,' insisting that it was not important, after all, if their daughter wanted to 'pluck her eyebrows,' that it was 'just one or two hairs.' Still, in a focus group, one Palestinian father reported that he was so upset about the 'bad words' his children had learned in school that the family had moved to a better neighbour-hood. Another worried about 'smoking at school' and youngsters 'doing drugs,' although, they added, 'boys are worse' because 'girls have more limits.' To these, a third Palestinian father, reflecting a dif-ferent attitude, sharply responded that the question of 'honesty' was much more important, that he told his son that 'if he wants to smoke cigarettes, he should bring it home and not to do it behind my back.'

How rules are applied differently to females and males is also a recurrent theme. In each community, young females who are still living at home are more likely than young males to report that they must return home immediately after school and must also be home earlier than their brothers. This is a rule applied to 48 per cent of young Palestinian females and 44 per cent of Afghan females, as compared to 29 per cent of young female Pakistanis and 18 per cent of young Iranian females in the study. But even for the more religious Pakistanis, Canadian conditions have had their impact, as illustrated below:

> Here, my mother always tells me not to go out, you are a girl. Take care of yourself; go out with your brother ... If someone comes and says that this culture is not good for children, then my mother also gets alarmed that her children may also get affected by this environment ... They think the same way as other people in Pakistan do. We cannot change their minds. In Pakistan, my sister [and I] never went to school alone. We never travelled in buses or taxis. My brother used to take us to school and bring us back. We never even went to bazaar alone. So when, in Canada, I go to school alone, it creates a difference. (Young Pakistani woman)

What is the effect of this daily struggle between parents and youth? Negotiating these small challenges, most of those interviewed – parents and children – claimed that these relationships had become 'warmer and more truthful' in the process, drawing on a foundation of common respect. In a sense, they had grown closer in coming to Canada. Note the following statements:

> ... [W]e now understand their emotions and feelings. We understand their intentions and we will not do anything to make them feel bad. [We are now taking this attitude], I think, because we are growing up. (Pakistani youth in Toronto)

> ... [T]he relationship between me and my mom has changed in a positive way, because both of us [now know] each other better. I don't call it mother-and-child relation; I call it the family of two. In Iran I was wondering if we [could] be like friends, here I believe that we are friends. I appreciate them for coming here for our sake. (Iranian youth in Toronto)

This optimistic or conciliatory view is perhaps more prevalent among educated Iranians and their children in cases where the parents were political refugees, but even here it is shaded and complicated by the challenge of Canadian ways. As the same young person said:

> ... [R]elations and family are more outspoken here. I don't know if I can call it closer but it is franker than Iran. Perhaps it is because I got older than then. They have to travel a lot and stay there for a long time so we can't be together that much. I would like to keep this relationship, try to talk to them more, especially to my dad.

While Iranians and Pakistanis do not distinguish between males and females in allowing their children to stay overnight at the home of a same-sex friend, Afghans do. These 'overnights' are permitted for 57 per cent of young males but only for 22 per cent of young females. Only 20 per cent of young Palestinian females and 24 per cent of young Palestinian males are permitted to do so; while the numbers are low, they are not gender-divided. Still, as a young Palestinian woman says, regardless of the rules, feelings about gender difference and women's greater need for protection persist. However, the youths try to see their parents' viewpoint:

> My mom, she obviously tries to be as fair as she can with all of us, but at the end of the day, if my brother wants to sleep out with his guy friend, it is all right; it is not [as big a] deal as [it is for] me. [For me,] sleeping over is in question unless it is my family's place ... When I was growing up I was [asking] all [the] time, 'So what's wrong with it? You know, all my friends, people in my school do it,' and it was easy for me [to say this]. It is still tough – I am not saying it is easy – but sometimes I think, okay, how would I feel about it as a mother? Sometimes, I take a step back. In general, for the first generation growing up here it is not easy, but you know, *inshallah*, if I get married and have kids, it will be easier for them because I've already been brought up here.

The same attitude of compromise is also found among parents, but not among all of them. An Iranian grandparent in Toronto complained:

> ... [I]n Canada, kids take their own parents to court! The father tells the kid, 'Do not stay in the street. Come home before dark.' But children do not listen. My grandchildren do not talk to me. Kids are very indifferent. They do not respect any values.

It should be emphasized that these issues are not just the result of 'family' disputes. Difficulties can also grow out of the serious problems the parents encounter outside, at work, and in finding work. A Pakistani woman in Toronto explained:

> ... [M]y husband is looking for jobs non-stop and hasn't found one yet. We have problems with our children's education. My husband has developed a kind of depression, and when the head of the family is in tension or trouble, then the entire family suffers.

Certainly, it is true that if a young person's parents find it hard to obtain employment, this will make family life tense. Within the family, these difficulties are always a stressor. Thus, the family can become a point of condensation for problems which originate elsewhere. The pressures build outside, but the family is the place where they often must find a resolution. As an Iranian youth explained:

> ... [In Canada] we see each other less, but hard life made us close to each other. I can't say it's better or worse, just different. Now, the whole family is under pressure.

Along with new problems, the pace of life has changed. Some parents worry that that they are unable to control their children at school, and, as a Palestinian parent explained, they don't like it when the children 'go out too much.' The changed physical environment also can yield contradictory effects. For a well-off Pakistani parent used to living in a large house in their home country, 'living in smaller places' in Canada prompts too much interaction, while a Palestinian from a poorer, rural family lamented:

> ... [B]ack home, maybe in the countryside, [the] family still sits and eats from the same plate, and how tasty is the food when you eat it together; even religiously it is blessed, and in it you teach your children the sharing and caring for others. [Here, by comparison, each child has his own room and] you are compelled by law to separate boys from girls.

The result is a dispiriting individualism:

> So the message they [the forces of the established culture] deliver to children is the love of your own self and the denial of the other, and this

breaks the tight relationship in the family. [The] new values contradict our religion and our Arabic tradition.

It is evident that these issues go beyond the simple confrontation of younger and older generations, and offer fewer escapes. Indeed, in respect to the generational conflict alone, as an Afghan youth says, it would perhaps be sufficient if parents were 'open-minded' and respected the 'personal freedom' that their children have now come to expect. Of course, they would still argue, explained a Palestinian youth, because:

... they [the parents] want us to have similar ideas, thoughts and behaviour as them. They do not really get it that we are influence[d] by two cultures.

But there is much more at play here than being old or young, or that some parents 'get it' and some don't. For one, not all parents are locked into the older culture, and we see that this adaptability can vary in strategic ways. Some parents, instead of fighting nostalgically for what is past, understand the change as beneficial and as part of an organic process in which they will learn from their children and, through them, from the new society in which they are now living. The following statements reflect these pressures to change:

I think this culture is ahead of my culture. People like me usually keep to our own culture and do not explore Canadian culture, but our kids are not like this ... [Still], seeing this difference does not make me feel depressed. I have accepted that our kids should be raised in and by this culture. However, my way of dealing with these differences is to allow them to live their life and not interfere with their affairs. Therefore, I do not try to learn their ways. I just live my life and let them lead theirs. (An Iranian parent in Toronto)

My beliefs have changed a lot since I have come to Canada. For example, I used to think it is extremely important for a girl to be [a] virgin at marriage. If somebody told me this is not an issue, I would think what a buster [bi-ghayrat] he must be! I no longer think that way. Now I think there are lots of other qualities that a woman should have which are much more important. Or, I see people here just live together without getting married. I like that; this is a very wise thing to do ... You live together as long as you wish and don't when you don't wish. In Iran, when you get married, you're stuck with it 'til the end of your life! But in Iran you cannot do that [just live together]; [*laughing*] they would stone you to death if you do! (Iranian father in Montreal)

The ability of parents to change in Canada has a powerful effect on the adjustment of their children. The insightful statement below, from an older Iranian woman in Toronto, reflects on this process of adjustment:

I see cultural differences between my children, grandchildren and myself. But I see it as a positive thing, and accept it. I do not have any irrational, nationalist fervour. I think Iranian culture has some positive aspects, but Canadian culture also has very good elements. I want my children to have whatever is good from both cultures. I accept the fact that my granddaughter has a boyfriend. She even brings him to our home. Iranian culture does not accept a woman to be free and independent. I do not agree with our culture on this ... I think we should raise our kids as decent and truthful human beings. I was a school counsellor in Iran. Many teenagers who had girlfriends or boyfriends used to come and talk to me. They could not talk to their own families about their problems. I used to tell them that they are not doing anything wrong. They should only try to keep their respect throughout. I used to teach them self-respect so no one could take advantage of them ... In Canada, Iranian families are making a huge mistake when they force their kids to follow traditional Iranian culture. They should teach their kids to be good human beings. These families do not teach their kids how to swim; then they expect them to jump in the 'big sea' [society]. We should talk to our kids about ethics, about the dangers of addiction, unwanted pregnancy, and so on. In Canadian culture, kids are more free and independent. (Iranian woman in Toronto)

Maintaining or Parting with the Original Culture

Like their parents or the older generation, youths in diaspora live within two cultural paradigms – one the dominant culture of their adopted country, the other the culture of their country of origin. Although physically distant from the old country for a good part of their lives, it still lingers in the memories of these youths, kept fresh by their families and by the community at large. Different cultural markers, such as retention and use of the mother tongue, religious

Table 5.1 Cultural markers – language, percentages

Youth and adult samples	Afghans		Iranians		Pakistanis		Palestinians	
	Males	Females	Males	Females	Males	Females	Males	Females
Mother tongue at home								
Youth	40.00	42.59	55.56	54.55	47.14	46.15	61.90	45.00
Adults	80.59	81.94	79.87	88.59	66.67	65.91	73.00	73.91
English at home								
Youth	3.33	1.85	5.56	2.27	10.00	4.62	30.95	37.50
Adults	0.59	0.00	5.84	0.54	4.40	4.55	15.5	8.70
Mother tongue and English at home								
Youth	53.33	46.30	30.56	34.09	32.86	43.08	7.14	17.50
Adults	13.53	6.45	7.14	3.26	20.13	21.02	3.00	6.96
Mother tongue always in public								
Youth	3.33	3.70	2.78	13.64	5.71	7.69	26.19	12.50
Adults	17.06	23.23	24.03	32.61	17.61	20.45	26.50	30.43
Mother tongue always to read								
Youth	0.00	0.00	2.78	0.00	1.43	3.08	0.00	2.50
Adults	10.00	8.39	12.99	15.76	8.81	11.93	27.00	6.09
Mother tongue always to write								
Youth	0.00	0.00	2.78	0.00	1.43	4.62	0.00	0.00
Adults	10.00	10.32	8.44	10.33	6.92	11.36	9.00	4.35

observance, attendance at cultural events, enjoyment of traditional music and food, adoption of religious or traditional attire, and interaction with others from one's community in social groups show the ways in which youths in the four communities are maintaining or gradually parting with the original culture of the older generation. To get a closer look at these trends, this section compares data for youths and adults on these cultural dimensions.

In terms of language (table 5.1), the results are straightforward, and are as expected. Youths in each community are much less likely than the older generation to use their heritage language exclusively in the home. While the percentage of adults who only speak their mother tongue at home ranges from over 73 to over 88 per cent, the range for youth is from 40 to about 62 per cent. Among Palestinian youths (one segment of which was born in Canada or the United States), a higher percentage speaks English at home. Otherwise, for Afghan, Iranian, and Pakistani youths, the pattern at home is either to speak the mother tongue only (from 40 to 55 per cent do so) or to combine it with English (this ranges from 31 to 53 per cent).

Smaller percentages of the youth of the four communities speak their mother tongue in public. As with many cultural activities and preferences, there is a gender gap; in most communities, young women are more likely than their male counterparts to speak their mother tongue in public. Among Iranian youths, for example, some 14 per cent of females say they 'always' speak Farsi in public, as compared to only 3 per cent of young Iranian males. But, perhaps as a demonstration of national identity (despite the fact that a larger percentage of Palestinians only speak English at home), some 27 per cent of young Palestinian males (as compared to 12 per cent of young Palestinian females) declare that they 'always' speak Arabic in public.

As for reading and writing in the mother tongue, it seems from the response to the question, 'How often do you use your mother language to read or write?' that the ancestral language has been lost among youth in all four communities, although this preference survives for about a tenth of the older population.

As for other cultural markers (see table 5.2), older respondents are more likely to express a nostalgic interest in cultural events and the 'music, dances and entertainment' from their own community. There is also a gender component to this, as young females more often than males declare that they 'always' attend cultural events from the country of origin and 'strongly prefer' music, dances and entertainment' from their own group. Even so, the frequency of such endorse-

Table 5.2 Cultural markers – cultural events, music, food, percentages

Youth and adult samples	Afghans		Iranians		Pakistanis		Palestinians	
	Males	Females	Males	Females	Males	Females	Males	Females
Attend cultural events from country of origin always								
Youth	3.33	3.70	2.78	13.64	2.86	3.08	9.52	17.50
Adults	17.06	8.39	5.19	4.89	5.03	5.68	15.50	21.74
Strongly prefer music, dances, and entertainment from my own ethnic group								
Youth	23.33	24.07	8.33	36.36	8.57	26.15	59.52	65.00
Adults	39.41	49.68	23.38	26.09	33.33	35.23	29.50	47.83
Strongly prefer food from my own ethnic group								
Youth	30.00	42.59	25.00	61.36	64.29	53.85	64.29	52.50
Adults	64.12	63.23	43.51	35.33	72.33	64.20	66.00	59.13

ments among the youths is not high. The exceptions are for young Iranian females, of whom 36 per cent stated that they 'strongly prefer' forms of ethnic cultural expression from their own community; similarly, about 65 per cent of young Palestinian females reported that they 'strongly prefer' their ethnic group's music, dances, and entertainment. About 60 per cent of young Palestinian males also declare their preferences for 'music, dances, and entertainment' from their cultural group, as compared, for example, to only about 8 or 9 per cent, respectively, of Iranian and Pakistani young men and 23 per cent of young Afghan males.

Young men in the four communities are generally much stronger in their preference for the food from their ethnic group than in their devotion to its cultural events or entertainments. This is especially the case for young Pakistani males, of whom only 9 per cent reported that they 'strongly prefer' the music but 65 per cent said they 'strongly prefer' Pakistani cooking. Another interesting case is the young Iranian women who more strongly express devotion to Iranian cultural events, music, dances, and entertainment than do older Iranian women. With 61 per cent expressing their fondness for Persian cuisine, these young Iranian women nearly match the home-cuisine commitments of young Pakistani males (65 per cent) and Palestinian males (64 per cent).

Table 5.3 compares the behaviour and attitudes of youths and older respondents from the four communities in terms of involvement in social groups, interaction with persons in other communities, and preferences for friendship and social mixing. With the exception of Iranian females (high at 41 per cent), young respondents tend to involve themselves less with groups from their country of origin than do older respondents. At the same time, young Iranian females, young Pakistanis, and young Palestinians are more likely than older respondents to 'strongly agree' with the statement that they 'like meeting with other ethnic groups.' Generally, the youths in our study overwhelmingly 'disagree or somewhat disagree' with the notion that it is 'better if different ethnic groups don't try to mix.' The measure of their disagreement ranges from about 73 per cent to over 98 per cent. But at the same time, with the exception of Palestinians, a large fraction of whom grew up in North America, most prefer friendships within their own community than to friendships with members of the majority group (that is, with white Canadians). While these youths, like older persons in the study, have no enthusiasm for cultural apartheid and firmly reject the idea that groups should live apart, at the same time

Table 5.3   Cultural markers – ethnicity and social integration, percentages

Youth and adult samples	Afghans		Iranians		Pakistanis		Palestinians	
	Males	Females	Males	Females	Males	Females	Males	Females
Very or somewhat active in social groups from country of origin								
Youth	20.00	14.82	8.33	40.91	34.29	43.07	45.23	52.50
Adults	39.41	34.20	27.27	27.72	41.51	44.31	56.00	65.22
Strongly or somewhat disagree with 'prefer friends from majority group'								
Youth	50.00	42.59	63.89	72.73	67.14	67.70	28.57	20.00
Adults	67.06	51.61	66.24	72.28	55.35	59.66	35.50	58.26
Strongly agree with 'like meeting other ethnic groups'								
Youth	26.67	24.07	41.67	38.64	48.57	43.08	45.24	67.50
Adults	28.24	26.45	40.26	30.43	37.74	35.23	39.50	44.35
Strongly or somewhat disagree with 'it's better if different ethnic groups don't try to mix'								
Youth	73.34	74.09	86.11	77.28	98.57	92.30	73.81	90.00
Adults	65.30	60.00	93.39	86.96	86.90	77.27	89.00	83.48

their exposure to racist and exclusionary attitudes seems to have made them wary of too close or too exclusive a connection to the culturally dominant majority.

Religion

Measures dealing with religious identity and religious practice for youths and older respondents are provided in table 5.4. There are two important themes, the first being the trend for youth as compared with the older population, and the second the differences among the various youth groups. The differences are uneven with respect to the respondents' claims regarding specific practices, such as 'always' eating halal, 'fasting on Ramadan and some other days,' or 'regularly' following the Islamic dress code. Claims about one's connection to Islam are also complicated, involving more of either a 'cultural' or a 'religious' identity. These will be considered below. But for the three key baseline measures – 'very strongly' identifying as Muslim; an increase in religious feeling (comparing one's feelings in Canada and what one remembers about one's feelings in one's country of origin); and 'always' or 'often' attending mosque – the greater religious involvement of the older population as compared to youths is clear. The differences involved are sometimes quite pronounced.

Thus, for example, among more religious men, 85 per cent of older Pakistanis as compared with 57 per cent of young Pakistani males and 71 per cent of older Afghans as compared to 50 per cent of young Afghan males say they 'very strongly' identify as Muslims. As well, for women, 77 per cent of older Afghan females as compared to 65 per cent of young Afghan females say they 'very strongly' identify as Muslims. The differences are smaller for Pakistani females, among whom 88 per cent of the older group compared to 86 per cent of female youths say they 'very strongly' identify as Muslims, and for older Palestinian women (56 per cent) compared to their younger counterparts (50 per cent). The scores for Palestinian males, younger and older, are practically tied at about 55 per cent. In sum, for all of these groups, while religious adherence is still important, none of the younger people are likely to claim a very 'strong' religious identity with greater frequency than persons of the older generation. Compared with their elders, the trend is either flat or downward for younger people.

As for individuals who testify that their religious feelings are 'much stronger' in Canada today than in their country of origin, this report-

Table 5.4 Religious identity and practice, percentages

Youth and adult samples	Afghans		Iranians		Pakistanis		Palestinians	
	Males	Females	Males	Females	Males	Females	Males	Females
Very strongly identify as Muslim								
Youth	50.00	65.45	11.11	13.64	57.14	86.15	54.76	50.00
Adults	70.59	77.42	16.23	23.91	84.91	88.07	54.50	56.52
More a religious than a cultural identity								
Youth	30.00	50.91	2.78	9.09	35.71	58.46	42.86	27.50
Adults	41.76	34.19	6.49	8.70	45.28	49.43	28.00	33.91
Religious feelings much stronger than in country of origin								
Youth	10.00	10.91	0.00	6.82	22.86	50.77	7.14	0.00
Adults	18.82	17.42	1.03	3.80	38.36	35.80	14.50	15.65
Always or often attend mosque								
Youth	26.67	10.91	0.00	0.00	60.00	63.08	33.34	10.00
Adults	51.76	23.22	4.55	5.43	72.95	51.70	41.00	14.79
Always eat halal								
Youth	46.67	49.09	5.56	13.64	47.14	84.62	83.33	85.00
Adults	79.41	68.39	12.99	11.96	73.58	78.41	72.00	73.04
Fast on Ramadan and some other days								
Youth	3.33	14.55	2.78	2.27	34.29	47.69	4.76	10.00
Adults	16.47	28.39	1.95	3.80	25.16	37.50	13.50	39.13
Regularly follow Islamic dress code								
Youth	6.67	25.45	0.00	2.27	47.14	75.38	23.81	5.00
Adults	25.88	24.52	1.95	4.35	47.17	50.00	26.50	28.70

ing is again found more frequently in older respondents among Afghans, Pakistani males – the one exception being young Pakistani females – and Palestinians. Older respondents, male and female, are also more likely to attend mosque 'always or often' than their youth comparators. Again, there is one consistent exception: some 63 per cent of young Pakistani females, as compared to 52 per cent of older Pakistani women, say they 'always' or 'often' attend mosque; likewise, 51 per cent of these younger Pakistani females, as compared to 36 per cent of their older counterparts, say that their religious feelings today are 'much stronger' than in Pakistan. But with that signal exception, these data definitely falsify the notion of an onrushing religious tsunami among youths of Muslim background.

Apart from age differences, the other religious theme concerns differences among youths in the four communities. Again, as in the discussion of religion among the older population (chapter 4), Iranian youths score very low on all the measures. Compared to the older group (already unreligious), even fewer Iranian youths 'very strongly' identify as Muslim. In fact, the number of young Iranian men in our sample who claim 'much stronger' religious feelings in Canada is exactly zero; and no young Iranian man or woman reports that he or she 'always' or 'often' attends mosque. This is in sharp contrast to the more religious sentiments expressed by young Afghans, Pakistanis, and Palestinians, of whom nearly half or more 'very strongly' identify as Muslim. This is certainly the case for 86 per cent of young Pakistani females, who also are likely (58 per cent) to see their involvement more as a 'religious' than 'cultural' identity – a view also held by 51 per cent of Afghan females and 43 per cent of Palestinian males. These young Pakistani females are consistent: some 63 per cent say that they 'always' or 'often' attend mosque; 85 per cent say that they 'always' follow Muslim dietary rules (they tie young Palestinian females on this count); 48 per cent say they fast on Ramadan and other days (the highest score in the study); and perhaps most importantly, 75 per cent say they 'regularly' follow the Islamic dress code – an incidence about 50 per cent higher than any other group.

In respect to dress code, the only other segment where the score for younger people is higher than the score for older people is Afghan women. But 25 per cent of young Afghan women follow the code as compared to 75 per cent of their Pakistani sisters. And although young Palestinian women lay claim often to a 'strong' Muslim identity and most eat halal, they come nowhere near older Palestinian women or young Pakistani females in fasting, or near the young Pakistani women in attending mosque. Finally, in contrast to the Pakistanis at 75 per cent, only 5 per cent of young Palestinian women claim to follow Islamic dress code, sharply down from the 29 per cent for their older counterparts.

Certainly, the tendency among a proportion of youths from Muslim background to hold onto their faith and its public expression is undeniable, and unlike previous generations, they don't want to be merely tolerated, but accepted and recognized. Still, with the noted exceptions, the shifts observed among the young are generally in the direction of less religion, not more. This calls into question the stereotyped images of a captured and fanatic 'Islamic' community. It also underlines the reasons these youths resent being put under constant political suspicion.

Other studies in Canada also point to the same reality. A similar dwindling and dissolving tendency can also be discerned for religious involvement among the 250 Muslim and Christian Arab CEGEP youth (aged 17–24) studied by Eid in Montreal (2003: 42–3). As with other Canadians, it was found that religion for this second-generation group had become more privatized. Indeed, comparing religious expressions of devotion and ethnic signifiers, Eid found that religious observance had 'lost much of its driving force as a structuring element of social interactions, being more confined to the realm of personal beliefs and self-consciousness.' Participation in religious affairs was limited largely to special holidays. While the Muslim subjects in this sample, like the Christian Arabs (French- and English-speaking) also included in it, continued to value religion as a way of finding 'general spiritual guidance,' with many continuing to pray, the greater importance of formal religious affiliation seemed to be in helping to fix ethnic identities as Arabs, or more particularly, as Syrians, Lebanese, Algerians, or Palestinians.

The commitment of some community members reported in this study to religious institutions is obvious, particularly among Pakistanis of the older generation. About 20 per cent of young Pakistani females and 21 per cent of young Pakistani males were sent to an Islamic school, numbers equalled only by young Afghan females; in about half of these cases, this was their 'regular school' and 'not just for Qur'an lessons.' In addition, some 91 per cent of young Pakistani females said that it was 'very important within their family' that they 'marry someone in the Islamic faith,' and 45 per cent said that it was also 'very important' that they 'associate with other Muslims' (the comparable figures for 'marriage to a Muslim' is 75 per cent for Pakistani males, 85 per cent for Palestinian females, 91 per cent for Palestinian males and 82 per cent for Afghan females; while the numbers for 'associating with Muslims' is 37 per cent for Pakistani males, only 2 per cent for Palestinian males and females, and 28 per cent for Afghan females). At the same time, some 19 per cent of young Pakistani females report that it is 'very important within their family' that they 'associate with people from the same ethnic background,' and another 51 per cent say that it is 'somewhat important' – bringing the total to nearly 70 per cent. The parallel percentage for young Pakistani males is 71 per cent, as compared to 43 per cent for young Iranian females and 28 per cent for young Iranian males.

The young Pakistani females who declare their strong adherence to Islam are adamant in insisting that this is not merely 'a cultural identity.' Some 59 per cent mark it as a 'religious' identity; but another 39 per cent see this commitment as a 'combination' of religion and culture. Indeed, for young Pakistani males, the proportions are reversed; 60 per cent see their adherence to Islam as a 'combination' of religion and culture compared to 36 per cent who say it is only religion. What differences can be seen between the women and the men? They are equally likely to attend mosque either 'always' or 'often' (in fact, the young men are more likely to say 'always'), and within their families, nearly all have been made to feel that it is 'very important' or 'somewhat important' to marry someone within the faith; but the young women are more likely to lay claim to a 'much stronger' religious identity (for 27 per cent of the young men, it is actually 'weaker' in Canada), eat halal, pray, and follow the Islamic dress code.

What tilts the women's adherence in the 'religious' direction is thus not only a shift in subjective experience but also a shift in 'the public performance' of ritual (Islamic dress, eating halal). These become important not simply as moral and religious signifiers but also as markers of 'family respectability' and 'honour' as well as cultural autonomy. In much the same way, young Iranian women (themselves resolutely non-religious) attend secular cultural and social activities, appreciate traditional music and 'entertainments,' literature and poetry and Persian cuisine, speak Farsi at home, and visit with family 'usually everyday' as ways to help establish a secure place in their circle of relatives and in their community. Thus, the religious commitments of the young Pakistani women do not separate them from their families or from parental discipline, but, on the contrary, make them even more respectable and dutiful daughters. Indeed, their parents are considered to have done their duty, even if, in the larger community, the young women's observance of religious ritual, and especially the wearing of hijab, positions them in an attitude of cultural dissent. Their integration within the family comes at the expense of a more challenging and dissonant relationship to Canadian society, but this is a price they are prepared to pay.

Not all religious parents have such success in terms of conformity; for those who remain committed to traditional values, the unwillingness of their children to carry on in this way can be quite upsetting. This, in fact, was the bitter complaint of a Pakistani father.

> ... [In moving to the new country] the relationship between parents and children got worse. My children are now sixteen, eighteen, and twenty-one years old. I brought them to hajj and tried to train them in [the] Islamic way, but the Canadian cultural environment spoiled them. They are not obedient now, and when I asked [them] to do this, they argue that they are Canadian and they want to live and do what they like and what their friends do. They do not care about Islamic and parental values. It is a big problem for me. (Pakistani father in Toronto)

In other testimony, a young Pakistani woman also commented on these difficulties, echoing and sympathizing with her parents' concern about morals, and even saying that this was a 'very Pakistani' thing for her to do. Her father was only visiting in Canada; the family had moved several times, including a stay in Saudi Arabia. In the meantime, she and her mother had taken up the task of policing her brothers but, identifying with her parents' values, she said that her brothers were 'getting out of hand':

> Porn ... Internet crap! That is my dad's major problem right now. Because in Saudi, it is very inconvenient. You get that trash in Pakistan as well. But in Saudi you have firewalls and you cannot get that stuff easily. Saudi is very, very clean. That's the major problem with my brothers, by the way. My mom has caught them, I have caught them, but my dad hasn't. Me and my mom were so Pakistani, we do not know what to do! My dad came for two weeks and I think my mom mentioned it to him, but the boys are getting out of hand. So he gave a lecture, while he [had] never done that before. (Young Pakistani woman)

How important such instruction (and ways of accommodation) is among Pakistanis is suggested by the two respondents below:

> When my eldest daughter was nineteen years old, she wanted to move out. She was quite unhappy living at home. I found out that she was in love with her high school sweetheart, a French-Canadian boy. But my elders had always told me that Muslim women can't marry non-Muslim men, so he became a Muslim to marry her. His parents didn't know about it. (Pakistani mother in Montreal)

> My mom worries that I won't marry a Pakistani girl. She's like, 'What are you going to do about food? Who's going to feed you?' Already, my brother is marrying a Romanian girl. For me, at this point, I don't care [about the ethnicity or nationality] of who I'll marry. I've thought about this and analysed this so much, that at some point, I'm like, it'll just happen, when the time is right. (Young Pakistani man in Montreal)

A young Montreal woman of an age and background that could make her his sister remarks, with considerably more heat:

> I am not married, but my parents are putting a lot of pressure on me to get married. They keep trying to arrange things, to find a guy for me through the arranged marriage route. It's really aggravating, because my big thing is that I do not want to marry someone born and raised in Pakistan who's never lived here. I've gotten used to the way of life here. I'm planning to settle in Canada; I want someone who can fit into that way of thinking and lifestyle along with me. I don't want to marry some typical Pakistani guy who expects me to cater to his every wish, and sacrifice myself for him and his family.

This testimony reminds us how much the key issues faced by youths in our sample often depend for resolution on their families. To an impressive extent, despite the political and social currents swirling about them, they are still caught up in struggles concerning independence and maturity, and obligation and rights within the smaller setting, a world in which ethnic and religious markers are so deeply connected to the opinions of their parents, and so, for example, to the worries their parents express, often, quite insistently, about 'getting married' and 'settling down.' At the same time, while many of the older respondents find the individualism of Canada to be daunting and corrosive of family and traditional cultural ideas, some parents have either led or followed their children on this point and found it to be a benefit, seeing the individual testing endemic to the society as a useful challenge.

> ... [R]ight now, I am finishing my last semester at York [University] and doing two jobs, paying bills and the loans. Living here is a constant struggle ... I am glad that I am in Canada. Most of my friends are Pakistani but I like to meet people from other groups ... I am grateful that I am living here. Getting an education and doing a job. I feel so much [more] independent and stronger now. Also, it feels like I have grown about fifty years and matured so much. (Young Pakistani woman in Toronto)

We recall the opinion of the Iranian woman that parents must teach their children to 'be good human beings,' to not shy away from controversy and responsibility, and that they should 'teach them to swim' before they are obliged to 'jump into the big sea.' Here was a young person who was in that big sea, and for whom coming to Canada had made a decisive difference.

Barriers to Integration

Youths in our study were asked whether they (or 'anyone they knew') had ever been discriminated against 'because of their ethnic origin.' Young Iranians and Pakistanis were more likely to answer 'yes,' with 47 per cent of Iranian males, 43 per cent of Iranian females, 41 per cent of Pakistani males, and 51 per cent of Pakistani females signalling this view; by comparison, no more than 19 per cent of the Afghan or Palestinian groups responded positively. Of those complaining of discrimination, about half of the Afghans, male and female, offered further comment, but only a very few Palestinians did so. Most vocal were Iranian males, of which 82 per cent of those responding 'yes' gave further testimony, along with 68 per cent of Iranian females, 41 per cent of Pakistani males, and 67 per cent of Pakistani females. These differences may suggest a greater determination to speak of rights and wrongs among the more educated – itself a testimony to their greater involvement with Canadian 'rights'-based thinking and ideas of justice.

More than a third of the young female Pakistanis registering a specific complaint spoke of bad treatment in the community because they wore 'traditional' dress, hijab or shalwar (or salwar) kameez; and among an additional third who complained of problems in getting a job or unfair treatment on the job, dress also figured prominently. They spoke of people 'passing comments' when 'they see my traditional clothes,' saying, 'Brown people, go back to your country,' and they also complained of being called 'Paki' and of being mocked for their accents or the food they ate.

Another cluster of responses came from young Iranian males, most of them secular and unreligious. More than half of those issuing a comment complained of discrimination at school or of being labelled a 'criminal' or a 'terrorist.' One said he was punished with 'bad words' because he was Persian, while another remembered that in high school he was forced to assume 'a double personality' if he wanted to fit in. An ESL teacher 'failed him twice,' said another, because he was convinced that people from the Middle East 'could not learn English.' An Iranian male youth, although saying he was 'not Muslim at all' in terms of identity, lost his job working in a house because he was discovered by a tenant to be reading a book by Ali Shariati (an Iranian sociologist of religion and religious reformer). 'People think that all of us,' he said, 'are Arabs and sons of Bin Laden.' In fact, said another young Iranian male, people think that 'you are more likely to do crime because of your ethnic background.' Another, who described himself as 'not strongly religious,' recounted distributing flyers in Toronto seeking support after the earthquake that in December 2003 killed at least 15,000 people in Bam, in south-eastern Iran. While he was doing so, he said, '[A] man came toward me and started to insult me by telling me that Iranians deserved to die, as they are terrorists.'

In this abusive and troubling type of experience, this young Iranian man was joined by a young Pakistani male who was accosted by a TTC driver because he was wearing traditional religious dress, and then found himself 'embarrassed' and 'humiliated' by being searched in public for a gun; by the two young Pakistani females in the study who report they were 'made fun of' or told to 'go back to your country' – and also, called 'terrorists' – for wearing hijab; by the young Iranian woman who complained that a police officer had attacked her cousin and beat him 'because he [the officer] was suspicious'; by a religious young Iranian female who said her father was given a 'very hard time' by an immigration officer and even 'had a heart attack' when seeking admission as a refugee; and by the young Iranian male, 'not at all' religious and unusual among Iranians in applying for welfare, who said he and his family were treated 'as criminals' at the welfare office.

The pattern that cuts across virtually all of the groups involves discriminatory experiences either when seeking a job or being on the job, occasions accounting for about one-sixth to one-quarter of all comments recorded. This is the most regularly occurring group of comments, along with difficulties in school (reported by all groups except Palestinians) and difficulties occasioned by religious dress (reported by male and female Pakistanis and by Palestinian males). One young Iranian male reported that because 'they didn't accept' Iranian credentials, 'my father had to study a number of courses in medical school again, although he was already a doctor for more than twenty years.' A young Iranian female said her mother 'worked very hard' when they came to Canada but 'they mocked her because of her English accent,' and a young Pakistani female reported that when her uncle, a security guard, tried to pick up something a lady had dropped, out of courtesy, she suddenly remarked, 'Why don't you go back to your country.'

More common are brief notes that describe how being perceived as Muslim or Middle Eastern, or simply as non-white, put the individual at a disadvantage. It is noteworthy that the group exhibiting the prejudice is often referred to as 'white' in these accounts. Thus, a young Iranian woman, not seeing herself as a strong Muslim (it was only a 'cultural' identity for her), said that even with a BA in computer engineering she could only get work as a computer laboratory assistant or technician while 'the whites' with the same degree were 'working at companies as professionals.' Another young Iranian female said that she 'applied for several jobs, and they refused me although in most cases I was the most qualified – it was always the "white" who got the job.' A young Pakistani man said that when he was in the UK they called him for a job, but when he came here there was 'nothing ... I think it's a big discrimination.' Another Pakistani man, failing to get a call, sent in his résumé 'with a white name like Bob Smith,' and got a call. A Pakistani female, who described herself as very religious, could not get a job until she took off her hijab; another who could not get work because she wore hijab simply gave up and went to work for her father. A religious Palestinian female, one of the few Palestinians to testify, said that 'in professional circumstances, like interviews,' she was 'repeatedly and jokingly called a "terrorist" or "Muslim fundamentalist."' A young Pakistani male working as a security officer said he was accused 'numerous times' by people at work of 'giving favours to "Pakis" and "Muslims."' A Pakistani woman simply stated, 'I am a Muslim; in my job place most of them do not like Muslims.' A young Palestinian woman said that when customers where she works find out her parents are Palestinian, they 'treat me different.'

The problems among Muslim youth of being caught between generations and between cultures took a sudden jump following the events of 11 September, as cultural and political pressures and use of the 'race' card intensified, moving these personal and generational issues into the public realm. After the attacks in the U.S., expressions of anti-Arab and anti-Muslim sentiment led to protests by different Muslim organizations as well as efforts by Muslim activists to 'reach out' in the schools and to youth, emphasizing the plural and diverse nature of the Islamic community (Zine, 2003).

No doubt, sensational press and television coverage of recurring 'terrorist' conspiracies deepened the anxiety around the Islamic presence. Alarming events were given front-page coverage but lacked evidence on the particulars when brought to court. The first of these, surfacing in 2003, was 'Project Thread,' in which twenty-two Pakistani immigrant students and refugee claimants were arrested on 'suspicion of terrorism.' The holding evidence was shown to be highly circumstantial. Indeed, spokespersons for Citizenship and Immigration Canada (CIC), the RCMP, and the Solicitor-General said flatly there was 'no known threat, what is being investigated is a reasonable suspicion' – even while the Ontario Provincial Security Minister complained that federal authorities were 'hogging vital anti-terror information' (Jimenez, Freeze, and Burnett, 2003; Freeze, 2003). Then came the spectacular 2 June 2006 arrests of seventeen individuals in Brampton in a 'homegrown terrorist cell,' with allegations that the group intended to 'blow up' the downtown Toronto headquarters of the Canadian Security Intelligence Service (CSIS) and then travel to Ottawa to 'storm Parliament' and 'behead' the prime minister. These claims were based, in part, on Internet intercepts. They were substantially compromised when two of those involved, including an older sharia law activist, were revealed to be informants in the pay of security forces and when a high-profile imam, acting as an 'unofficial public spokesperson' for individuals accused in the case, became known to have previously fingered others for arrest (Shepard, 2006; Campion-Smith and Shepard, 2006; Friesen, 2006; Grewal and Shephard, 2006; El-Akkad and Freeze, 2006; El-Akkad, 2007: 76, 80). In an

IPSOS poll immediately following the arrests in June, some 61 per cent of those interviewed in Ontario and 59 per cent in Quebec felt the incidents were just 'the tip of the iceberg,' not merely the work of an 'isolated group of fanatical individuals' – alarming views that were not affected by the gender of the respondent and only slightly affected by differences in age. About half felt that authorities should 'more strongly focus their anti-terrorism surveillance on the Canadian Muslim community than other ethnic communities.'[1]

These incidents suggest the unsettled environment in which young people of Muslim background try to get on with their lives. On balance, the situation in Canada, despite economic pressures and recurrent public scares, appears to be less intense than in Europe and the United States. Still, even without the fevered nationalism and concentrated political overlay noted elsewhere, the disciplining of everyday life offers a hard lesson for people, so many of whom have moved to escape political persecution or to enjoy a good life.

These pressures are also instructive for their children, who otherwise seem protected from Europe's pattern of harsh conflicts and day-to-day agitation. Still, for a substantial segment of youth whose parents came from the region, the violence in Afghanistan, the unjust and tormenting treatment of Palestinians in the Occupied Territories, and the continuing devastation in Iraq cause deep concern – not to mention fears of a new U.S. intervention in Iran, or escalating troubles involving India and Pakistan.

Others are deeply troubled and frightened by reports of terrorist activity in Canada in which young people like themselves are implicated, provoking a backlash in which they are rendered 'guilty by association,' while another group, embittered by these events and caught by deep divisions within the community, have been encouraged in mosques to separate themselves from the Canadian mainstream and to adopt an enclosed 'Muslim' identity. This worries their parents, alarmed by stories of radical Islamists recruiting suicide bombers among the disoriented and unemployed youth of Paris and London, or in the poorest areas in the UK such as Oldham, Bradford, or Leeds, or agitated by the visits to Canada of radical clerics invited to speak on what they picture as an 'utterly evil' and condemning world and who are accused of publicly vilifying liberal Muslims, Jews, and Hindus (Freeze, 2005; Campion-Smith, 2006; Yelaja and Yelaja, 2006; Bhattacharya, 2006; Shepard and Teotonio, 2006; Saunders, 2005, 2006). At the root of the problem is the suspicion (or worry) that young people have succumbed to the constant 'Islamic' propaganda and become susceptible to dangerous pleas.

The racial framing and victimization of youth may take curiously divergent paths. Described as a confused and uncertain 'jihadist' generation 'in search of roots,' it is even said that young Muslim men, caught in a compelling cultural transition, would rather 'slurp iced cappuccino' and talk about the basketball playoffs like good Canadians, but instead are being drawn to radical Islam and being contaminated (or 'warped') by disreputable teachers (Teotonio and Leeder, 2006). Absurd or at least dubious in their particulars, these stories help cement a hostile political attitude. The overall view is instilled that a familiar and comforting Canada is now under attack. In addition, Muslim youths must endure the added stigma of a suspect cultural and religious identity imposed upon them even if they are non-believers and never practise the faith. So it is a double and often contradictory cultural lesson that must be absorbed, inviting active participation and achievement in Canada – finding oneself encouraged by the fresh mingling of people from every corner of the globe – but, at the same time, reminded of deeper liabilities and risks.

Notwithstanding these challenges, the majority of Muslim youths appear to have held firm in their aim to find a foundation for personal security and achievement through hard work in school and staying close to their family, but trying at the same time to learn new Canadian ways. Despite the prevalence of racism and Islamaphobia in the media, the youths in our study overwhelmingly accept and endorse Canadian values of political and cultural tolerance; they are opposed to dividing up the country into separate cultural enclaves. They also feel they belong in Canada. Roughly two-thirds to three-quarters of respondents say that the decision to migrate to Canada was 'the right one.' More importantly, a significant percentage of them responded that Canada is their 'home' country (table 5.5) in response to the question, 'Which country do you consider as your "home country"?' Like their elders (see chapter 7), the majority of these youths consider their country of origin to be their 'home,' but the percentage of youths who consider Canada to be their 'home country' is higher. The exceptions are Palestinians, for whom the Palestine homeland is an undeniable part of their psyche and politics.

The great majority of Muslim youth, despite the challenges recorded above, tend to become part of the fabric of Canada. They learn the lan-

Table 5.5 Which country is considered as the 'home' country (youth)?

Youth	Original home	New country of residence	Original and new country	Other	N/A
Afghans	64.09	31.50	1.82	0.00	3.40
Iranians	63.50	26.60	6.19	0.00	2.27
Pakistanis	63.70	20.80	8.02	2.20	5.16
Palestinians	82.90	7.32	4.90	3.60	2.38

guage and customs, take on Canadian views on many topics, assimilate into the culture, the democratic political commitment, and modern social outlook of their new country – even though nearly all of them (except some of the Palestinians) were born outside the country. Indeed, for roughly one-fifth to one-third of the youths interviewed, this commitment goes so far that Canada now has become their 'new place of primary identification.'

6 Social and Economic Integration

Undoubtedly, tension is increasingly felt between Muslim populations in the West and the governments and larger societies of Europe and North America. This tension is the result of conflicting aims on both sides, and the inability, so far, to find a way to accommodate them. For the majority of Muslims, the key issues are the removal of barriers to their full involvements and integration in the economic, social and political life of their new adopted country. For the minority with a strong religious commitment, it is getting recognition for their right to a public expression of faith and maintaining cultural continuity. The chief concern for Western governments is to accommodate Muslim demands without promoting the formation of separate, isolated, and private communities immune from the normative expectations of the larger society and its laws. Realistically, no democratic, multi-ethnic society can ignore the legitimate religious rights of its population, including Muslims. However, the fact remains that some practices advocated by Muslim organizations are not as benign as others. As Sawitri Sharso (2003) rightly argues, accommodation of some practices would not only compromise the social and legal principles of societies in which Muslims live but could also infringe upon the rights of individuals within the Muslim community itself, particularly with regards to principles of gender equity.

In fact, an accommodation to such demands may sharpen cultural divides, disadvantage Muslim women, create more tensions, and lead to the formation of Muslim ghettos. Taken to an extreme, Muslims' links to the larger society would then be reduced to the bare minimum of legal residency and the securing of citizenship documents needed to benefit from some social services. This would only lead to further isolation of the population. The lack of involvement in the social and cultural life of the new country would obstruct the development in the Muslim community of a sense of attachment, warmth and loyalty to it. However, contemplating such possibilities forces us to ask whether such tensions are inevitable. We need to then consider what constitutes the successful integration of any migrant group and, specifically, of Muslim migrants, in a new country. Are Muslims, as is sometimes suggested, the hardest group to integrate?

This study's general assumption in this regard is that social integration for any minority group is a multifaceted process, and that for it to be effective and lasting, it must also be reciprocal – a genuine 'two-way' process in which there is give-and-take on both sides. But the reality is that migrants from various countries differ markedly in their ability to create a niche in the new country that rewards them with personal satisfaction, a sense of confidence, psychological comfort, economic achievement, and social respect. As well, integration may be understood quite differently by the majority society and by immigrants. As Muhammad Anwar (2005) suggests with regards to the British context, immigrants may understand 'integration' as acceptance of their separate ethnic and cultural identity by the majority, while from a majority point of view, the concept may reflect a demand for the acceptance of the ideology of the dominant group.

From this point of view, integration means the insertion of the group into a social arrangement taken to be permanent and unchangeable, and any group or social segment that is unabsorbed or 'not assimilated' is considered as upsetting the equalization of social relations (Anwar, cited in Roald, 2002: 105). Against that notion one can argue that the integration of ethnocultural minorities only becomes a reality when it occurs gradually, reflecting growth in the migrant's self-confidence and sense of self-worth. If this happens, then abandoning certain cultural practices and adopting new ones does not threaten a person's ethnocultural identity. This can be contrasted with the more common situation, where an imposed identity is reluctantly accepted in the new country by individuals subject to public scrutiny within the host society but shed like a badly fitting uniform when the individual is safely at home in the private domain of family.

We remarked in chapter 1 that as groups in diaspora are confronted with new realities and new opportunities, their identities are merged in an interactive process that involves not only the circumstances in which an individual or a group finds itself but also the claims made upon it by others. In other words, migrants' identities are reconstructed in the new country, and the process involves both the passive experience of 'being made' by external forces and the active process by which a group 'makes itself' (Cornell and Hartmann, 1998: 80, quoted in Kibria, 1998: 941; Nagel, 1994). It follows that the production of social identities involves the interaction of material factors and cultural ideals, including the assertion of older values drawn from one's country of origin and the reproduction or transformation, in the new country, of these ideas of self. Often, this is thought of as a process of choice, as migrants come to embrace social values or beliefs in the new society or reject and resist such values. That is how a group 'makes itself.' But we also need to direct attention to the more coercive and sometimes punishing aspects of this process, the side of 'being made' that involves socio-economic pressures and power relations in which choice does not play a role.

Within this context, the development of a sense of confidence and contentment can be seen as an essential precondition for voluntary accommodation to the new society's codes of conduct and social values. But for this to happen, it is not enough to make allowances for a minority group to maintain its religious and cultural practices and separate identity. Without taking responsibility for the socio-economic and political barriers to the integration of Muslim populations, neither the concerns of the larger society nor those of Muslim minorities will be addressed. The increasing frustration and discontent of the second and third generations of Muslim populations, and the extreme forms through which such discontents are sometimes expressed – often to the surprise of the first generation – show that the process of integration cannot be taken for granted. Thus, 'internalizing the values of society' and finding 'access to the values of the institutionalized organizing social system,' as suggested, for example, by Andreas Goldberg (2002: 35), depend on factors not limited to the access 'foreign' children have to education and the provision of vocational training and more professional chances. Along with the crucial reduction in structural barriers, integration should be viewed as a process that involves making allowances for Muslims to preserve and affirm their identity free from harassment, disrespect, or unreasonable hardships. This will justify the expectation, in return, that the universal laws, democratic principles, and social values of the society be accommodated and respected.

The reciprocal nature of the process needs to be emphasized. That is to say, true social integration requires a *two-way* exchange, and a *two-way* openness to cultural change. For Muslim populations, it involves a process of adjusting and accommodating that would involve learning the language, social skills, and social norms required for functioning in the new country; reconsidering and abandoning certain cultural practices that do not oppose their faith; and learning to abide by the universally applicable laws of the host society. It also includes reconfiguring one's identity, removing the emphasis on some aspects of it, and opening a mental space for the inclusion of others.

But social integration also depends as much on the receiving society's psychological capacity to overcome its fear of difference and to accept pluralism in beliefs, principles, visions, and ways of life, and its preparedness to accept the possibility that the familiar and accepted norms are not always the only suitable ones, or the best ones. Above all, it depends on the willingness to open a space for practical initiatives and socio-economic policies that promote social integration into the host society as a positive change that will yield an improvement in the life of individuals. It means making conscious and determined efforts to make it possible for migrants to live a decent and satisfying life, free from disrespect and discrimination, without having to give up their faith or disguise or denounce their ethnic identity, nationality, and religious and cultural values. The adoption of clearly stated and consistently implemented policies with regards to societal expectations regarding social codes of conduct will overcome confusions regarding the integration of Muslims in their new country.

How effectively has this been accomplished to date? Until very recently, for example, resettlement and integration policies in the Netherlands, based on that country's Pillarization tradition, combined the expectation that immigrants participate in the labour market and in social and political sectors of the society with a rather generous policy geared to accommodate migrant demands, such as public funding of Muslim schools and establishing an Islamic infrastructure. Adopted in the early 1980s, it seemed to be a democratic compromise that would allow for the integration of the Muslim population. The emphasis, as Sunier and Kuijeren (2002) have noted, was not only on the importance to minorities of preserving cultural and religious identity but also on programs for combating poverty and deprivation, without which 'integration was bound to fail' (149).

These efforts, overall, were assumed to be acculturative and integrating rather than expressing a wish by Muslims to separate from the rest of Dutch society. Even though these initiatives were naturally bound to lead to more demands by raising the sense of entitlement as permanent residents, it was felt that the push for improvement through schooling and employment would be unlikely to provoke hostile reactions from the larger society (Statham et al., 2005: 444). But this liberal and promising policy has now reached a deadlock as a result of increasing anti-Muslim racism and discrimination. Policy towards Muslims in the Netherlands has now come into line with the non-liberal policies of other European countries, notably Britain and France.

A similar situation, but perhaps worse, prevails in the UK. The Muslim population in Britain now constitutes the most economically marginal of the country's minority ethnic groups. Worse, its *Race Relation* and *Fair Employment Acts* do not protect Muslims, as they do Sikhs and Jews, from religious discrimination, hence subjecting them to both religious as well as racial discrimination (Anwar, 2005: 40–1). This situation leads Tariq Modood (2005) to argue that South Asian Muslims in Britain suffer from 'a double or a compound racism' that combines 'colour racism' and 'cultural racism' (7). The same is true in France, where an assimilationist approach refuses to recognize Muslims' presence in the country and considers their cultural practices a threat to the French way of life.

This persistent drive for conformity, as evidenced in the Netherlands, Britain, and France, is in sharp contrast to the condition of peaceful co-existence, which Bassam Tibi describes as the concept of Euro-Islam. For Tibi, Euro-Islam draws upon the early Islamic Enlightenment and Islamic rationalism, and is 'an interpretation of Islam that makes it compatible with the four European constitutional standards: laicism (that is, the separation of religion and politics); secular tolerance, based on individual human rights (this includes the freedom of dissent and belief); democratic pluralism; and civil society' (Tibi, 2001: 226). In Tibi's view, an 'open-minded cultural and political adjustment of Islam to European standards' and learning by Muslims that 'their belief is only one of many others and does not have the monopoly over truth' are as important to the integration of Muslims as the adoption by leaders in the new countries of integration policies that go beyond the rhetoric of acknowledging cultural differences and try to supersede European arrogance and xenophobia.

Along the same lines, Tariq Ramadan (2002) points to the need for Muslims to re-examine their religious practices and to be mindful of the dual dimension of Islam as well as the distinction between worship (*ibadat*) and social affairs (*mu'amalat*). In matters related to worship, he suggests, Muslims have to do what has been prescribed in the Qur'an and Sunna, for example, in how they pray; but in matters related to social affairs, they should be able to do as they wish. At the same time, if certain actions are considered impermissible, then there is a need for a reliable text that would back that prohibition. This means that Muslims must make a distinction between what is essential (*sabit*) and non-negotiable, and what is subject to change (*mutaghayr*) or context-related (Ramadan, 2002: 212–13). Such a distinction would also mean taking a rational attitude towards the cultural environment, accepting change and embracing it, and thus allowing the integration into a secular society without fear of contradicting or contravening the essentials of the faith. By this, Ramadan does not mean just social and political integration, but also religious and philosophical integration. He advocates adopting and learning from what is good in Europe, such as the concepts of justice and equality, as these ideas, in his view, are also spiritual and philosophical aspects of Islam. This, of course, requires formidable efforts on both sides. But, as Ramadan argues, mutual fear and suspicion – fear of assimilation or loss of Islamic identity on the part of Muslims, and the fear of the Islamization of Europe on the part of Europeans – prevent the process of integration of Muslims in their new countries, something that is in the interest of both Muslim and European ideals.

In today's tense atmosphere, however, the divisions between Muslim communities and their new countries are not reducible to cultural practices and beliefs, inviolable to one side and objectionable to the other; Muslims also face prejudicial and exclusionary treatment in public life, and this has a strong practical effect. The majority of migrants from Islamic cultural backgrounds live in precarious conditions that inevitably determine the quality of their housing, schooling for children, access to health care, social benefits, and other social services. According to the United Kingdom's 2001 Census, for example, Muslim populations accounted for 2.7 per cent of the total population, and the majority were of Bangladeshi or Pakistani nationality. These groups, the most economically marginalized among Britain's ethnic minorities, suffer from poor education, a high rate of unemployment along with a low level of labour-force participation, inadequate

housing (in terms of ownership), and a higher rate of dependence on
social housing than other religious groups. In 2001, the figure for
Muslims in the UK who had never worked or were long-term unemployed was 16 per cent, compared to the average of 3 per cent, more
than five times higher than that for the population as a whole (Peach,
2005). Similarly, in France, unemployment among Muslims is more
than double the national average, especially among the young, and
even including those who have completed secondary education.
According to Remy Leveau and Shireen Hunter (2002: 9), the rate of
unemployment among North African Muslims stands at 33 per cent,
and is even higher in the suburbs. In general, French Muslims have a
much lower socio-economic status than the national average.

Finally, in Sweden, a state with a tradition of governmental obligation to 'take care' of its citizens, notions of equality and uniformity,
along with a well-established social security system, mean that society
should provide for the material well-being of the Muslim population
in terms of housing and meeting daily needs. But despite the implementation of the *Law Against Ethnic Discrimination* in 1994 and the
much-debated establishment of the National Office of Integration in
the late 1990s, Muslims, as immigrants *per definition*, live in ghettoized
suburbs. There is massive unemployment, and Muslim children go to
schools in 'immigrant areas' with much lower standards. Moreover,
the population has hardly any contact with ethnic Swedes and, as a
consequence, an inadequate knowledge of the Swedish language and
its cultural codes. This situation has led Anne Sofie Roald and other
scholars to suggest that it is not Muslims who do not want to integrate,
but the Swedish social structure that does not allow them to do so
(Sander, cited in Roald, 2002).

Taken together, these experiences suggest that far from making
immigrants feel welcomed and appreciated, 'difference' is sometimes
made the object of an inquisitor's concern, the basis for suspicion and
a police file, or justification for a broad, censorious intervention in
everyday life. That is, difference does not invite an even-handed integration, but instead a punitive and regulatory disciplining of ethnicities. The situation of Muslims in the West is made even more precarious because of an essentializing process in which culture and
religion are taken to determine social practices. In such an understanding, 'culture' is radically disconnected from social conditions
and social practices, and thought to be produced and reproduced in
isolation – outside of time and space, daily experience, and struggle,

as well as local and global influence – all of which might positively or negatively impact Muslim diaspora. This is a narrow and reified understanding of culture. So entrenched are perceptions about Muslim cultural values, religious institutions, and traditional mind-sets that it is assumed they are shared by all members of the various communities; this gives these institutions a quasi-natural or biological character that is taken to be inherited, automatically reproduced, and unchangeable (Modood, 2005). Hence, the problem of integration is seen as simply the matter of Muslims not having the right ingredients for adaptation to modern, secular life in contemporary Western societies. They are judged to be unassimilable. In this way, in effect, culture is racialized, and there is no need – or possibility – of considering a two-way conversation.

To be sure, this essentialist perception does not only target Muslims but also the presumably well-integrated groups, such as the economically successful Chinese migrants to North America. They, too, are pressured to adopt a cautious, fragmenting strategy, allowing themselves to be praised but also effectively isolated as a 'model minority' (Ong, 1996, 1997). At the same time, those who are successful are asked to accept some of the premises of the dominant culture, in effect asking them to turn against their own people and their own past (Portes and Sensenbrenner, 1993: 1343). Ironically, the well-integrated often lose credibility, particularly outside their own communities. This is often the case for individuals coming from Muslim-majority countries who fit in too well and do not appear 'authentic' in the eyes of seemingly well-intentioned individuals who, blinded by the seduction of the notion of 'authenticity,' cannot recognize it as a construct invented by outsiders or by an elite. Indeed, as Juliet Peteet (1993) argues, as an appeal to 'tradition' and past culture, 'authenticity' establishes the parameters of dialogue with outsiders; it is flexible and dynamic. Following Radhakrishnan (2003), one should ask: 'Authenticity' for whom, for whose satisfaction and for what purpose? Who is checking people's authenticity, and by whose authority?

In any case, at a minimum, social integration may be looked at as a process that is marked by language change in public, some shifts in cultural tastes and patterns of association, and the relearning by a migrant group of specific codes of conduct. At a basic level, this allows members of the group to participate in the social, economic and political life of the new society. For the integration to be effective, however, there must also be a mutuality of sacrifice, a willingness to change on both sides. That is to say, integration is not possible if the cultural definitions imposed by dominant groups remain frozen and untouchable, or if some groups (but not others) are systematically subjected to humiliation, or worse, interrogation, surveillance, and reprimand while other groups are treated (and treat themselves) as perfectly entitled; one cannot be integrated if one is always the object of suspicion. Integration also involves practical accommodation within a political and economic structure in which institutional responsiveness is critical and equality of outcomes for equal effort has to be demonstrated. Thus, integration, as distinguished from mere assimilation or acculturation, or the induction of individuals as permanent subordinates in an ongoing organization, always invokes and measures against the equality agenda. Integration is only possible in an open society that is involved in and welcomes change.

In what follows, we will address these points with reference to migrants from the four communities studied, and specifically in the Canadian context. We discuss whether or not they feel 'at home' in Canada, and what external factors determine their perception. The survey includes consideration of structural integration related to educational and occupational satisfaction (or dissatisfaction) in Canada compared to the respondents' countries of origin, and estimates of their overall situation in Canada. We will also explore whether they feel included in the social and cultural life of the country, or if they feel instead that they are outside the mainstream and turning, as a result, to more local and private identities and practices linked to feelings of a separate ethnic belonging.

Education as a Tool for Economic Success

As has been mentioned, a significant number of members of the four communities surveyed came to Canada with a relatively high level of education. Many had also pursued further education at different levels. Over 23 per cent of Palestinians, 16 per cent of Iranians, about 13 per cent of Pakistani, and 4 per cent of Afghans obtained university degrees, some at the graduate level. Many also continued their education at community colleges and received certificates and diplomas: about 30 per cent of Pakistanis, over 25 per cent of Iranians and Palestinians, and over 18 per cent of Afghans fall into this category. Again, the same trend, but with lower percentages, is observable in relation to spouses.

Generally, both men and women respondents in our sample have pursued further education in Canada. But more men than women have enhanced their education at the university level. The percentages vary widely from one community to another and from one level of education to another. For example, as compared to the men in their communities, larger percentages of Iranian, Pakistani, and Palestinian women have continued their education at the college level, receiving college certificates or diplomas; but more men in these communities have completed master's degrees. Over 22 per cent of Iranian men (as compared to about 11 per cent of Iranian women), over 18 per cent of Pakistani men (as compared to about 9 per cent of Pakistani women) and about 26 per cent of Palestinian men (as compared to about 21 per cent of Palestinian women) have added to their educational qualifications by completing a BA or a post-graduate degree in Canada. Even for Afghans, who show lower percentages in educational attainment, the per centage of men going to university is double that of women (6.4 per cent versus 3.2 per cent).

The interesting point is that while the pattern of more men than women obtaining a university education also exists in the respondents' countries of origin, the gender differences were not as sharp as in Canada. For example, 54 per cent of Iranian males had a 'high' level of education in the home country, as opposed to about 50 per cent of Iranian women. Among Pakistanis, the difference was between 74 and 67 per cent, respectively, for men and women. In understanding these data, we must take into account Canadian immigration practices. Education in one's country of origin is a strong determinant of admission to the country, establishing a preference for applicants with degrees. This biases the selection of individuals – both men and women – in the direction of the highly educated, thus affecting the cohort admitted to Canada. It also affects the education reported by respondents in our sample regarding their experience in their home countries.

The pattern changes, however, once people are in Canada. A sexual division of labour appears to develop within immigrant families so that, irrespective of the level of education achieved prior to migration, women go to community college. Presumably, their aim is to attain a certificate, find a job, and support the family, while men go to university for a better career. Exhibiting a survival strategy common to many migrant groups, the women must postpone or give up their career aspirations. However, the gender bias in education also puts a woman at a strategic disadvantage should the marital relationship come apart;

it can encourage her to stay in a poor relationship if she lacks qualifications. The overall pattern, then, is that some women are streamed towards the college system and go to work early, albeit at an entry level, while other women, as housewives, are likely to avoid paid employment altogether, reinforcing traditional expectations. In either case, they miss the opportunity for a university-based career. Other factors, such as pregnancy and family responsibility, also negatively affect women's educational chances in the new country.

Consider the following statements by Afghan, Pakistani and Iranian females, which also show the ways in which education and work intersect with family relations:

> My husband continued his education and finished his master's studies but he never worked outside home. He used to do some sort of business within a small circle of Iranians in order to earn some money ... His desire for imposing the control showed up immediately after our arrival in Montreal. I remember, during the first days, we saw an immigration counsellor to help us settle down. The counsellor wanted to send me to French language school and my husband kept insisting I should go to housekeeping and sewing courses instead. Finally, with much argument and tension, I did go to the French school. Not only that, at nights I attended CEGEP, and later the university, and so many other independent courses ... until I finally finished my higher education in medical technology and started working in my field. As far as I can remember, for each and every step that I wanted to take, I had to fight so hard and argue my way out, but at the end I always did what I wanted to do. (Iranian female)

> I wanted to continue my education in Canada, but after having children and other responsibilities, I could not go back to school. My husband was not supportive either, so I decided not to continue my education. My husband got his college diploma and now he has his own business. (Afghan female)

> I want to work and want to pursue something [career-wise]. But right now, my priority is my baby. I will try to fit my career to my baby. I'm looking at working from home. I'll start full-time when he starts going to school. For now, I just want to be there for him. Sometimes I feel like I missed out [because I had a baby and stopped working]. Life becomes monotonous at home sometimes. But then I think you have to sacrifice sometimes. You can't have everything in life. (Pakistani female)

The point is that even though, as the study shows, the majority of individuals in our samples were educated to different degrees, many of them in each group furthered their education in Canada, obviously in the hope of enhancing their employment opportunities. This might be the right perception, as the study also shows that in many cases a positive relationship exists between level of education and type of occupation. The analysis of the data, based on the typology we created for the levels of education in the country of origin and in Canada (types A, B, C, and D, discussed in chapter 3) show that type A persons (those with a university degree in their country of origin plus a university degree in Canada) are more likely to be engaged in professional and other white-collar positions than persons of other types; type D persons (those with no university degree in their country of origin or in Canada) are more likely to be situated in blue-collar occupations, trades, and crafts. The situation varies considerably from one community to another. The pattern is also differentiated by gender.

Employment

Access to financially and psychologically rewarding employment is perhaps the most important factor in determining a sense of self-worth and confidence for any individual moving to a new country. The picture we get from the respondents in this regard, however, shows a dramatic change in occupational pattern from white-collar positions to blue-collar wage work, a shift that can be interpreted as a sort of *proletarianization* of the Muslim immigrant communities in Canada.

Although, as mentioned in chapter 2, sizeable percentages of the four communities came from managerial, professional, and other white-collar occupations in their countries of origin, only a portion of our respondents were able to continue in the same occupational categories in Canada. A comparison between respondents' occupations in the country of origin and in Canada, shown in figures 6.1 to 6.5, clearly demonstrates the changes in occupation that they experienced.[1] In the managerial and professional category, there are fewer Iranian and Pakistani men and women and Afghan men working in these fields in Canada compared to the countries of origin. Only Afghan women and Palestinian men and women have increased their share in this category. As shown in figure 6.1, the sharpest decline is observable among Iranian men, as only 21 per cent work in this category, compared to over 38 per cent in the country of origin. Iranian women and Pakistani

Figure 6.1   Managerial, professional, and business occupations in the country of origin and in Canada, percentages

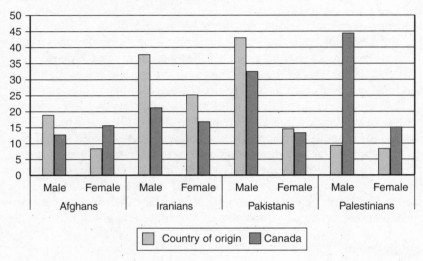

men have also experienced a sharp decline in their professional status. In their countries of origin, the highest percentages of Iranian men and women, as well as of Pakistani men, were doctors, lawyers, and engineers. Because of tough requirements for entry into these professions in Canada, and the lack of recognition of the educational credentials of these individuals, many of them cannot practise their professions in this country. The only sharp rise in the category is for Palestinian men (from over 9 per cent in the country of origin to over 44 per cent in Canada). This may be explained by their longer history in the country and younger age at the time of immigration to Canada.

We also see a decline in the professional status of other white-collar occupations, including civil servants, military personnel, teachers, and technicians, for the majority of respondents in our sample. As shown in figure 6.2, with the exception of Palestinians (whose percentages in these occupations have doubled in Canada compared to those in their country of origin), a smaller number of individuals from other communities are present in the white-collar category. The sharpest decline is for Afghan men and women.

Conversely, the data show a sharp increase in the number of persons of both genders from all four communities whose occupations include various categories of trade, craft, and small business, the latter charac-

Figure 6.2   Other white-collar occupations in the country of origin and in Canada, percentages

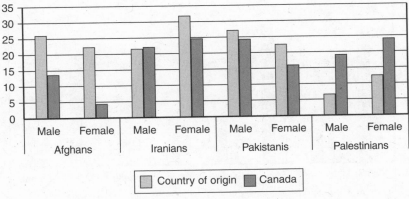

terized as having fewer than five employees (figure 6.3). For example, while only 5.7 per cent of Afghan men were in these occupations in their country of origin, over 16 per cent of them now work in these fields in Canada. The shares of Iranian and Afghan women have more than doubled and that of Pakistani women more than tripled in trades, crafts, and small businesses in Canada. The reason in all cases is obviously the inability of these individuals to find employment in Canada in occupations comparable to what they did at home, despite their education and experiences.

Moreover, we see a sharp rise in the percentage of individuals who have entered blue-collar occupations as wage workers in Canada. As shown in figure 6.4, very small percentages of men and women from the four communities were wage workers in their countries of origin. That is, only about 3 per cent of Afghan women and Pakistani and Palestinian men, less than 2 per cent of Iranian men and Pakistani women, and no Iranian and Palestinian women were wage workers before coming to Canada. Yet there has been a dramatic rise in the number of community members in these professions since moving to Canada, the sharpest increases shown for Afghan men (reaching over 33 per cent) and Pakistani men (over 22 per cent), followed by Afghan women (over 18 per cent) and Iranian men and Pakistani women (over 15 per cent for both).

Another important shift in the socio-economic status of members of the four communities relates to homemakers. As shown in figure 6.5,

Figure 6.3   Trades, crafts, and other small-business occupations in the country of origin and in Canada, percentages

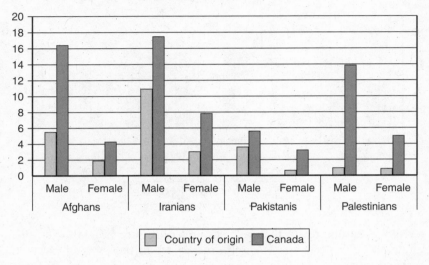

Figure 6.4   Blue-collar occupations in the country of origin and in Canada, percentages

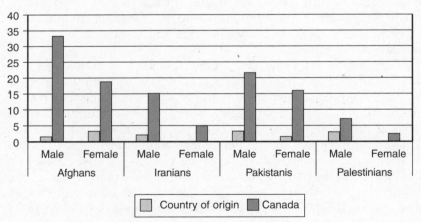

in line with the traditional sexual division of labour, a significant number of women in the four communities were homemakers before coming to Canada (over 30 per cent of Pakistani and Palestinian women, over 25 per cent of Afghan and 22 per cent of Iranian women).

Figure 6.5   Homemaker occupations in the country of origin and in Canada, percentages

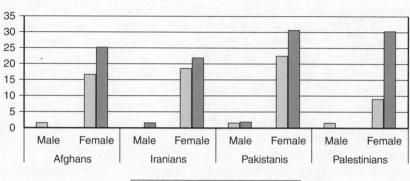

The same division of labour by gender persists after coming to Canada, where not only do women represent a higher percentage than men in the homemaker occupation category, but their percentages in this occupational category have also increased. This is despite the fact that a significant number of women in the four communities have also entered trades and blue-collar wage work, and some have succeeded in maintaining their white-collar occupations. A combination of the continuing sexual division of labour and disadvantages in the job market explains this situation.

The situation in Canada seems to reflect a broader trend. Studies of employment of communities from Muslim-majority countries in Britain also show that a much lower per cent of Muslim women, particularly Pakistani and Bangladeshi women, work outside the home (29 and 25 per cent, respectively) compared to their white counterparts (at 60 per cent), or women of African descent (62 per cent), and Indian women (at 57 per cent) (Anwar, 2005: 34). In fact, Britain's Pakistani and Bangladeshi women have the lowest economic participation rates of any ethnic minority in the UK, presumably in part because of traditional Islamic values that protect women from and limit their contact with men outside their immediate family (Peach, 2005: 29). However, the small number of men in the four communities who have moved to the homemaker category after moving to Canada speaks to their disadvantaged position in the job market and to their restricted access to lower-end occupations.

A substantial number of men and women from the four communities were students in their country of origin. Since moving to Canada and growing older, many have moved into various job categories. As a result, there are fewer respondents who list themselves as students in Canada. The exception is the Iranian women, who have slightly increased from 9 per cent as students in the country of origin to over 10 per cent in Canada. The share of Iranian men who are students has just about stayed the same. Finally, there are also small numbers of retirees in Canada in the four communities, ranging from 1.1 per cent of Pakistani women to 5.1 per cent of Iranian men.

Overall, comparisons between the occupations of the men and women of the four communities in their countries of origin and in Canada show a significant shift away from their middle-class professions at home to traditional middle-class occupations in Canada in trades and small businesses, and particularly to blue-collar wage work. However, there is variation by community and by gender. Afghan women and Palestinian men and women increased their share in professional categories in Canada, but both males and females in the other communities experienced a decline in the numbers able to maintain white-collar status. For males and females in all communities, we witness a sharp rise in trades and blue-collar workers, signifying a class shift and a change in social status.

Perceptions about Life in the New Country

Except for refugees, who are escaping a life-threatening situation and often are understandably less concerned about what will await them at their destination, the decision to migrate to a new country is usually made in the hopes of pursuing better living standards and job prospects or to secure a better future for one's children. The perception of success in the new country is also relative to the socio-economic conditions the migrant experienced in the country left behind.

The responses of the participants in this study reflect retrospective data, and thus are subject to the vagaries of remembering, forgetting, and filtering as one tries to establish a new identity in the host country. The psychological need to 'put on a good face,' as well as an element of nostalgia, are also often present, although it seems that it is more men than women who have fond memories of the situation in their home countries, and that this is more true of some communities than others. For example, remembering their jobs at home, about 55 per cent of Afghan males, as opposed to about 29 per cent of Afghan females, reported that they were 'very satisfied' with the work in their main occupation in their country of origin (the percentage for Afghan males was the highest among the eight community–gender groups). The percentages are somewhat lower for Iranian males (38 per cent) and females (27 per cent), as well as Pakistani males (41 per cent) and females (28 per cent). By contrast, they are much lower at about 7 and 14 per cent for Palestinian males and females.

This variation in level of satisfaction must be examined in the context of the reasons given for leaving the country of origin. As discussed in chapter 2, between 83 and 85 per cent of Afghan males and females list 'war or civil war' as their reason for emigrating – a much higher percentage than for Palestinian males (58 per cent) or Palestinian females (41 per cent) or for Iranian males, 43 per cent of whom also give 'political persecution' as one of the main reasons they left Iran. Still, reflecting on their experience under the Israeli occupation in the West Bank or Gaza (for those remaining in the homeland) or their situation in a third country, Palestinians are much less likely than respondents from other groups to report 'high' satisfaction in the country of origin on a summary measure[2] which registers occupational, educational and financial satisfaction in country of origin (see table 6.1). Over 8 per cent of Palestinian males and 10 per cent of Palestinian females register 'high' satisfaction with the situation they remember from home, as compared, for example, to 59 per cent of Afghan males and 35 per cent of Afghan females. About 54 per cent of Palestinian males and 43 per cent of Palestinian females report satisfactions on this summary measure to be 'low,' by far the highest figures for all groups.

These figures are supported by the following statements by Palestinian respondents:

I was born in Nablus. My father used to work in a bank; my mother is a housewife. I have three brothers and two sisters. Most of my relatives used to live on the same avenue. However, the Israeli occupation makes our lives there impossible. The Israeli troops used to give us such a hard time, for many times they search our home in a violent way. People are not working, children are not attending school, and life is so difficult there. After getting married in 1985, we went to Saudi Arabia; then we came here in 1995. (Palestinian female)

In 1985 we went to Jordan looking for a safe and better place for our chil-

Table 6.1 Occupational, educational, and financial satisfaction in country of origin, percentages

Responses	Afghans		Iranians		Pakistanis		Palestinians	
	Male	Female	Male	Female	Male	Female	Male	Female
N/A	0.00	1.29	1.28	0.00	0.0	1.14	6.5	6.96
Low	9.94	20.65	19.87	22.28	19.5	23.86	53.5	43.48
Medium	30.99	42.58	43.59	45.11	47.8	46.02	31.5	39.13
High	59.06	35.48	35.26	32.61	32.7	28.98	8.5	10.43
Total	100	100	100	100	100	100	100	100

dren, but we were not doing well financially. In 1993, we came to Canada for our children's education. We want them to have a better chance than what we had in everything. We chose Canada because Canada has an easier migration process compare[d] to other countries. (Palestinian male)

My father left in 1948 due to the Israeli occupation. He went to Kuwait, and found a good job there, so he got married and had all of his children in Kuwait. Due to the 1991 Gulf War, my family went back to Gaza, but I did not; instead, I applied to come to Canada. I came to Canada in 1992. In 1997, I sponsored my parents and they are here now. The most important reason I came to Canada is that I wanted to have an identity. As a Palestinian from Gaza, I have no identity and it is very hard on us to move from one place to another, so I wanted to find a solution to that problem. Now I have a Canadian passport. (Palestinian male)

We left Palestine because the situation there was too bad because of the Israeli occupation; also, the economical situation was very bad. Furthermore, education opportunities were rare and my family income was so low as there was no work available. People were suffering in every way. For these reasons, as soon as we got the chance to leave we did ... The occupation makes it hard for people to live a normal life; for example, the kids could not play as any other kids at their age without us worrying about them. The main decision to leave Jenin for me was the education; for my family it was to live a better life and to find better job opportunities. (Palestinian male)

Thus, for Palestinians, coming to Canada is understood as an urgent economic need, quite apart from the gain in personal and political freedoms that they share with the other three communities. Nonetheless, economic needs area also important for other groups. While the 'peacefulness' of the country is unchallenged, these responses by individuals from Afghanistan, Pakistan, and Iran also indicate disappointment and, in some instances, real frustration in the opportunities found in Canada.

Canada as a peaceful country was the first preference for me as an Afghan coming from a war zone. It's very peaceful and quiet. But before coming to Canada I was thinking life here would be very easy, there would be a lot of employment opportunities and I will be able to find a job of my interest easily, which was not correct. It is very difficult to find a job and the wages [are] also very low. (Afghan female)

My father is staying in Saudi [Arabia] because he's not getting a job here. I mean I really hate the Canadian system ... First they say for us to come and then they say we want experience. I mean my dad has 40 years of experience in his field but none Canadian ... [I just] read in the newspaper that there is a scientist who sent a rocket to the moon and he is selling doughnuts in Canada. That's horrible! That's just pathetic, like they have no value here. (Pakistani female)

When I was working in the company in Iran, I had a good position and earned lots of money, I mean real good money. But I felt I had to go on doing my PhD, improving myself. I felt that there in Iran, because of the government restrictions and all that, my potentials were not recognized. I felt I could be recognized and [flourish] in somewhere like Canada. But I was wrong: now that I am here, I see there are other restrictions that do not allow my potentials to be recognized, like the problem of race. (Iranian male)

To assess the situation in Canada, a set of eight questions was used to estimate each respondent's perception of her or his occupational success and educational and financial achievement since arriving in the new country compared to what they remembered from their main jobs in their countries of origin. The questions included the skill level, financial and educational situation, and the educational opportunities for themselves and their spouses and generally how they saw the situation for women and men in Canada (table 6.2).

Here again, the conditions experienced in the home country and the reasons for departure affect the level of satisfaction. We see that,

Table 6.2 Occupational, educational, and financial satisfaction in Canada, percentages

Responses	Afghans		Iranians		Pakistanis		Palestinians	
	Male	Female	Male	Female	Male	Female	Male	Female
N/A	0.00	2.58	0.64	1.09	0.63	2.84	1.5	0.87
Low	43.27	45.81	50.64	35.87	26.42	29.55	23.0	40.00
Medium	38.01	38.06	32.69	43.48	47.8	39.20	39.5	36.52
High	18.71	13.55	16.03	19.57	25.16	28.41	36.0	22.61
Total	100	100	100	100	100	100	100	100

overall, Palestinians score high in their assessment of life in Canada, with 36 per cent of Palestinian males reporting 'high' satisfaction and only 23 per cent reporting 'low.' What is surprising is that Pakistani males (about 25 per cent) and females (about 28 per cent) also continue to report their satisfaction in Canada as 'high,' compared to their experience with what they remember from the past. This is noteworthy, since the literal meaning of the questions asks for an estimate of improvements over a previous experience that was already judged to be favourable. But while the percentage of Iranian males and females who reported occupational, educational, and economic satisfaction as 'high' in the home country was about 35 per cent for males and 33 per cent for females, these figures are now reduced in Canada to 16 per cent for males and less than 20 per cent for females. Even allowing for the relatively modest size of community samples, the uncertain role of nostalgia in shading one's memory of the past and the fact that the scoring for the 'home' and 'host' indexes is slightly different, the downward trend in reported satisfactions is suggestive.

The sense of disappointment with opportunities in Canada is strengthened when we turn to the individual questions that serve as components of these indexes. Fully 20 per cent of Iranian males report job satisfaction as being 'much worse' in Canada than at home and 17 per cent of Iranian females report that job satisfaction is 'much worse' for their spouse, as compared to 12 per cent of Afghan males, 6 per cent of Pakistani males, and only 2 per cent of Palestinian males. The figures for females reporting 'much worse' job satisfaction for their spouses are 9 per cent for Afghan females, 6 per cent for Pakistani females, and 3 per cent for Palestinian females. Indeed, if we combine the two lower categories, 38 per cent of Iranian males indicate 'worse' or 'much worse' job satisfaction in Canada. As well, 16 per cent of Iranian males report skills in their current job to be 'much lower' than in their home country, and 16 per cent of Iranian females report skills for their spouses' job to be 'much lower.' The same applies to the work of Iranian women themselves, although to a smaller degree: 8 per cent of Iranian women record their own job satisfaction in Canada as 'much worse' and 9 per cent say the skill level is 'much lower' than at home. If we look more broadly at these Iranian women, fully a quarter say that their jobs in Canada are 'worse' or 'much worse' than they were at home, and about one-fifth say that the skill level of their jobs is 'lower' or 'much lower' in the new country. For a group that puts great emphasis on educational achievement and making use of one's education on the job, these are significant declines.

Similarly, looking at table 6.1 and table 6.2, less than 19 per cent of Afghan males report 'high' satisfaction in Canada as compared to 59 per cent reporting 'high' satisfaction for occupation, education, and financial satisfaction at home. The rate for Afghan females in this category is about 14 per cent. This is not surprising, as only 27 per cent of Afghan males (and 17 per cent of Afghan females) find job satisfaction in their current job to be 'better' or 'much better' than at home, and 26 per cent of Afghan males find their skill level in Canada to be 'higher' or 'much higher.' At the same time, 32 per cent of Afghan males record their job satisfaction to be 'worse' or 'much worse' in Canada, and 28 per cent say the skill level is 'lower' or 'much lower.'

Overall in Canada, the stable and continuing 'high' satisfaction for Pakistanis, the sharp declines for Iranian males and females, and the mixed results for Afghans all contrast sharply with the strong upward trend for Palestinians. This is consistent with the Palestinians' low level of satisfaction in their country of origin or transit country (table 6.1). The advance in overall 'high' levels of satisfaction for Palestinians (about 36 and 22 per cent, respectively, for male and female) is supported by the fact that 61 per cent and 34 per cent, respectively, of males and females from that community rate their job satisfaction in Canada as 'much better' or 'better' than in the home country, and 54 and 31 per cent, respectively, regard the skill levels of their current job to be 'much higher' or 'higher' than in their country of origin, while only 3 per cent report skill levels in Canada to be 'lower' or 'much lower.'

We can say that both Pakistanis and Palestinians feel more satisfied in Canada with their economic situation – the Pakistanis building from a firmly anchored 'high' base in the country of origin, and the Palestinians from a very low one. By contrast, many Iranians are acutely conscious of economic retrogression – including downward mobility on the job and performing below skill level – in the new country. Afghans are split between those experiencing an improvement on the job and others who feel a decline in satisfaction at work and in the skill level of their job in Canada.

This is not surprising, as our data show (see fig. 6.1 and fig. 6.2) that both Iranians and Afghans have experienced a decline in numbers in the category of professional and other white-collar occupations in Canada. But so have Pakistani men, although the rate of decline is not quite so steep. For Palestinians, male and female, and for Afghan and Pakistani women, moving to Canada has provided economic opportunities, even though this relatively favourable advance must be balanced against the fact that nearly one-third of Palestinian, Afghan and Pakistani women, following 'traditional' practices (or reflecting the judgment that a good job would be hard to find), are absent altogether from the labour force.

The relatively greater dissatisfaction of Iranian males as compared to their Pakistani counterparts is not explained by differences in income. Financially, the two groups are on a par with each other. About 32 per cent of Iranian males received individual incomes of $40,000 or more, compared to 34 per cent for Pakistani males; but for roughly 45 per cent of Iranian males – as compared to 42 per cent for Pakistani males – total household incomes exceeded $40,000. The highest income category ($70,000 and above) found about 19 per cent of Iranian males in such households, as compared to about 13 per cent of Pakistani males. The reason for the greater disappointment among Iranian men is therefore not to be found in financial success per se but in less tangible differences based on professional self-esteem and involvement in community life. The different political trajectories of Iranian and Pakistani males, in terms of the reasons for their migration, helps explain to a great extent the continued dissatisfaction of the Iranians, even when they have left behind the economic and financial hardship of exile or self-exile.

From all this, what conclusions can one draw with regard to the problems and prospects for social integration of Canada's migrants and citizens originating in Muslim-majority countries? First and foremost, that integration must be looked at as a process in which the socio-economic status of immigrants plays an enormous part. As such, the processes of adaptation and integration can be assisted or stalled depending on the active involvement or cynical disengagement of the host society and its immigration and settlement policies. As well, the equitable and fair treatment of members of Muslim populations in terms of education, jobs, housing, and social services, along with the adoption and implementation of serious anti-racist policies, are bound to have a significant impact on the sense of confidence, inclusion, and belonging of the population.

There is an important dialectic here, however, that needs to be underlined. First, the state's determined effort to redress problems of poverty, discrimination, and social exclusion can provide Muslim migrants with a renewed sense of confidence and integrity. This means the state must avoid giving too much weight to 'culture,' or rather, treating 'culture' in isolation, as somehow separate from social life. If we are to foster a healthy integration, we need to see clearly the links between a migrant's painful entry to a new country and the efforts she or he makes to attain economic security and a psychologically reassuring place in the larger society. The process of integration is not to be detached from its material moorings or disguised by a seemingly 'liberal' ideology that masks inequality through the language of cultural difference. At the same time, it is important to bear in mind that the legitimate rights and demands of these populations regarding religious beliefs and practices can be protected and reasonably accommodated without bowing to the demands of the conservative, self-appointed Muslim leaders in the name of respecting citizens' rights to practise their cultural heritage.

normative – in the sense of a two-way street,

7 Sense of (Not) Belonging

We have argued so far that structural and socio-economic discrimination are major factors in instilling a continuing sense of 'not belonging' among minority groups, including the four communities from Muslim-majority countries that we have studied.

Our concern has been that when persons from ethnic or religious minorities feel they are not included in the social and cultural life of the receiving society, they may look back to their country of origin for inspiration, a sense of connection, and the social and political involvement they feel they have been denied. This can lead to the formation of separate ethnic enclaves. The feeling of social exclusion and, perhaps even more, a sense that one is excluded from the rewards of social and economic activity in a society that puts such a premium on material success are measurable through the reflections of individuals on their day-to-day experience. This includes their reports on their experience in the job market and the connection they see between education and work: whether individuals feel good use has been made of their efforts to obtain an education; whether their work provides them with a true opportunity to exercise their skills; and whether they feel they are treated fairly and decently on the job. But a general sense of being valued and respected as a person is also related to how ethnic minorities are treated by society at large, how the media understands and presents to the larger public their religious and cultural practices, and whether members of the group encounter direct discrimination.

Diaspora and a Sense of Belonging

The statement below captures the complex, multifaceted, and contradictory feelings of a dislocated individual from our Iranian sample in the UK, and the emotional roller-coaster ride that is involved in her feelings about immigration in general:

> I can say that I am well adapted in the British society. I owe my present situation to several factors: I found a full-time job, which gives me a lot of satisfaction; [it] connected me to the outside world and opened my circle of relationships that I missed after arriving in Britain. I have been keen to work with and for women, and my work here gives me this opportunity. Then I married a man with whom I have a good under-standing; he is a constant help, not a burden. We have enough financial resources to live a fairly comfortable life ... [But] this does not mean that I am happy here. I don't really like the British weather and [the British] mentality ... They don't really accept foreigners and [they] look down on you. You may go as far as one can in terms of education and training, [but] the glass ceiling is always there to prevent you [from going] further. I live here because of my children, who are completely integrated into the British society, but I am not sure that I will stay here all my life. (Iranian female in the UK)

To be sure, separation from one's homeland, particularly when the 'race' factor acts as a constant reminder of who you are and who you are not and can never be, inevitably involves continuous emotional vulnerability, distrust of others and clinging to a hope or a dream of the impermanency of the situation. This tortured existence seems to be embedded in any involuntary separation from one's homeland. A moving passage in Eva Hoffman's *Lost in Translation* (1990) powerfully portrays the psyche of the nostalgic diaspora: 'Loss is a magical pre-servative. Time stops at the point of severance, and no subsequent impressions muddy the picture you have in mind.' Hoffman points to a very common psychological need in the individual who has been involuntarily severed from his or her homeland: not only does every-thing that has been lost remain forever as one remembers it, but that it is 'made more beautiful by the medium in which it is held and by its stillness' (115).

Narratives of exile and dislocation sometimes reflect the psycholog-ical troubles of dislocated individuals, even some sort of irrational hos-tility towards the place of refuge. During his exile in the United States in the 1940s, Bertolt Brecht would complain about everything Ameri-can; he claimed, for example, that he was not able to open his windows in the morning, as he had in Germany, because nothing in California was worth breathing and smelling (Lyon, 1980: 30–5). Theodor Adorno also shared Brecht's strong distaste for American culture and way of life, saying he was 'offended by the easy camaraderie that allowed strangers to address each other by their first names' (Heilbut, 1983: 161–3).

Is nostalgia a form of fidelity, as Eva Hoffman suggests? Perhaps. For a person in the diaspora, nostalgia is an antidote to the humdrum of life in a physically and culturally foreign and inhospitable land. The longing for the familiar and the known can reach such absurdity that · at times everything about the host society is rejected as heartless, inhuman, and damnable. Hence, it should not be surprising to hear some expatriates, particularly from Muslim-majority countries, lament the lack of friendliness, emotional warmth, caring, and family ties in Europe or Canada, or criticize what they see as excessive 'immoral' behaviour among women and youth – things that in their imagination represent values opposite to those cherished in their own homeland.

Many individuals try to minimize these feelings by maximizing connections with people from their own ethnic or religious backgrounds, and in doing so are sometimes dragged into other people's agendas. The majority live day to day, without making any particular attempt at being integrated, and in this way wall themselves up against all possible intrusions. Note the following statements from individuals in our study:

It is the situation in Iran that pushes everyone to leave the country ... After lots of headache and living in various refugee hotels and camps in Derby [I landed here], got shelter, plus £40 for food. When I complained, the manager in the Refugee Council told me, 'Go back to your country. Why are you here if you don't like it?' That really hurt. Finally, the Home Office accepted my refugee claim and I am now living with my boyfriend. He works, but I don't, and I have absolutely no connection with the British society and British people. It's true that the situation in Iran is bad, but at least no one feels lonely. (Young Iranian female in the UK)

I have bad, bitter experiences living in Iran, being displaced and dealing with legal regulations. In the past there were not so many Afghans in Iran, and the government provided more facilities, like ration cards. [In the past] there were some clear rules and regulations. Now dealing with the government offices has become very difficult; for example, it will take two or three months to get a reply to your letter. In 1379 [1999] my father was not in Iran, so the authorities took our ID cards, and since then we have not been able to continue our schooling. (Afghan female refugee in Iran)

People weren't very religious before the diaspora; only some elderly men were religious. But young people weren't religious, and there were no religious parties. But because of the diaspora, there were more [religious] political parties and people thought that what happened to them was a consequence of not being religious. That is how many became religious, and it is understandable. When we came to El-Ezareyeh, the number of people who did pray was very small; however, today thousands go to pray in the mosques, and most of them are youth. Every time they face a tragedy they go to God. (Palestinian male refugee in the West Bank)

... About success, yes, you can say that I am a successful person, having made a life for [my]self in this country. But it depends how we define success. Do I feel I belong here? No. And no one can blame me that I did not make an effort to be part of this society or to make friends with [Anglo-European] Canadians. I did volunteer work with several social service organizations, participated in non-ethnic cultural and political events, and made a few friends. But it took me almost two decades to realize that I will always remain the Iranian and the Muslim, even though I am a non-believing person who has turned her back on the Iranian patriarchal culture ... I now see myself going back to my own culture for a sense of belonging, reclaiming my relations with old acquaintances and friends [because] sadly, cultural gaps, language barriers – and by this I don't mean language skills, but differences in emotional meanings – will always separate me from Canadian friends and colleagues. How could one cross the [interpersonal] borders (marz'ha) that forbid touching, hugging, crying, [where] friendship is just for having fun, and does not include mutual dependence, giving without calculation and loyalty? (Iranian female in Toronto)

Nonetheless, what needs to be borne in mind is that generally, the depth in which refugees and migrants plunge into a sense of nostalgia is determined more than anything else by how they are received and treated in the new country, and that today, the populations that originate in Muslim-majority countries seem to be in a worse position than other racialized minority groups. For at present, no other groups are so systematically, willfully and tirelessly stereotyped, essentialized, feared, and hated as those which comprise Muslims in the West.

Muslimphobia – like anti-Semitism, which continues to infect humanity and has reached appalling intensity in certain historical periods – is a poison that has afflicted Western political culture. The increase in surveillance of Muslims, arbitrary arrests, and identity checks at borders and within states post-11 September has inevitably taken away what small sense of security and confidence was enjoyed in all Western countries by ethnic minorities, and particularly those coming from Muslim-majority countries.

After 11 September, the notion of an overpowering Muslim religious commitment driven by frightening, radical ideas was implanted in the psyche of the citizens in Western societies, providing a connecting thread that went beyond apprehensions regarding the exotic to justify the need for a watchful, regular, and insistent suspicion. However, it is crucial to emphasize that the planting and accumulation of stereotypes is a historical process that reaches beyond the media to involve the actions of ordinary people, and that Muslims were targets of suspicions that harboured hostility against them even before the events of 11 September.

During the First Gulf War, for example, researchers found that Arab-Canadians, both Christian and Muslim, felt 'silenced, devalued, misunderstood, and misrepresented.' Public school teachers in Edmonton, rather than calming the situation, allowed 'Iraqi bashing' to turn into 'Arab bashing,' and Arab-Canadians, portrayed as 'irrational' and driven by 'raw emotions' and equally raw 'instincts' ('sex' and 'violence'), were made to feel that they were 'guilty until proven innocent.' The situation only got worse after 11 September. Women wearing hijab said they were afraid to leave their homes. Non-Muslims of colour also sensed an upsurge of prejudice. Parents felt they had to escort their children to school. Because a woman wore hijab, she and her husband were evicted from their apartment. Because their customers believed they were 'Arab' or 'Muslim,' darker-skinned taxi drivers found that people would not ride in their cars (Khalema and Wannas-Jones, 2003: 26, 28, 32–3, citing Khalema and Mungall, 2001; El-Yasir, 2001: 9–10).

In a study conducted in late December 2006 by Leger Marketing and Sun Media (Sun Media, 2007: 3, 7), some 47 per cent of Canadian respondents surveyed expressed the view that they were 'strongly,' 'moderately,' or 'slightly' racist, with only 53 per cent holding a 'somewhat good' or 'very good' opinion of Arabs, as compared to 76 per cent holding such views of Jews and 88 per cent holding these views of Italians.[1] An earlier poll conducted by Ipsos-Reid agency in March, 2005 (Ipsos News Center, 2005a; 2005b: 4) agreed that these numbers indicated a high incidence of prejudice. It reported that close to one in six Canadians said they had personally been victims of racism, with 41 per cent of respondents in Ontario and 47 per cent in Quebec indicating that 'Muslims' or 'Arabs' were the groups which were most likely to be targets or victims in their community.[2]

This view was regionally particularized, however. Muslims and Arabs were identified as the main targets in central Canada, but in Alberta, 47 per cent felt 'aboriginals or First Nation peoples' were so marked, while in British Columbia, 46 per cent said 'East Indians' were the most victimized group. In another study, conducted for the Association for Canadian Studies by the Environics Research Group in 2003, some 68 per cent of respondents were 'concerned' about anti-Arab sentiment in Canada, while 30 per cent felt that Arabs and Muslims 'projected a negative image.'[3] In Toronto, the Police Service Hate Crime Unit (HCU), a subunit of Intelligence Services, noted a 66 percent increase in 2001 with 121 incidents related to the 11 September attacks. Most involved 'mischief to property' (such as graffiti plastered on TTC trains), followed by 'threats and assaults.' After the attacks, the Refugee Housing Task Force in Toronto issued a report saying that some landlords were refusing to rent to Muslims (cited in Zine, 2003). In 2001, the Toronto HCU listed fourteen attacks on Muslim places of worship. From Halifax to Vancouver, at least one incident of vandalism was reported at each Islamic centre. In Moose Jaw, services were discontinued because of the attacks. In the weeks immediately following 11 September, almost every Canadian city reported a protective police presence for Friday prayers (Hussain, 2002).

There is no doubt that Muslimphobia is a problem in Canada and the 11 September fallout for Muslims in the form of surveillance of the population, closure of bank accounts, and interrogation and arrest of individuals who are considered potential terrorists are undeniable facts. The most famous or infamous case relates to Maher Arar, a Canadian citizen and wireless technology consultant in Ottawa. Arrested at a U.S. airport and deported to Syria, Arar was jailed and tortured for ten months before he was finally released and returned to Canada. In the course of the campaign to clear his name and a public inquiry ordered by the Canadian government into the circumstances of his detention, it became evident that Arar had become a target of the

Canadian Intelligence and secret service agencies because of his acquaintance with another individual who had also been tortured in Syria. The formation of the public inquiry and the final report of the judge, exonerating Maher Arar from any wrongdoing, and the payment by the Canadian government of $10.5 million in compensation along with a formal apology, are other sides to the Arar case.

Nonetheless, having said all this, hate crimes in Canada directed against Muslims have been few, and compared to other Western societies, Canadian anti-Muslim agitation is milder and less violent. In the United Kingdom, by contrast, racist attitudes are often openly expressed and racial appeals have been consciously deployed by both mainstream parties and by movements on the Right. For example, in 1988, anti-Muslim feelings deepened when some UK Muslim leaders reiterated Ayatollah Khomeini's threatening fatwa against British author Salman Rushdie. In 2001, the growing, cumulative anger among the diaspora about Britain's anti-Muslim policies led to widespread riots. In 2007 the Rushdie controversy was rekindled when he was granted a knighthood. As well, in Britain, unlike Canada, there are open confrontations between the leaders of Muslim religious communities and the authorities. As with other highly visible migrant populations, the Muslim concentration in particular cities and districts, along with mosques and 'ethnic' food shops, made the impact more obvious in the UK.

Aside from the Rushdie controversy, the 2001 riots in Bradford, Oldham, Burnley, Leicester, Southall, and Birmingham showed the devastating effects of mounting segregation and the de-funding of youth services by the Thatcher government, and made the 'depth of polarization' evident in 'educational arrangements, community and voluntary bodies, employment, places of worship, language [and] social and cultural networks' (Community Cohesion Unit, 2003). With this background, it was no surprise, then, that when the white paper *Secure Borders, Safe Haven* passed into law in 2002 as the *Nationality, Immigration and Asylum Act*, it focused almost entirely on measures to tighten entry, identifying asylum-seekers as intruders and the cause of Britain's racial problems. In July 2002, asylum-seekers' right to work legally was entirely revoked (Sales, 2005: 446–7, 454).

By the end of 2006, the European Monitoring Centre on Racism and Xenophobia concluded in a comprehensive survey of Muslim experience that 'Islamophobia, discrimination, and socio-economic marginalization' were generating disaffection and alienation, that Muslims felt their acceptance was increasingly premised on 'assimilation' bound up with an enforced loss of Muslim identity, and that events had put the Muslim populace 'under a general suspicion of terrorism.' Noting the alarming impact of hostile media and violent physical assaults on Islamic communities, the study also recorded disturbingly negative patterns of employment and educational attainment, finding that Muslims were disproportionately represented in areas with poor housing conditions, that educational achievement among Muslim youth fell below average, and that with high rates of unemployment (for example, in 2004 reaching 13 per cent among males and 18 per cent for females in the UK) Muslims were often forced to work at jobs requiring lower qualifications and for low pay (European Monitoring Centre on Racism and Xenophobia, 2006: 3, 8, 11–12, 22). Within this context, it should not be a surprise that a 2007 study of economic conditions of ethnic minorities in Britain revealed that 74 per cent of Bangladeshi and 60 per cent of Pakistani children, compared to one in four white children, were living in poverty. This sad truth prompted the chair of the Commission for Racial Equality in the UK to speak of an invisible apartheid that separates modern Britain (*Guardian Weekly*, 5 April 2007).

Britain's involvement in the second invasion of Iraq and the government's continuing support for the Bush administration's aggressive stance angered many Muslims, leading to the disastrous London bombings. Inevitably, the bombings then led to a further deterioration in relations between Muslim communities and the British public. Street attacks increased, together with vandalism directed against Muslim-owned stores and the desecration of mosques (now numbering some 1,200) throughout the UK. The British government was forced to pass legislation against religious hatred. Some say this act has only inflamed Islamophobia further (Gelb, 2005: 11). According to the Home Office's *British Crime Survey*, Pakistanis and Bangladeshis are consistently more at risk in racially motivated crime. During 2003–4, some twenty-two of the forty-four incidents reported to the director of Public Prosecutions gave the victim's 'actual or perceived religion' as Muslim, and in 2004–5 the ratio increased to twenty-three out of thirty-four, including fifteen criminal assaults in two years. In the wake of the 7 July 2005 bombings in the London Underground and of a double-decker bus that killed fifty-two people and injured hundreds, 'faith hate' incidents surged, a six-fold rise from forty in 2004 to 269 in the first three weeks after the event (BBC, 2005) – that is, more than sixty incidents each week into mid-August.

In contrast to the UK, in Canada in general there have been fewer and less serious confrontations between Muslims and the rest of society and the government. Most Canadian Muslims are supportive of Canada's liberal democracy and appreciate its multicultural tolerance and benefit from it. A growing number of Muslims have willingly assimilated into the culture of the larger society and have distanced themselves from the conservative, politicized religious groups. In fact, a secular or moderate Muslim minority has become the target for verbal and physical attack by conservatives for exactly the same reason. Also, in contrast to the UK, the majority of non-Muslim Canadians are less inclined to use aggression or violent language to express their dislike for the Muslim presence in the country. In Canada more than in any other society in the West, a 'live-and-let-live' stance still seems to be the dominant trend. Since 2001, self-identified Muslims in Canada have become more politically engaged at the provincial and federal levels, hoping to influence top politicians and the general public (*Time*, 3 May 2004).

Discrimination and Social Exclusion

In chapter 1 we described some of the key factors that have emerged in the increasingly difficult relations between Muslim communities and their new countries of residence. The difficulty may primarily be that, as Max Frisch suggests in the European context, governments 'had asked for workers, but human beings came,' and that the dynamics of chain migration, one cohort pulling along another and setting up a home, could not be stopped by administrative fiat. Getting numerically larger and more collectively conscious of discriminatory and humiliating treatments they had for too long received in the new countries, Muslim populations finally found the confidence and the courage to start pressing these societies to recognize their presence, sometimes by radical and, more recently, by violent means not acceptable to the host societies.

Going back to the idea, discussed in chapter 6, of social integration as a two-way street, it is reasonable to assume that faced with hostile or embittering attitudes, minorities close themselves off and withdraw to their own group and to its language, media, and past cultural practices. At a minimum, the sense of separation from the mainstream diminishes a group's sense of belonging and moral agency. In some cases, the sense of separation is taken a step further and is reflected in

Table 7.1   Commitment to culture of country of origin, percentages

Responses	Afghans		Iranians		Pakistanis		Palestinians	
	Male	Female	Male	Female	Male	Female	Male	Female
N/A	0.58	1.29	0.00	1.09	0.63	0.57	0.50	0.87
Low	15.20	16.77	20.78	23.91	23.90	18.75	4.50	6.96
Medium	61.99	65.16	60.39	58.15	56.60	60.23	47.00	33.91
High	22.22	16.77	18.83	16.85	18.87	20.45	48.00	58.26
Total	100	100	100	100	100	100	100	100

intolerant or exclusionary gestures towards other ethnic and cultural groups. An interesting example is how many Iranians in Canada continue to identify Anglo-Europeans and, generally, non-Iranians as 'foreigners' (*khareji*). The term, used in the homeland in reference to outsiders and particularly to those of Western origin, in a sense connotes a sense of power associated with being an insider. Now one must ask whether the continued use of this term – even when Iranians, at least emotionally, live as 'foreigners' in Canada – is simply a matter of lingual habit or if it signals a more profound meaning that reflects the individuals' need to deny their new situation and new identity (externally assigned by the larger society) and to resist letting go of a pre-diasporic sense of autonomy and power.

In any case, being interested in the issues, events, and news in one's new country and considering them important for the individual and the society can be taken as a marker of integration and a sense of connection to the place in which one lives. For diasporas originating in non-democratic and autocratic states, for example, living in a society with established traditions of respect for individual liberties and political and religious freedoms should reasonably generate a sense of security and appreciation that would develop, in combination with other social and economic factors, into a sense of belonging. By contrast, attending cultural events relating to the home country only; having an exclusive interest in home-related events, music, and movies; following the home country's news on television; and always speaking one's native language at home or in public are measures that indicate a continuing attachment to one's cultural origins. Data reflecting these issues are reported in table 7.1.[4]

Among community–gender groups, Palestinian females (about 58 per cent) and males (48 per cent) most frequently scored 'high' on these nostalgic cultural descriptors, saying that they 'always' listened to music from their home country and followed the news on TV from Palestine. Otherwise, the 'high' score for other communities was about the same, ranging from about 18 to 22 per cent. Aside from the Palestinians, the most common response for cultural commitments was at the 'medium' level, with about 58 to 65 per cent of Afghans, Iranians, and Pakistanis scoring 'medium' on this measure. Over 92 per cent of Palestinians, male and female, scored either 'high' or 'medium' in their commitment to activities reflecting an attachment to their culture of origin, a very high level when compared to other groups. As well, drawing from another set of cultural markers, about 36 to 40 per cent of Palestinian males and females said they 'always' use their mother tongue, compared to other groups which averaged about 14 to 22 per cent.

The average social involvement of individuals with their own community is fairly uniform for each of the four groups. About three-quarters of each group in our samples scored 'high' or 'medium' on an index that combined friendships with members of one's own group, living in a neighbourhood with individuals from the same ethnic background, and being 'active' in social groups, which include people mostly from their country of origin.[5] However, a substantial group of Iranians – 28 per cent of males and 23 per cent of females – also lived in neighbourhoods where none of the people were from Iran. This relative dispersion was exceeded only by Palestinian males, 30 per cent of whom said that none of their neighbours were Palestinians.

Participation in the politics of the new country is usually taken as a sign of integration, or the desire by a migrant community to be involved in a new county's political institutions and public life. The measures we use include expressions of the sense that Canada (as opposed to one's country of origin) is understood as the 'home country,' along with the habit of 'following the news' in Canada on television and radio, in newspapers and magazines, whether respondents regard political events in Canada as 'really important' to them or whether they feel that political and religious freedoms are better defended in Canada as compared to what they remember from their country of origin.[6] Taken together, these elements suggest a commitment to the country and an interest in day-to-day politics as well as a commitment to widely endorsed ideas in Canada of tolerance and civic culture, including the defence of individual political and reli-

Table 7.2   Involvement in Canadian political culture, percentages

Responses	Afghans		Iranians		Pakistanis		Palestinians	
	Male	Female	Male	Female	Male	Female	Male	Female
N/A	1.18	2.58	1.30	1.09	0.00	1.14	0.50	0.00
Low	18.24	38.71	34.42	36.41	16.35	26.14	22.00	26.09
Medium	57.06	47.10	53.90	52.72	57.86	53.41	64.50	69.57
High	23.53	11.61	10.39	9.78	25.79	19.32	13.00	4.35
Total	100	100	100	100	100	100	100	100

gious rights. This bundle of attitudes and activities, in turn, provides a contrast to the expression of ethnocentric and intolerant, self-isolating, or exclusionary viewpoints.

Data on involvement in Canadian politics and Canadian political culture are reported in table 7.2. Generally, we observe a low level of participation in political and civic activities in our samples with males showing greater interest than females in politics. The population segments more involved in Canadian political culture were Pakistanis (male and female), together with Afghan males and Palestinian males; close to 26 per cent of Pakistani males and slightly over 19 per cent of Pakistani females scored 'high' in their involvement, followed by Afghan males at about 24 per cent. At the other extreme, only about 10 to 11 per cent of Iranians (male and female) indicated a 'high' involvement in Canadian politics and political life; most scored at the 'medium' level.

Most respondents followed Canadian news, and the majority from each group said that political freedom was 'much better' or 'somewhat better' in Canada than in their country of origin. Among those 'turned off' by Canadian politics, some 9 to 15 per cent of Afghan, Iranian and Pakistani females said that what happened in Canada really didn't matter to them. Iranian males provide the only instance of males exceeding females with this negative view (12 per cent). Some 30 per cent of Afghan females, 42 per cent of Pakistani males, and 37 per cent of Pakistani females felt that freedom of religion was 'much better' in Canada than in their country of origin. By contrast, only 11 per cent of Iranian males held this view. Indeed, 50 per cent of Iranian males and 43 per cent of Iranian females said that the right to 'exercise freely your religious convictions' in Canada and Iran were 'about the same.' A dis-

senting minority of 16 per cent of Iranian females felt that these pro-
tections were 'much better' in the new country.

Iranian respondents, better educated and more 'modern' in their
gender and family attitudes, are resolutely non-religious and, on
average, are less involved in Canadian politics, indicating only a
'medium' interest. The contrary case is provided by Pakistani males –
the group most committed to Muslim ceremony, food restrictions, and
dress – who nevertheless exhibit a keen interest in Canadian politics
and praise political and religious freedoms in the country. One possible explanation is the continuing mental or actual involvement of
Iranian males with politics in their home country as well as their
general disillusionment with politics, resulting from the disappointing
consequences of the 1979 revolution and substantial losses incurred in
the migration process, all of which can lead to political scepticism,
weariness, and even rejection. Cultural nostalgia can spill into suspicion of other communities or a reluctance to get involved in the public
life of the new country, which is the basis for committed, democratic
politics. Another plausible explanation for the difference is the more
extensive involvement of Pakistanis in their own community and their
greater reverence for religious leaders who, particularly more recently,
have become involved in Canadian politics and policymaking institutions in an effort to gain specific faith-based rights. This kind of politics has had less appeal for the more secular Iranians.

The tendency to rely on the family rather than getting involved with
the larger society is a continuation of patterns that began when
respondents moved with their families from the country of origin. In
Canada, they live with family members and extended kin; and when
dealing with problems involving one's marriage or financial and job-
related issues, they seek help from family members, relatives, and
friends rather than from community or religious organizations, social
organizations, or governmental services (see table 7.3).[7] In this regard,
Palestinian females (at about 25 per cent) lead other respondents in
their 'high' dependence on help from parents, siblings, adult children,
other relatives, and friends. Also indicating strong reliance on personal
support are Pakistani males at about 21 per cent. Among those who
replied to questions concerning help in all three areas, at least 65 per
cent from each of the four communities – males and females – indicated a 'high' or 'medium' dependence on family and friends to help
them out, with about 78 per cent of Palestinian females giving this
response. But the results varied by issue, as about one-third to one-half

Table 7.3   Seeking support from relatives and friends, percentages

Responses	Afghans		Iranians		Pakistanis		Palestinians	
	Male	Female	Male	Female	Male	Female	Male	Female
N/A	30.41	30.32	30.13	29.89	32.08	39.77	40.50	27.83
Low	17.54	22.58	21.15	21.74	21.38	21.02	17.50	15.65
Medium	43.86	33.55	37.18	29.89	25.79	23.30	22.50	31.30
High	8.19	13.55	11.54	18.48	20.75	15.91	19.50	25.22
Total	100	100	100	100	100	100	100	100

of those interviewed claimed that they had sought help from 'no one' (at the 'high' end, about 51 per cent of Pakistani females, 54 per cent of Afghan males, and 56 per cent of Iranian males said that 'no one' helped them with family or marital problems).

Turning to the specific areas, the percentage of respondents who depended on help from relatives alone on marital issues ranged from a low of 15 to 16 per cent for Iranian males and females and Afghan males to a high of about 37 per cent of Palestinian females – again emphasizing the importance of family support for Palestinian women. On financial problems, as an exception, support from social service agencies was sought by 19 per cent of Afghan females and 9 per cent of Afghan males; for all other groups, those depending on social service agencies never exceeded 7 per cent. Religious organizations provided virtually no help on marital problems or on financial or job-related matters among all the groups, with less than 1 per cent of each group reporting that they seek help from these sources. Community organizations, however, were more active on job-related issues, with about 10 per cent of Afghan females and 10 per cent of Palestinian females indicating they had sought help from them in this area. The data for Canadian youth (see chapter 5) also shows a low dependence by younger people on help from community service agencies or religious organizations.

Having noted these patterns for Canada, the question inevitably arises as to whether life is any easier for displaced individuals who end up living in a society that is culturally, religiously, and linguistically closer to their country of origin. If we take the example of Afghans in Iran, we can see that the response to the question is complex. In fact, the increasingly harsh conditions of Afghans' lives in

Iran, their hard work in professions not acceptable to Iranians, and, more recently, their mass deportation testify to one sad reality – that closing borders to outsiders, or the grudging acceptance of displaced populations without much concern for their dignity, well-being, and human rights, are not exclusively Western practices. Even where the source and destination countries share key aspects of geography, culture, and religion, immigrants still have to endure the chilly reception given to 'outsiders.' It might indeed be true that 'there is no place on earth where an uprooted population can live in peace and harmony without its sense of dignity being threatened' (Ashrafi and Moghissi, 2002: 95).

For more than two decades, Iran hosted Afghan refugees with very limited or no international assistance at all, initially adopting a very liberal approach to displaced Afghan (and Iraqi) asylum-seekers, and issuing resident cards, work permits, and government assistance such as monthly allowances or food coupons to all without completing the standard legal procedures (Ebadi, 1373/1995). However, the fact should not be overlooked that the Iranian government's hospitality derived from an ideological hostility towards the then-existing Soviet Union and the West rather than the principle of providing dignified refuge to those in need of protection as acclaimed in the 1951 Refugee Convention, signed by Iran in 1967, and as emphasized in Article 26 of the country's post-1979 Revolution Constitution. As well, Iran's confusing bureaucratic approach to providing legal documentation to Afghan refugees created much discomfort and uncertainty for the refugees, negatively affecting their right to protection and to a sense of security and dignity. While Iranian law grants the possibility for naturalization to persons born in Iran of foreign nationals if they have lived in Iran for up to one year after their eighteenth birthday, it has been very hard for Afghan children with valid documents to benefit from the right to obtain Iranian citizenship (ibid.: 164). This has had tremendous negative consequences for Afghans in the country in terms of access to education and health care, freedom of movement, obtaining travel documents and work permits, and marriage, particularly since the mid-1990s. True, Afghan refugees were regarded as 'brethren' and 'guests' with access to free education and health services. Nonetheless, an overwhelming majority of Afghan migrants and refugees have had to work in low-paying, manual jobs such as construction, brick-making, well-digging, and labouring on poultry and dairy farms, and often living with up to twelve family members or friends in a three- or four-room apartment or house (Ashrafi and Moghissi, 2002). Since the 1990s, increasing social and economic pressures on the native population have made Afghans the target of prejudicial attitudes and even the animosity of the general public. Accentuating the problem was the withdrawal of state subsidies and the government's corruption and loss of legitimacy, as well as the use of Afghan refugees as an ideological tool, including their coerced participation in the Islamic government's propaganda machinery, such as Friday prayers and other political events, particularly during the bloody war with Iraq in the 1980s.

The passing in the *majlis* (parliament) of Article 48 as an annex to Iran's Third Five-Year Economic Development Plan in April 2000 is a case in point. Article 48 instructed the Ministry of the Interior to round up all foreigners without work permits and deport them to their countries of origin. In June of 2001, the Ministry of Labour announced that all illegal foreign workers in Iran should be dismissed; otherwise, the employers would be subjected to heavy fines and/or imprisonment. The persecution of Afghans has resulted in a 'revolving-door' phenomenon of departure and return across Iranian borders, causing much hardship for the Afghan population in Iran and blocking their access to health care and education. The following statements, taken from a focus group discussion conducted in Iran, capture the sentiments of Afghan refugees in the country:

From a financial point of view, we own land in Afghanistan and we can have a bank account. Here, there is no financial saving. The only support we have here is that we have to work to live. We can invest in our work when we go back. If we had spent half the time we worked here [in Iran] in Afghanistan, we could have bought a piece of land there. (Afghan male in Iran)

There are two kinds of immigrants (*mohajer*): the first group came because of war and political reasons, the second group to find work and earn an income. Those who came to Iran to seek work made a lot of progress. But those who left Afghanistan because of political reasons, their life has become much worse. In immigration the first generation is destroyed ... (Afghan female in Iran)

From an educational point of view, and social relations, we have a lot of restrictions here. Our growth and advancement were stopped in many ways. If we were in another country we could have achieved more. (Afghan female in Iran)

The freedom we had in Afghanistan, we don't have in Iran. Here I cannot go anywhere. We lived in a village in Afghanistan; therefore, girls could easily go everywhere. (Afghan female in Iran)

My parents are educated. In Iran for one year they worked as teachers, but they can't work any more, not as teachers nor as office workers; they are under great emotional and economic pressure. My father says I got an education so that I don't have to do whatever work is available, but here I have to go for any kind of work I find. (Afghan female in Iran)

My father was a colonel, but when we came to Iran, he was doing construction work. For us, we live a much worse life in Iran. (Afghan female in Iran)

The point is that racism and discrimination against Afghan refugees in Iran cannot be attributed to dramatic differences in religious beliefs and cultural practices (as might be the case with Muslim diasporas in Western societies), or to historical ethnic conflicts or mutual incomprehension due to different linguistic or behavioural patterns. Instead, the experience of Afghans in Iran reflects the constitution of an ethnic hierarchy and an intraracial racism, which does not use religion, culture, or language as a determinant but rather lower economic status, which in times of economic hardship accentuates the fear of having to share scarce social and economic resources with those who are marked as 'outsiders.' This form of prejudice must be distinguished from discrimination traditionally justified in Islamic states by appeals to religious difference, such as that experienced in the country by Jews or Armenians (Sanasarian, 1995; Sarshar, 1996).

The Afghan experience in Iran seems to suggest that, at least at present, in host societies in a non-Western context, lower levels of social and economic development, along with political underdevelopment, are inevitably translated into stronger tribalism, a lower level of tolerance for 'outsiders' and less generosity towards displaced populations, who by the force of circumstances have left their homelands only to live where they are constantly made to feel they do not belong. The recent, callous mass deportation from Iran of Afghans, many of whom had lived in the country for over a quarter of a century and had

married Iranian women, is a case in point: beginning in 2000 and cul-
minating in 2007, these continual, forcible expulsions led to the breaking up of families and the loss for Afghans of modest livelihoods. No
amount of protest and pleading from international organizations, nor
a collective letter signed by a group of Iranian intellectuals inside the
country, could soften the heart of the government of the Islamic
Republic that once welcomed Afghans into the country and then
exploited them for its own political purposes.

It is important to note that the media and its sensational reporting
on refugees, migrants, and aliens, be they Pakistanis in Britain or
Afghans in Iran, are strong forces in the racialization process and in
shaping public opinion against diasporas. The role of the media is particularly important when emotionally charged symbols are coupled
with the dramatic force of 'breaking' events.

This reality is reflected in the responses of the individuals interviewed, even though perceptions of hostility by the media are different among the groups in the study and also depend on the specific
target involved. For example, among those who said they followed
news on television and radio and in the print media, about 29 per
cent of Pakistani males and 28 per cent of Pakistani females in the UK
said the media coverage of Muslims was 'very unfair.' The numbers
are lower in Canada, where about 20 per cent of Pakistani males and
about 17 per cent of Pakistani females said media coverage of
'Muslim communities in Canada' was 'very unfair.' But these complaints increase sharply to 30 per cent for males and 28 per cent for
females if these Pakistani respondents are asked about how the
Canadian media treats 'Islam in general,' and to 37 per cent for males
and 27 per cent for females for Canadian media coverage of the
Middle East. By comparison, a smaller percentage of Iranians in
Canada (about 12 per cent of males and 7 per cent of females) find
media coverage of Muslims in Canada to be 'very unfair.' About 5
per cent of Palestinian males and 11 per cent of Palestinian females
and about 9 per cent of Afghan males and females in Canada said the
media treatment of 'Muslim communities' in the country was 'very
unfair.' Finally, in Iran, about 41 per cent of Afghan males and 20 per
cent of Afghan females also found the media coverage of 'other'
Muslim communities (including their own) to be 'somewhat' or 'very
unfair.' These figures are high, and for males, even higher than the
high figures for Pakistani males in the UK, confirming the view that
living in a country with shared religious values and cultural practices

Table 7.4   Perception of discrimination and social exclusion, percentages

Responses	Afghans		Iranians		Pakistanis		Palestinians	
	Male	Female	Male	Female	Male	Female	Male	Female
N/A	6.47	26.45	7.05	6.52	4.40	8.52	2.00	2.61
Low	54.71	49.68	42.95	58.70	51.57	54.55	71.50	67.83
Medium	27.65	15.48	32.69	20.11	24.53	23.30	19.00	20.87
High	11.18	8.39	17.31	14.67	19.50	13.64	7.50	8.70
Total	100	100	100	100	100	100	100	100

does not necessarily provide protection against a chilling or outright hostile reception by the receiving society.

We created an index to measure a respondent's sense of being subject to discrimination and social exclusion. The index combines questions on media bias, a respondent's report on discriminatory experience, testimony that one is not able to use their education effectively at work, and the feeling of being treated unfairly on the job (table 7.4).[8]

Those most likely to perceive a 'high' level of discrimination based on these questions are Pakistani males (about 20 per cent) and Iranian males (about 17 per cent). Among groups registering the greater complaints, about 54 per cent of Afghan males and 41 per cent of Afghan females, 48 per cent of Iranian males and 45 per cent of Iranian females, 36 per cent of Pakistani males and 27 percent of Pakistani females (as opposed to about 25 per cent of Palestinians, male and female) feel that their jobs do *not* make good use of their education. In Britain, a somewhat smaller percentage of Iranian males and females (about 39 and 25 per cent, respectively) and an even smaller percentage of Pakistani male and females (over 14 and 28 per cent, respectively) express this complaint.

Among Afghans in Iran, the percentage of male respondents who do not feel their education is being put to good use is higher (over 62 per cent, as compared to 54 per cent in Canada). It is also somewhat higher for females (47 per cent in Iran, compared to 41 per cent in Canada). Of those in Canada who indicated that their qualifications had not been recognized, about 14 per cent of Afghan males and females, 11 per cent of Pakistani males, and 6 per cent of Pakistani females (but only about 3 or 4 per cent of Iranians and Palestinians) said their degree or diploma from the home country had not been accepted. The percentages are similar in Britain – about 3 per cent for Iranian males, 2 per cent for Iranian females, and 6 per cent for Pakistani males.

Some 24 per cent of Iranian males, 19 per cent of Afghan males and 14 per cent of Iranian females in Canada felt they were not treated fairly on the job. About 47 per cent of Iranian males, 42 per cent of Iranian females, and 34 per cent of Pakistani males reported that they or someone they knew had been discriminated against because of their ethnic origin. Of those reporting such experiences, about 25 per cent of Iranians, male and female, and about 18 per cent of Pakistani males complained of discrimination in an institutional setting, including the workplace, while 15 per cent of Iranian males, 12 per cent of Iranian females and about 9 per cent of Pakistani males and females complained of specific overt acts. The following samples from our interviews range across the different sorts of discrimination felt by the respondents:

> Here [in Montreal], francophones are the first choices for everything. But it is not all about language barriers. Just because I am coming from Iran, it means that I fall behind. Why? Because the educational system here does not know our system and so they don't give it much weight when they want to evaluate our academic standing. (Iranian male in Montreal)

> I didn't feel that much difference where I worked after 9/11, but my husband had some problems. He started to notice that people would always ask him for his opinion on what had happened and the political situation; they would single him out for it. This was difficult for him. People would start insulting Muslims at a [corporate] dinner or at a meeting and he had to say something. He had to choose a middle ground to say something. (Pakistani female in Toronto)

> I worked as a pharmacist trainee to obtain Canadian experience for nine months in Calgary. I met people who were very conservative and did not like immigrants. I experienced discrimination at work throughout the duration of my stay. My work supervisor, who was older than the other employees, made me very uncomfortable with negative comments about immigrants. He was tough and harsh with me and asked me to do twice as much work as the others. He made comments about customers: 'Why do they come to this country?' 'We pay taxes and they take them.' 'They cannot speak English.' I complained to the boss, to no avail. (Palestinian male in Toronto)

> In Canada people are very biased and it's hard to practise my religion
> here. When I wear my head-covering during Ramadan [the Fasting
> Month], people treat me totally different and I know how some people
> are Islamophobic here. Even my own friends ask me not to wear [the]
> scarf, or [they ask me] why I am wearing [a] head-cover. (Afghan female
> in Toronto)

Having said this, it is important to emphasize that, taking into
account the majority of comparisons among the four groups surveyed
in other settings and in Canada, Canada still seems to provide the
more hospitable and, generally, the less discriminatory environment.
For example, close to 85 per cent of Afghan males and over 58 per cent
of Afghan females in Iran, compared to 24 per cent of Afghan males
and 20 per cent of Afghan females in Canada, said they had been discriminated against because of their ethnic origin; over 57 per cent of
Iranian males in the UK said they had experienced discrimination,
compared to 44 per cent of Iranian males in Canada; and, among Palestinians, over 35 per cent of males and close to 41 per cent of females of
respondents in our sample living in West Bank refugee camps said
they had been discriminated against as compared to 12 per cent of
Palestinians, male and female, who said they were discriminated
against in Canada. In some cases, the record in Canada is about the
same or slightly worse than elsewhere. In the UK, about 32 per cent of
Pakistani males and 23 per cent of Pakistani females mention discrimination, compared with the 34 per cent of Pakistani males and 23 per
cent of Pakistani females in Canada with the same complaint. About 36
per cent of Iranian females in the UK reported discrimination against
themselves or someone they knew, as compared to complaints of discrimination by over 41 per cent of their counterparts in Canada.

The following statements by Palestinian refugees in the West Bank
and by Afghan refugees in Iran help give substance to the record of
discrimination:

> Before we were forced to leave, life was hard. I was working at home and
> also on the land. People didn't have money, but here whatever you do
> people look at you as a refugee, and not as an original dweller, and some-
> times people moved from this village when there were troubles between
> refugees and original people. (Palestinian female refugee in the West
> Bank)

[One] negative aspect of diaspora is problems between people, and discriminations: this is a refugee and this one is not. And hatred becomes common between people. (Palestinian male from Jerusalem)

The fact that immigrants have no rights turns some Iranians very hostile towards us. They don't treat us very well in Iran. My children cannot go to school because they don't have ID cards; I don't like the Afghan schools because they [don't] get a lot of money and there is one teacher for every 100 students. I send my children to school by themselves, because I am not well and I have to go to work. (Afghan female in Iran)

At the outset of this study, we pointed out that a chilly reception by the host country would be the single most important factor that determines the sense of belonging for a refugee and may force members of a diasporic community to seek refuge in a folkloric 'Islamic' identity. The responses of several individuals interviewed in Palestine support this argument:

I remember people [in the past] wore normal clothes, not religious ones. Today people wear more conservative clothes. It has to do with the situation people live in. Women in cities were less conservative than in villages. Now this has changed, now you don't recognize if women are from cities or villages; everyone now wears fashionable Islamic clothes. (Palestinian female in the West Bank)

Maybe today people pray more; today, those who pray know a lot about the religion, but those who do not, they run after pleasure and leisure, and there [are] more of them than before. (Palestinian male in the West Bank)

Still, not all experiences are negative, as the following excerpts from the interviews confirm:

I got to know a lot of people in Iran. It was because of immigration that I met and got to know Afghans from different ethnic groups and cultures. If it was not for the war and migration, I would have never met Afghans from different places and ethnic groups. Now I can say Afghanistan is our land. It was in Iran that we learned to put aside our conflicts that existed for years among different ethnic and religious groups. We became closer in Iran. (Afghan male refugee in Iran)

I regret that I wasted many years in my country, Iran. The first few years in the UK, I was asking myself who I was, why I was here. Then I analysed my situation and realized that I lagged behind in my life because I always lived in [one] place but my thoughts were in another. So I must settle, stop the nomadic life, and spread my roots in this country. Iran is my motherland, but I [am] married to this country. When I got my citizenship I was truly happy. I have respect for my new identity and I am thankful to Britain for giving me this possibility. Many Iranians cannot bring themselves to say or hear this. But I have made my choice. I will do whatever I can for Iran, always, but this is my country, and that is why I am doing my utmost best to make a change here by joining the Labour Party, and [I] was elected as a councillor. I am an Iranian and a Muslim, but a modern Muslim. At present I am working with one of the MPs to create a committee, that is, Muslims for Labour, in order for Muslims to have some influence in Parliament. The only way to change the mentality of the fundamentalists [and] conservatives is to make the possibility for them to intermingle with the enlightened individuals. The more isolated a culture, the more conservative it [will] be, increasing the risk of extremism. (Iranian female in the UK)

There are cultural values that are imposed here. And you have to be a part of it. There's no way out, even if you think it's painful inside ... But you have to make your peace with this. Of course, sometimes you feel like you want to run away. You think this is not your world; you don't belong to this place. But then, what you say there, now you have to perform here. Over there I used to speak of [gender] equality, but there is no equality there ... The problem is that you don't belong there anymore ... Your roots are torn up and planted here, and for that plant to grow it takes a long time. (Pakistani male in Montreal)

I feel Canada is a very good place ... people come here just to make good living for themselves. Most of them have escaped trouble in their home countries and they do not want to see [any] here. (Afghan male in Toronto)

[In the past], a woman worked near her husband in the fields. But they didn't give her rights. I mean ... she didn't get what she deserved, like inheritance ... She was also ashamed to ask for her rights from her brothers. And this of course affected her afterwards. After 1948, when she went out of the village and saw life out there and she mixed up with other

people, she changed her opinion on life a bit. Even her husband and children started to conceive her differently. They do so since they also suffered from the diaspora, and they had to help each other and build a new type of cooperation in order to remake themselves again. So, many women could work in trading, or in building the house, and go outside.
Q: You mean women have more rights now?
A: Yes, as a result of the mixing [with each other]. Girls went to schools, they became educated and worked. A large number became teachers, and this affected the family, which could have better social quality.
Q: That's what you think happened to women after the diaspora?
A: Yes, [they are] more valued.
(Conversation with a Palestinian female in the West Bank)

What conclusions can we draw from the comparative data in Canada and in other settings? Certainly, these data provide suggestive results with regards to the 'sense of belonging,' which is so important in providing an anchorage for a migrant community. To be sure, liberal democratic states insist, as a point of principle, that they recognize the rights of Muslims to maintain their religious practices and cultural heritage. As we know, the actual policies for accommodating these rights vary substantially. Still, our data show that, as far as this can be tapped by a simple, direct question in the interview, the emotional experience in the post-11 September period was nearly identical in Canada and the United Kingdom. For example, among Pakistanis, about 32 per cent of males and 31 per cent of females in the UK as compared to about 30 per cent of males and 34 per cent of females in Canada said they had been forced to confront 'more hostile attitudes and suspicion' after the attacks in New York City and Washington, DC.

This stance can perhaps explain why an overwhelming majority of respondents from each of the four groups in Canada and in other settings identified their original country as 'home' in answering the question, 'What country do you regard as your home country?' This sobering reality – in addition to the fact that only a minority are throwing themselves into politics and civic activities in the new country with the hope of finding a niche in its political and cultural life – seems to suggest that the integration of Muslim diasporas into their new country is so far an illusive reality in every host society. Only a minority are making connections with like-minded individuals in the host society, taking up new social commitments or welcoming the opportunity for learning and unlearning certain values, ideas, and vocations

Table 7.5 Which country is considered the 'home country', percentages

	Afghans		Iranians		Pakistanis		Palestinians	
	In Iran	In Canada	In UK	In Canada	In UK	In Canada	In W.Bank/Gaza	In Canada
Original home country	91.06	79.08	83.70	78.60	84.70	67.16	N/A	82.20
New country of residence	2.78	12.92	0.00	14.21	0.00	13.73	N/A	2.86
Original and new country	0.00	3.69	6.86	5.47	9.26	15.22	N/A	5.08
Other	3.40	0.62	6.62	1.14	2.00	0.90	N/A	5.40
N/A	2.08	4.00	3.33	1.14	4.00	2.69	N/A	3.49

that are necessary for adjusting to new circumstances. The majority, as Eva Hoffman would put it, 'can't afford to look back and can't figure out how to look forward' (1989: 115–16). Will the passage of time change this situation? Perhaps.

Nonetheless, as mentioned earlier, on balance, Canada seems to be doing better in providing these communities with a sense of belonging, as the percentages of the respondents that identified Canada as their 'home country' were higher than those in other settings. As shown in table 7.5, while only about 3 per cent of Afghans in Iran considered Iran their 'home country,' the percentage for Afghans in Canada was about 13 per cent. Neither Iranians nor Pakistanis in the UK considered the UK their 'home,' but in Canada about 14 per cent of each group considered Canada to be their place of national belonging. In the case of the Palestinians, by contrast, given their traumatic experiences since 1948, their emotional and political attachments to Palestine and the connection of Palestinian statehood to a sense of loyalty and personal honour, it is not surprising that a much smaller percentage (only about 2 per cent of males and 3 per cent of females) thought of Canada as their home country.[9]

In addition to the important differences one can observe between migrant communities in Canada and elsewhere, the element of age and generation is also crucial in thinking about the question of an individual's sense of 'home.' As discussed in chapter 5, the percentages of respondents who identified with Canada as their 'home country' was much higher for youth in each of the communities as compared to older persons from their background. This, by itself, is perhaps a sign that Canada's efforts to provide a home for migrants is making some progress among individuals who have moved from Muslim-majority countries – but modest progress only.

Conclusions

The peoples of the Muslim diaspora are varied and are of various opinions. But Western governments, Canada included, have developed the habit of talking only or mainly to the most conservative and religiously orthodox elements in the community, and this has helped reinforce the notion – contested in this volume – that these many communities from Muslim-majority countries have been welded together to form a population that is culturally homogenous and religiously driven. As we have emphasized throughout this book, the most important questions facing migrants and refugees of Muslim cultural background are practical ones. Indeed, if culture and religion had such a unilateral and determining impact on the sense of contentment and belonging in diaspora communities, then Afghans in Iran, because of linguistic, religious, and cultural similarities with the receiving country, should have had a much more positive experience in Iran than their counterparts in Canada. The evidence we have assembled shows the contrary. The singular, crude, and naive reductionist notion of 'culture' obscures the reality that many different factors shape the migrant experience. It also blocks the effort to identify and redress the urgent problems individuals face in finding a secure place in the new society. Reducing everything to 'culture' causes confusion when there is a need for the Canadian state to stand up firmly and clearly to the pressures exercised by Muslim conservative factions in seeking 'special' or 'exceptional rights' for religiously zealous constituents that would trample upon the individual rights of other community members and should have no place in an open and democratic society.

The message springing from such policies should be simple to understand – that Canadian society, in defence of its liberal and constitutional values, welcomes migrants from the world over and will do everything it can to make room for them and to protect their rights and dignity; but, at the same time, members of these groups are expected to accept and respect the social contract and codes of conduct that have been developed and guaranteed in the society in which they have chosen to live, in the interest of all. As always, it must be a two-way process. Only through this process of give-and-take can the larger society be reassured that its cherished social and political values and commitment to legal equality are not threatened by the presence of the Muslim minority and that, in fact, Canada will benefit from its presence.

The great majority of the populations of Muslim cultural background came to Canada, as to other Western countries, in the hope of finding a decent life free from violence, disrespect, discrimination, and harassment. Many paid a high price in getting here – leaving behind loved ones, and the feelings of warmth of being at home. Many, in fact, were forced to leave. Determined to live by the sociocultural codes of the society at large, they were eager to be accepted and included here. We find it remarkable that despite dissatisfaction with the low levels of occupational and economic achievement expressed by the respondents in the four communities, the great majority (70 per cent) of men and women in our Canadian samples think the decision to migrate to Canada was the right one. This is something that the larger community can use to promote an equitable, multicultural, and socially cohesive society. If people live on the margins and feel that the future is unknown, uncertain, and insecure, they may easily be driven to cling to the past as a means of preserving their sense of identity, dignity, and self-worth. For the diasporas, moving from the past into the future is one of the most complex and challenging issues facing them and their new countries.

Notes

1 Introduction

1 See *International Herald Tribune*, 3–4 December 2005; *Die Zeit*, 10 November 2005, *Frankfurter Allgemeine Zeitung*, 24 November 2005, and Associated Press report, 17 November 2005. These are just a few of many reports on violence among poor youth in suburban Paris in the fall of 2005, in which young women became targets in a racial and colonial battlefield. A recent case in Toronto region involves the death of a teenage girl, allegedly at the hands of her father, a Pakistani taxi driver, who it is said became enraged because she refused to wear hijab (El-Akkad, 2007; Henry and Mitchell, 2007).

2 Community Profiles, Social Origins, and Status

1 More detailed data of the four communities are available in the Diaspora, Islam, and Gender Project (2005).

2 For occupation data for other cities, see Diaspora, Islam, and Gender Project (2005): 38–9, 51–3.

3 Employment income here refers to the total income received by persons fifteen years of age and over during the calendar year 2000 as wages and salaries, net income from a non-farm unincorporated business and/or professional practice, and/or net farm self-employment income.

4 Census of Canada, 2001, Special Interest Tables (SITs), Data Matrix 97f0010xcb01043.

5 Average income is the weighted mean of the total income (income from all sources, including employment income, government benefits, and 'other' sources of income). This considers people working either full-time or part-time and also includes those not working.

6   Median income constitutes a better measure of equity, since it gives us the income that leaves half of the population on each side of the distribution.
7   The standard error is a measure of the size of the variation in the sample statistic over all samples of the same size as the study sample. The greater the study sample size, the smaller the variation across samples. The size of the standard error determines the range of values that will include the population parameter. Smaller standard errors lead to more precise estimates of the characteristic in the population. For more, please refer to www.thewager.org/glossary.htm.
8   The income figures in this section have also been deflated to 1996.
9   Refers to a group of two or more persons who live in the same dwelling and are related to each other by blood, marriage, common law, or adoption, as defined by Statistics Canada in 2001 Census Dictionary, Economic Family, available online at www12.statscan.ca/english/census01/Products/Reference/dict/ fam011.htm.
10   These are income levels at which families or unattached individuals spend 20 per cent more than average on food, shelter, and clothing. The low-income cut-offs are determined by the size of the city in which one lives and the number of members in the family. The following is an extract, relevant to this chapter, of the year 2000 matrix of low-income cut-offs from Statistics Canada, as retrieved 20 May 2008 from www12.statcan.ca/english/census01/Products/Reference/dict/fam021.htm.

Family size	1	2	3	4	5	6	7+
LICO for a city of 500,000 or more (CDN)	18,371	22,964	28,560	34,572	38,646	42,719	46,793

11   United Nations, Economic and Social Commission for Asia and Pacific (ESCAP), 2004 ESCAP Population data sheet, retrieved 28 May 2008 from www.222.unescap.org/esid/psis/population/database/data_sheet/2004/index2.asp.
12   1991 Census Local Base Statistics, ONS (from Nomis, 19 April 2005); Census, April 2001, Office for National Statistics. 1991 data is adjusted for under-enumeration using OPCS/GRO(S) 1994 adjustment factors (ONS, 2005a: 41, sec. 6.2; 42, table 17). 1.44 per cent of population in England is self-reported as Pakistani; as compared to 0.29 per cent in Wales; 0.63 per cent in Scotland; and 0.04 per cent in Northern Ireland (ONS, 2001a: table

3.7). ONS; General Register Office for Scotland; Northern Ireland Statistics and Research Agency. In 2001, persons of mixed parentage were excluded from Pakistani count – this 'mixed' white and Asian count (including mixed Pakistanis, Bangladeshis, Indians and 'Other') is 189,000 or 0.4 per cent (ONS, 2005a: 41, sec. 6.2; 42, table 17). Nearly half of the mixed white and Asian group declared itself to be Christian (only 1.86 per cent are Hindu, 16.08 per cent Muslim) (ONS, 2001b).

13 For ONS series (2004) indicates data was issued in 2004; no publication date was given.

14 Equivalised contemporary household disposable income before deduction of housing costs. Institute for Fiscal Studies, ONS: Department of Work and Pensions.

15 Annual Local Area Labour Force Survey.

16 Data of the number and age of Afghan refugees in Iran are from UNHCR Tehran office provided by our research colleagues in Tehran.

17 UNRWA defines Palestinian refugees as 'persons whose normal place of residence was Palestine between June 1946 and May 1948, who both lost their homes and means of livelihood as a result of the 1948 Arab–Israeli conflict.' Their descendants are also included in this category. The number of registered refugees has grown from 914,000 in 1950 to more than 4.4 million in 2005. See www.un.org/unrwa/refugees/whois.html.

5 Youths

1 Ipsos News Center, 'Canadians react in wake of terror-plot arrests,' 10 June 2006 (N=1005). Available online from www.ipsos-na.com/news/pressrelease.cfm?id=3108. Detailed tables at www.ipsos-na.com/news/client/act_dsp_pdf.cfm?name=mr060610-1tb.pdf&id=3108.

6 Social and Economic Integration

1 To determine occupation of respondents, the questionnaire offered twenty choices (including 'other'). For the purpose of analysis, they were divided into nine categories: (1) managerial, landowning, conducting own business and employing more than five workers, and professionals (including doctors, lawyers, engineers); (2) other white-collar workers, such as civil servants, military personnel, teachers; (3) blue-collar wage workers; (4) trades, crafts, small business employing less than five workers; (5) homemakers; (6) peasants, farmers; (7) students; (8) unemployed, retired; (9) other occupations and no answers.

2 This measure is based on the respondents' answers to questions on satisfaction with their main occupation in their country of origin and their assessment of economic and educational opportunities at home, and whether lack of economic or educational opportunities at home was one of their 'main reasons' for leaving the country. A parallel set of questions is used in the summary measure on satisfactions in Canada (see table 6.2).

7 Sense of (Not) Belonging

1 Sun Media, Racial Tolerance Report (January 2007), 3, 7, retrieved 3 May 2008 from www.legermarketing.com/documents/SPCLM/070119ENG.pdf. Survey conducted 27 December 2006 – 5 January 2007 (N=3092).
2 Ipsos News Center, 'International day for the elimination of racial discrimination,' 21 March 2005, retrieved 15 April 2007 from www.ipsos-na.com/news/pressrelease.cfm?id=2602. Citing Canadian Ipsos-Reid Express, Racism Study, 15–17 March 2007, detailed tables (N=1001), 4. Retrieved 15 April 2007 from www.ipsos-na.com/news/client/act_dsp _pdf.cfm?name=mr050321-2tb.pdf&id=2602.
3 Poll conducted 15–23 March 2003 (N=2002), reported in Khan (2003).
4 Based on responses to questions on attendance at cultural events and listening to music from home country, following news from country of origin and watching movies or videos from country of origin. A related index is based on commitment to the use of the mother tongue and includes language used at home and in public by members of the family, and use of mother-tongue television, radio, magazines, and newspapers.
5 Respondents were asked to describe the cultural background of most of their friends, whether most of their neighbours were from their country of origin, and how active they were in social groups that included mostly people from their country of origin.
6 Respondents were asked which country they considered to be their 'home' country today (with the option of being able to select Canada *and* another country), whether they 'follow the news' on television and radio or in newspapers and magazines in Canada, about their attitude towards politics in Canada, and how they compared political freedoms and the opportunity to exercise freely their religious convictions in Canada to their country of origin.
7 Respondents were asked where they sought help on family or marital problems, financial problems, or job-related issues, with the option to select family, relatives, friends, community or religious organizations,

social service agencies, medical authorities or the police, or 'no one.' A respondent who indicated a preference for family, relatives, or friends in preference to other supports was given a higher score, and these scores were then totalled over the three areas.

8 These questions were used: Does your job make good use of your education? Have your educational qualifications been recognized? Do you feel you have been treated fairly on the job? Have you ever been discriminated against because of your ethnic origin? These aspects of discriminatory treatment were combined with respondents' views on the 'fairness' of the media in its treatment of Muslims in Canada, Islam in general, and the Middle East.

9 Our Palestinian colleagues in the West Bank and Gaza chose not to include this question in the questionnaire, and so their percentages are not available.

Bibliography

Afshar, Haleh. 1994. Muslim women in West Yorkshire: Growing up with real and imaginary values amidst conflicting views of self and society. In *The dynamics of 'race' and gender: Some feminist interventions*, ed. Haleh Afshar and Mary Maynard. London: Taylor and Francis.

Afshar, Haleh, Robin Aitken, and Myfanway Franks. 2006. Islamophobia and women of Pakistani descent in Bradford: The crisis of ascribed and adopted identities. In *Muslim diaspora: Gender, culture and identity*, ed. Haideh Moghissi. London: Routledge.

Ahmad, Farah, Sarah Riaz, Paula Barata, and Donna E. Stewart. 2004. Patriarchal beliefs and perceptions of abuse among South Asian immigrant women. *Violence Against Women* 10: 262–82.

Allport, Gordon W., and J.M. Ross. 1967. Personal religious orientation and prejudice. *Journal of Personality and Social Psychology* 5: 432–43.

Anthias, Floya. 1998. Evaluating 'diaspora': Beyond ethnicity? *Sociology* 32: 557–80.

– 2001. New hybridities, old concepts: The limits of 'culture.' *Ethnic and Racial Studies* 24: 619–41.

Anwar, Muhammad. 2005. Issues, policy and practice. In *Muslim Britain, communities under pressure*, ed. Tahir Abbas. London: Zed Press.

Ashrafi, Afsaneh, and Haideh Moghissi. 2002. Afghans in Iran: Asylum fatigue overshadows Islamic brotherhood. *Global Dialogue* 4: 89–99.

Bartels, Edien. 2000. 'Dutch Islam': Young people, learning and integration. *Current Sociology* 48, part 4: 59–73.

Bechir, Saleh, and Hazem Saghieh. 2005. The 'Muslim community': A European invention. *Open Democracy*. Retrieved 15 August 2007 from www.opendemocracy.net/conflict-terrorism/community_2928.jsp.

Bhattacharya, Surya. 2006. A British imam has divided local Muslims. Are his words a danger to impressionable youth? *Toronto Star* (Metropolitan edition), 27 June: B5.

Bilgrami, Akeel. 2003. The clash within civilizations. *Daedalus* 132: 88–93.

Bowen, John Richard. 2004. Beyond migration: Islam as transnational public space. *Journal of Ethnic and Migration Studies* 30: 879–94.

Brah, Avtar. 1996. *Cartographies of diaspora: Contesting identities.* London: Routledge.

Braziel, Jana Evans, and Anita Mannur. 2003. *Theorizing diaspora.* Oxford: Blackwell.

Brinkerhoff, Merlin B., Elaine Grandin, and Eugen Lupri. 1992. Religious involvement and spousal violence: The Canadian case. *Journal for the Scientific Study of Religion* 31: 15–31.

British Broadcasting Corporation (BBC). 2005. Hate crimes soar after bombing: Religious hate crimes, mostly against Muslims, have risen six-fold in London since the bombings, 4 August. Retrieved 6 August 2007 from http://news.bbc.co.uk/2/hi/uk_news/england/london/4740015.stm.

Brubaker, Rogers. 2005. The 'diaspora' of diaspora. *Ethnic and Racial Studies* 28: 1–19.

Buijs, Gina. 1993. Introduction. In *Migrant women: Crossing boundaries and changing identities*, ed. Gina Buijs. Oxford: Berg.

Campion-Smith, Bruce. 2006. Help us weed out extremists, Muslims tell governments. Politicians support idea of summit. Youth feel marginalized, groups say. *Toronto Star* (Ontario edition), 9 June: A10.

Campion-Smith, Bruce, and Michelle Shepard. 2006. Former soldier accused of plan to 'behead' PM. Brampton court hears of plot to storm Parliament Hill and take politicians hostage. *Toronto Star* (Metropolitan edition), 7 June: A01.

Cesari, Jocelyne. 2003. Muslim minorities in Europe: The silent revolution. In *Modernizing Islam: Religion in the public sphere in Europe and the Middle East*, ed. John L. Esposito and François Burgat. New Brunswick, NJ: Rutgers University Press.

Cherribi, Osama. 2003. The growing Islamization of Europe. In *Modernizing Islam: Religion in the public sphere in Europe and the Middle East*, ed. John L. Esposito and François Burgat. New Brunswick, NJ: Rutgers University Press.

Clifford, James. 1997. Diaspora. In *The ethnicity reader: Nationalism, multiculturalism and migration*, ed. Montserrat Guibernay and John Rex. London: Polity Press. Originally published in *Cultural Anthroplogy* 9 (1994): 302–38.

Cloud, David S. 2006. Rumsfeld says war critics haven't learned lessons of history. *New York Times*, 30 August. Retrieved 30 July 2007 from www.nytimes.com/2006/08/30/washington/30rumsfeld.html.

Cohen, Adam B., Daniel E. Hall, Harold G. Koenig, and Keith G. Meador. 2005. Social versus individual motivations: Implications for normative definitions of religious orientation. *Personality and Social Psychology Review* 9: 48–61.

Cohen, Phil. 1999. *New ethnicities, old racisms*. London: Zed Press.

Cohen, Robin. 1997. *Global diasporas: An introduction*. Seattle: University of Washington Press.

Community Cohesion Unit, 2003. Community cohesion: A report of the Independent Review Team chaired by Ted Cantle. London: HMSO. Retrieved 19 July 2007 from http://image.guardian.co.uk/sys-files/Guardian/documents/2001/12/11 /communitycohesionreport.pdf.

Congressional Research Service, Library of Congress. 2005. *Islamist extremism in Europe* (29 July). Order Code RS22211. Retrieved 27 May 2008 from http://fas.org/sgp/crs/terror/RS22211.pdf.

Cornell, Stephen E., and Douglas Hartmann. 1998. *Ethnicity and race: Making identities in a changing world*. Thousand Oaks, CA: Pine Forge Press.

Diaspora, Islam, and Gender Project. 2005. *Selected communities of Islamic cultures in Canada: Statistical profile*. Toronto: York University.

Eastmond, Marita. 1993. Reconstructing life: Chilean refugee women and the dilemmas of exile. In *Migrant women: Crossing boundaries and changing identities*, ed. Gina Buijs. Oxford: Berg.

Ebadi, Shirin. 1373/1995. *The rights of refugees: A study of the legal rights of refugees in Iran (Hoquq-e panahandegan)*. Tehran: Ganj-e Danesh Publications.

Eid, Paul. 2003. The interplay between ethnicity, religion, and gender among second-generation Christian and Muslim Arabs in Montreal. *Canadian Ethnic Studies* 35: 30–48.

El-Akkad, Omar. 2007. The enigma. He's tied to alleged terrorists and the notorious Khadr family. He claims 9/11 was an American conspiracy. And yet some Muslims suspect Aly Hindy of being a CSIS informant. A portrait of Canada's most controversial imam. *Toronto Life* (May): 74–80.

El-Akkad, Omar, and Colin Freeze. 2006. Police had a second mole in terror plot. *Globe and Mail*, 14 October: A1.

El-Akkad, Omar, and Kenyon Wallace. 2007. Teen tried to leave strict family. 16-year old's love of dancing, fashion and photography brought her into conflict; father now faces murder charge. *Globe and Mail*, 12 December: A1.

El-Yasir, Nada. 2001. *Arab Canadians through the Decades*. Toronto: Canadian Arab Federation.

Elsayed-Ali, Sherif. 2006. Palestinian refugees in Lebanon. *Forced Migration Review* 26: 13–14.

Esposito, John L. 1998. Muslims in America or American Muslims. In

Muslims on the American Path? ed. Yvonne Yazbeck Haddad and John L. Esposito. Atlanta, GA: Scholar Press.

European Monitoring Centre on Racism and Xenophobia (EUMC). 2006. *Muslims in the European Union. Discrimination and Islamophobia.* Retrieved 18 July 2007 from http://eumc.europa.eu/eumc/material/pub/muslim/ Manifestations_EN.pdf.

Fanon, Frantz. 1967. The fact of blackness. In *Black skin, white masks.* Trans. Charles Lam Markmann. New York: Grove Press. Originally published as *Peau noire, masques blancs.* Paris: Editions du Seuil, 1952.

Fatah, Tarek. 2006. Race and religion at the Liberal Party convention. *Globe and Mail,* 6 December: A31.

Flynn, Karen Carole, and C. Crawford. 1998. Committing 'race treason': Battered women and mandatory arrest in Toronto's Caribbean community. In *Unsettling truths: Battered women, policy, politics, and contemporary research in Canada,* ed. Kevin D. Bonnycastle and George S. Rigakos. Vancouver: Collective Press.

Freeze, Colin. 2003. 19 terror suspects arrested, fear grows of Canadian 9/11. *Globe and Mail,* 23 August: A1.

– 2005. Leaders clash over who speaks for Muslims in Canada. *Globe and Mail,* 29 July: A4.

Friesen, Joe. 2006. Shocking revelations as terror suspects appear in court. *Globe and Mail,* 7 June: A1.

Gelb, Norman. 2005. Britain's Muslim question. *The New Leader* 88: 11–13 (January–February).

Gilroy, Paul. 2003. The Black Atlantic as a counterculture of modernity. In *Theorizing diaspora,* ed. Jana Evan Braziel and Anita Mannur. Oxford: Blackwell.

Goldberg, Andreas. 2002. Muslims in Germany. In *Islam, Europe's second religion: The new social, cultural, and political landscape,* ed. Shireen T. Hunter. London: Praeger.

Goldwasser, E. 1998. Economic security and Muslim identity: A study of the immigrant community in Durham, North Carolina. In *Muslims on the American Path?* ed. Yvonne Yazbeck Haddad and John L. Esposito. Atlanta, GA: Scholar Press.

Goodman, Mark J. 2006. Diaspora, ethnicity and problems of identity. In *Muslim diaspora: Gender, culture and identity,* ed. Haideh Moghissi. London: Routledge.

Grewal, San, and Michelle Shephard. 2006. Terror suspect a 'nice guy.' 18th man charged appears in court. *Toronto Star* (Ontario edition), 5 August: A40.

Grmela, S. 1991. The political and cultural identity of second generation Chilean exiles in Quebec. In *Immigrants and refugees in Canada: A national perspective on ethnicity, multiculturalism and cross-cultural adjustment*, ed. Satya P. Sharma, Alexander M. Ervin, and Deirdre Meintel. Saskatoon: University of Saskatchewan, and Montreal: Université de Montréal.

Haddad, Yvonne Yazbeck. 1998. Introduction. In *Muslims on the American path?* ed. Yvonne Yazbeck Haddad and John L. Esposito. Atlanta, GA: Scholar Press.

Hall, Stuart. 2003. Cultural identity and diaspora. In *Theorizing diaspora*, ed. Jana Evans Braziel and Anita Mannur. Oxford: Blackwell.

Harvey, Mary R. 2000. In the aftermath of sexual abuse: making and remaking meaning in narratives of trauma and recovery. *Narrative Inquiry* 10: 291–311.

Heilbut, Anthony. 1983. *Exiled in paradise: German refugee artists and intellectuals in America from the 1930s to the present.* Berkeley: University of California Press.

Helly, Denise. 2004. Are Muslims discriminated against in Canada since September 2001? *Canadian Ethnic Studies* 36: 24–42.

Henry, Michele, and Bob Mitchell. 2007. Muslim teen was abused, friends say. *Toronto Star* (Metropolitan edition), 12 December: A10.

Hoffman, Eva. 1990. *Lost in translation: A life in a new language.* New York: Penguin Books.

Hojat, Mohammadreza, Reza Shapurian, Danesh Foroughi, et al. 2000. Gender differences in traditional attitudes toward marriage and the family: An empirical study of Iranian immigrants in the United States. *Journal of Family Issues* 21: 419–34.

Hunter, Shireen. 2002. *Islam, Europe's second religion: The new social, cultural, and political landscape.* London: Praeger.

Husain, Fatima, and Margaret O'Brien. 2000. Muslim communities in Europe: Reconstruction and transformation. *Current Sociology* 48, part 4: 1–13.

Hussain, Samira. 2002. Voices of Muslim women: A community research project. Gananoque, ON: Canadian Council of Muslim Women (July). Retrieved 25 April 2005 from www.ccmw.com/publications/ Voices_of_Muslim_Women_full.htm.

Ipsos News Center. 2005a. International day for the elimination of racial discrimination. One in six Canadians says they have personally been the victim of racism. News release, 21 March 2005. Retrieved 15 April 2007 from www.ipsos-na.com/news/pressrelease.cfm?id=2602.

– 2005b. Racism Study (N=1001), 15–17 March 2005. Detailed tables.

Retrieved 15 April 2007 from www.ipsos-na.com/news/client/act_dsp
_pdf.cfm?name=mr050321-2tb.pdf&id=2602.

Janhevich, Derek, and Humera Ibrahim. 2004. Muslims in Canada: An illustrative and demographic profile. *Our Diverse Cities* 1: 49–56. Retrieved 10 August 2007 from http://canada.metropolis.net/research-policy/cities/publication/diverse_cite_magazine_e.pdf.

Jimenez, Marina, Colin Freeze, and Victoria Burnett. 2003. Case of 19 terrorists starts to unravel. *Globe and Mail*, 30 August: A5.

Khaksar, Nasim. 1999. *The world of exile and us (Ma va jahan-e tabeed)*. Stockholm: Baran Publisher.

Khalema, Ernest Nene, and Jenny Wannas-Jones. 2003. Under the prism of suspicion: Minority voices in Canada post-September 11. *Journal of Muslim Minority Affairs* 23: 25–39.

Khalema, Ernest Nene, and M. Mungall, 2001. *Alberta youth against racism – campaign, 2001: Report in preparation of the United Nations World Conference against Racism, Racial Discrimination, Xenophobia, and Related Intolerance*. A research report prepared for the Department of Canadian Heritage and the Northern Alberta Alliance on Race Relations. Retrieved 22 July 2007 from www.naarr.org/pdf/yarr.pdf.

Khan, Muqtedar M.A. 2003. Constructing the American Muslim community. In *Religion and immigration: Christian, Jewish and Muslim experiences in the United States*, ed. Yvonne Yazbeck Haddad, Jane I. Smith, and John L. Esposito. Walnut Creek, CA: AltaMira Press.

Khan, Sheema. 2003. Canadians still nasty to Muslims. *Globe and Mail*, 1 May: A19.

Khan, Zafar. 2000. Muslim presence in Europe: The British dimension, identity, integration, and community activism. *Current Sociology*, 48, part 4: 29–43.

Kibria, Nazli. 1998. The contested meanings of 'Asian American': Racial dilemmas in the contemporary United States. *Ethnic and Racial Studies* 21: 939–58.

Kocturk, Tahire. 1992. *A matter of honour: Experiences of Turkish women immigrants*. London: Zed Press.

Leonard, Karen. 2003. American Muslim politics, discourses and practices. *Ethnicities* 3: 147–81.

Leveau, Remy, and Shireen T. Hunter. 2002. Islam in France. In *Islam, Europe's second religion: The new social, cultural, and political landscape*, ed. Shireen T. Hunter. London: Praeger.

Lyon, James K. 1980. *Bertolt Brecht in America*. Princeton, NJ: Princeton University Press.

Malik, Iftikhar. 2004. *Islam and modernity: Muslims in Europe and the United States*. London: Pluto Press.

Mamdani, Mahmoud. 2004. *Good Muslim, bad Muslim*. New York: Three Leaves Press, Double Day.

Mashkoor, M. Javad. 1980. *Tarikh-e shi'eh va fergheh hay-e an ta gharn-e chaharom* (History of Shi'a and its factions until the fourth (tenth) century). Tehran: Eshraghi Publishers.

Mishler, Elliot George 1986. The joint construction of meaning. In *Research interviewing: Context and narrative*. Cambridge, MA: Harvard University Press.

– 1995. Models of narrative analysis: A typology. *Journal of Narrative and Life History* 5: 87–123.

Modood, Tariq. 2005. *Multicultural politics: Racism, ethnicity, and Muslims in Britain*. Minneapolis: University of Minnesota Press.

Moghissi, Haideh. 1999. Away from home: Iranian women, displacement, cultural resistance and change. *Journal of Comparative Family Studies* 30: 207–17.

– 2006. Introduction. In *Muslim diaspora: Gender, culture and identity*, ed. Haideh Moghissi. London: Routledge.

Moghissi, Haideh, and Mark J. Goodman. 1999. 'Cultures of violence' and diaspora: Dislocation and gendered conflict in Iranian-Canadian communities. *Humanity and Society: Journal of the Association for Humanist Sociology* 23: 297–318.

Nagel, Joane. 1994. Constructing ethnicity: Creating and recreating ethnic-identity and culture. *Social Problems* 41: 152–76.

Nassehi-Behnam, Vida. 1991. Iranian immigrants in France. In *Iranian refugees and exiles since Khomeini*, ed. Asgar Fathi. Costa Mesa, CA: Mazda Publications.

Ong, Aihwa. 1996. Cultural citizenship as subject-making: Immigrants negotiate racial and cultural boundaries in the United States. *Current Anthropology* 37: 737–62.

– 1997. 'A momentary glow of fraternity': Narratives of Chinese nationalism and capitalism. *Identities-Global Studies in Culture and Power* 3: 331–66.

ONS (Office for National Statistics, United Kingdom Statistics Authority). 2001a. Resident population by ethnic group, 2001. Retrieved 3 May 2008 from www.statistics.gov.uk/StatBase/Expodata/Spreadsheets /D7666.xls.

– 2001b. Ethnic group by religion. Retrieved 3 May 2008 from www.statistics.gov.uk/StatBase/Expodata/Spreadsheets/D6891.xls.

– 2001c. Individuals in households with incomes below 60 per cent of median disposable income: by ethnic group of head of household. Retrieved 3 May 2008 from www.statistics.gov.uk/StatBase/Expodata/Spreadsheets/D7451.xls.

– 2001d. People in employment who were in the higher managerial and professional group: by ethnic group, 2001–2. Retrieved 3 May 2008 from www.statistics.gov.uk/StatBase/Expodata/ Spreadsheets/D7380.xls.

– 2001e. Unemployment rates: by ethnic group and age, 2001–2, United Kingdom. Retrieved 3 May 2008 from www.statistics.gov.uk/StatBase/Expodata/Spreadsheets/D6282.xls.

– 2004a. Ethnic group. Retrieved 3 May 2008 from www.statistics.gov.uk/StatBase/Expodata/Spreadsheets/D8287.xls.

– 2004b. Income and Wealth. Retrieved 3 May 2008 from www.statistics.gov.uk/downloads/there_social/Social_Trends36/ST36_Ch05.pdf.

– 2005a. A guide to comparing 1991 and 2001 Census ethnic group data. Retrieved 3 May 2008 from www.statistics.gov.uk/articles/nojournal/GuideV9.pdf.

– 2005b. Inner London, ethnic group of residents. Newham dataset, CM07J. Updated 18 February 2005. Retrieved 3 May 2008 from www.statistics.gov.uk/StatBase/xsdataset.asp?More=Y.

– 2005c. West Midlands, ethnic group of residents. Birmingham dataset, CM07J. Updated 18 February 2005. Retrieved 3 May 2008 from www.statistics .gov.uk/StatBase/xsdataset.asp?More=Y.

Osler, A., and Z. Hussain. 2005. Educating Muslim girls: Do mothers have faith in the state sector? In *Muslim Britain: Communities under pressure*, ed. Tahir Abbas. London: Zed Press.

Peach, Ceri. 2005. Muslims in Britain. In *Muslim Britain: Communities under pressure*, ed. Tahir Abbas. London: Zed Press.

Peek, Lori. 2005. Becoming Muslim: The development of a religious identity. *Sociology of Religion* 66: 215–42.

Peteet, Juliet. 1993. Authenticity and gender. In *Arab women: Old boundaries, new frontiers*, ed. Judith E. Tucker. Bloomington: Indiana University Press.

Pollitt, Kathy. 2006. Wrong war, wrong word. *Nation*, 11 September. Retrieved 9 June 2006 from www.thenation.com/doc/20060911/pollitt.

Portes, Alejandro, and Julia Sensenbrenner. 1993. Embeddedness and immigration: Notes on the social determinants of economic action. *American Journal of Sociology* 98: 1320–50.

Radhakrishnan, Rajagopalan. 2003. Ethnicity in an age of diaspora. In *Theorizing diaspora*, ed. Jana Evan Braziel and Anita Mannur. Oxford: Blackwell.

Rahnema, Saeed. 1992. *Organization structure: A systemic approach, cases of the Canadian public sector*. Toronto: McGraw-Hill/Ryerson.

– 2006. Islam in diaspora and challenges to multiculturalism. In *Muslim diaspora: Gender, culture and identity*, ed. Haideh Moghissi. London: Routledge.

Ramadan, Tariq. 2002. Europeanization of Islam or Islamization of Europe. In *Islam, Europe's second religion: The new social, cultural, and political landscape*, ed. Shireen T. Hunter. London: Praeger.

Reis, Michele. 2004. Theorizing diaspora: Perspectives on 'classical' and 'contemporary' diaspora. *International Migration* 42: 41–60.

Rex, John. 1996. *Ethnic minorities in the modern nation state: Working papers in the theory of multiculturalism and political integration*. Houndmills, Basingstoke, UK: Macmillan.

– 2002. Islam in the United Kingdom. In *Islam, Europe's second religion*, ed. Shireen T. Hunter. London: Praeger.

Ristock, Janis, and Joan Pennel. 1996. *Community research as empowerment*. Toronto: Oxford University Press.

Roald, Anne Sofie. 2002. From 'people's home' to 'multiculturalism': Muslims in Sweden. In *Muslim minorities in the West: Visible and invisible*, ed. Yvonne Yazbeck Haddad and Jane I. Smith. Walnut Creek, CA: AltaMira Press.

Rockhill, Kathleen. 1986. *The chaos of subjectivity in the ordered halls of academe*. Toronto: Centre for Women's Studies in Education, Ontario Institute for Studies in Education.

Runnymede Trust. 1997. *Islamaphobia: A challenge for us all*. Retrieved 27 May 2008 from www.runnymedetrust.org/publications/17/74.html.

Saeed, Abdullah. 2002. The American Muslim paradox. In *Muslim minorities in the West: Visible and invisible*, ed. Yvonne Yazbeck Haddad and Jane I. Smith. Walnut Creek, CA: AltaMira Press.

Safran, William. 1991. Diasporas in modern societies: Myths of homeland and return. *Diaspora* 1: 83–99.

Saharso, Sawitri. 2003. Culture, tolerance and gender, a contribution from the Netherlands. *European Journal of Women's Studies* 10: 7–27.

Sales, Rosemary. 2005. Secure borders, safe haven: A contradiction in terms? *Ethnic and Racial Studies* 28: 445–62.

Salih, Ruba. 2004. The backward and the new: National, transnational, and post-national Islam in Europe. *Journal of Ethnic and Migration Studies* 30: 995–1011.

Sanasarian, Elise. 1995. State dominance and communal perspective: The

Armenian diaspora in the Islamic Republic of Iran, 1979–1989. *Diaspora* 4: 243–66.

Sardar, Zia-uldin. 1995. Introduction. In *Muslim minorities in the West*, ed. Syed Z. Abedin and Ziauddin Sardar. London: Grey Seal.

Sarshar, Homa. 1996. *The history of contemporary Iranian Jews.* Beverly Hills, CA: Center for Iranian Jewish Oral History.

Saunders, Doug. 2005. Radical Islam sows its seed in Europe's fertile soil. *Globe and Mail*, 10 September: A3.

– 2006. You better watch out. Here come the TJ brothers. *Globe and Mail*, 14 October: F3.

– 2007. Muslims find their voice outside religion. *Globe and Mail*, 10 March: A1.

Scott, Joan. 1987. Women's history and the rewriting of history. In *The Impact of feminist research in the academy*, ed. C. Farnham. Bloomington: Indiana University Press.

Shadid, Wasif A.R., and P. Sj. van Koningsveld. 1991. *The integration of Islam and Hinduism in Western Europe.* Kampen, The Netherlands: Kok Pharos · Publishing House.

Shakeri, E. 1998. Muslim women in Canada, their role and status as revealed in hijab controversy. In *Muslims on the American Path?* ed. Yvonne Yazbeck Haddad and John L. Esposito. Atlanta, GA: Scholar Press.

Shepard, Michelle. 2006. Terror cops swoop. How Internet monitoring sparked a CSIS investigation into what authorities allege is a homegrown Canadian terror cell. *Toronto Star* (Metropolitan edition), 3 June: A1.

Shepard, Michelle, and Isabel Teotonio. 2006. Portraits emerge. Trio underwent swift transformation from popular kids to devout, depressed. *Toronto Star* (Metropolitan edition), 5 June: A1.

Smith, Jane I. 2002. Introduction. In *Muslim minorities in the West: Visible and invisible*, ed. Yvonne Yazbeck Haddad and Jane I. Smith, 102–20. Walnut Creek, CA: AltaMira Press.

Smith, Timothy B., Michael E. McCullough, and Justin Poll. 2003. Religiousness and depression: Evidence for a main effect and the moderating influence of stressful life events. *Psychological Bulletin* 129: 614–36.

Soltanpour, Saeed. 2005. 'Iranian–Islamic Centres in Toronto,' part 2. *Shahrvand Weekly* (926), 11 February.

Soper, J. Christopher, and Joel S. Fetzer. 2003. Explaining the accommodation of Muslim religious practices in France, Britain, and Germany. *French Politics* 1: 39–59.

Spellman, Kathryn. 2004. *Religion and nation: Iranian local and transnational networks in Britain.* Studies in Forced Migration, vol. 15. Oxford : Berghahn Books.

Statham, Paul, Ruud Koopmans, Marco Giugni, and Florence Passy. 2005. Resilient or adoptable Islam? Multiculturalism, religion and migrants' claim-making for group demands in Britain, the Netherlands and France. *Ethnicities* 5: 427–59.

Sunier, Thijl, and Mira van Kuijeren. 2002. Islam in the Netherlands. In *Muslims in the West: From sojourners to citizens*, ed. Yvonne Yazbeck Haddad. Oxford: Oxford University Press.

Sun Media. 2007. Racial tolerance report. Survey (N=3092) conducted 27 December 2006 through 5 January 2007. Report issued January 2007. Retrieved 3 May 2008 from www.legermarketing.com/documents/ SPCLM/070119ENG.pdf.

Syed, Naseer (Irfan). 2004. Who speaks for Muslims in Canada? *Globe and Mail*, 27 October: A25.

Teotonio, Isabel, and Jessica Leeder. 2006. 'Jihadist generation' in search of roots. *Toronto Star* (Ontario edition), 10 June: A12.

Tibi, Bassam. 2001. *Islam between culture and politics*. Houndmills, Basingstoke, UK: Palgrave.

Travis, Alan. 2008. Officials think UK's Muslim population has risen to 2 million. *Guardian*, 8 April. Retrieved 3 May 2008 from www.guardian.co.uk /world/2008/apr/08/population.islam.

Van der Lans, J.M., and M. Rooijackers. 1992. Types of religious belief and un-belief among second generation Turkish migrants. In *Islam in Dutch society: Current developments and future prospects*, ed. Wasif A.R. Shadid and P. Sj. van Koningsveld. Kampen, The Netherlands: Kok Pharos Publishing House.

Wagtendonk, K. 1991. Islamic schools and Islamic religious education: A comparison between Holland and other West European countries. In *Islam in Dutch society: Current developments and future prospects*, ed. Wasif A.R. Shadid and P. Sj. van Koningsveld. Kampen, The Netherlands: Kok Pharos Publishing House.

Waters, Mary C. 1998. American identity and culture. In *Race, class and gender: An anthology*, ed. Margaret L. Andersen and Patricia Hill Collins. Belmont: Wadsworth.

Watt, William Montgomery. 1998. *The formative period of Islamic thought*. Oxford: One World.

Weber, Max. 1997. What is an ethnic group? In *The ethnicity reader: Nationalism, multiculturalism and migration*, ed. Montserrat Guibernay and John Rex. London: Polity Press.

Yelaja, Prithi, and Tabassum Siddiqui Prithi Yelaja. 2006. And who speaks for Muslims? Many are talking and delivering the 'sound bite,' yet there is no unified voice. Amid rivalry, there is some consensus. *Toronto Star* (Ontario edition), 12 June: A4.

Zine, Jasmin. 2003. Dealing with September 12th: the challenge of anti-Islamophobia education. *Orbit* 33: n.p. Retrieved 28 July 2007 from http://ezproxy.library.yorku.ca/login?url=http://proquest.umi.com .ezproxy.library.yorku.ca/pqdweb?did=688972661&sid+45& Fmt=2&clientld=5220&RQT+309&VName+PQD.

About the Authors

Haideh Moghissi is a professor of sociology and women's studies at Atkinson Faculty of Liberal and Professional Studies and the Faculty of Graduate Studies, York University, Toronto. She was a founder of the Iranian National Union of Women and a member of its first executive board and of the editorial boards of *Barabari* (Equality) and *Zanan Dar Mobarezeh* (Women in Struggle). Her previous books are: *Muslim Diaspora, Gender, Culture and Identity* (ed.) (2006); *Women and Islam: Critical Concepts in Sociology* (ed.) (2005); *Feminism and Islamic Fundamentalism: The Limits of Postmodern Analysis* (2000); and *Populism and Feminism in Iran: Women's Struggle in a Male-Defined Revolutionary Movement* (1994).

Saeed Rahnema is a professor of political science at York University, and has served as the director of the School of Public Policy and Administration and as Atkinson's Political Science coordinator. He has worked as a senior officer in the United Nation's Development Program and was a director of the Middle East Economic Association of the Allied Social Science Association, and has been on the editorial board of several journals. He is a frequent commentator of Middle Eastern politics in Canadian and international media. His previous books in English include *Selected Communities of Islamic Cultures in Canada: A Statistical Profile* (2005); *Iran after the Revolution: Crisis of An Islamic State*, co-edited (1995); *Re-Birth of Social Democracy in Iran* (1996); and *Organization Structure: A Systemic Approach: Cases of Canadian Public Sector* (1993).

Mark J. Goodman is a professor of sociology in the School of Social Sciences, Atkinson Faculty of Liberal and Professional Studies, York

University, Toronto. His previous publications include 'Cultures of Violence and Diaspora: Dislocation and Gendered Conflict in Iranian-Canadian Communities,' *Humanity and Society* (November 1999), co-authored with Haideh Moghissi; and 'Diaspora, Ethnicity and Problems of Identity,' in H. Moghissi, ed., *Muslim Diaspora, Gender, Culture and Identity* (2006). He is presently conducting a study of forced migration and cultural change among African-Americans from slavery onwards.

Index